LIGHT OUT OF DARKNESS

Light out of
Darkness

Kathleen O'Sullivan SSL

Hodder & Stoughton
LONDON SYDNEY AUCKLAND

British Library Cataloguing in Publication Data
A catalogue record for this book is
available from the British Library.

ISBN 0-340-58225 1

Published by Hodder and Stoughton,
a division of Hodder and Stoughton Ltd,
Mill Road, Dunton Green, Sevenoaks, Kent TN13 2YA.
Editorial Office: 47 Bedford Square, London WC1B 3DP.

Typeset by Hewer Text Composition Services Ltd, Edinburgh.
Printed in Great Britain by Clays Ltd, St. Ives plc.

Dedication

To Sheila and Dennis Wrigley,
whose constant prayer, practical support and faith in me
made this book possible.

Contents

Acknowledgements

I owe a debt of gratitude to all who have allowed God transform their lives through the various stages of these programmes. They continue to be an inspiration to me.

I thank Sheila Wrigley for her fidelity, encouragement and expert typing of the manuscript.

To Hodder & Stoughton and the editor of religious books, Carolyn Armitage, I express my thanks and appreciation.

Foreword

The Christian believer is often challenged with the question: if the world is created and sustained by a just, loving and merciful God, why is there so much suffering and evil in it? To this the believer can only reply: our religion does not offer an easy, glib answer to this question, such as can be grasped by the mind alone. The meaning of suffering and evil in the providential design of God is a mystery which cannot be plumbed simply by sitting in an armchair and talking about it, but only by living through it. Faced with this mystery, the human intellect breaks down, unable to make sense of the apparent meaninglessness and purposelessness of it all. The human will snaps too, unable to overcome its natural repugnance to pain and death. Only those who have launched out into the darkness in a spirit of faith and trust in God have managed to pierce the heart of this mystery, and to emerge triumphantly from the other side. If we want guides in this unknown territory, it is not the professional thinkers who will be able to help us. It is Job. It is Christ, above all, who has drunk the bitter cup to the dregs, yet lives on, even more gloriously than before.

Our religion does not claim to be able to *explain* suffering and evil. It does claim to show us how to carry it, how to live through it, how to *use* it. These dark areas of our human experience, when accepted in faith, become an instrument for spiritual growth. When our natural faculties break down, then God can step in. When all else proves useless, then the power of God can act unimpeded. We cannot hope to know God, or to be united with Him, until we have learned to surrender to Him. The seeming pointlessness and unbearableness of suffering brings us to that point by the quickest possible road. There are insights, glories and triumphs which can only be gained by treading this path.

It is essentially a path of transformation. By treading it, we change our experience of the world, our view of reality. More important still, we ourselves are changed. We become different people, Children of the Light. That is why it is extremely appropriate that the present book should be called Light out of Darkness. It is describing a process of alchemical transformation, whereby all that is dark in our experience of ourselves and the world can be transmuted into light. It shows us that instead of flinching from the dark, instead of running away from it, we can use it as fuel, which can be ignited, and become a source of light and warmth. There is nothing morbid, melancholy or masochistic about this. There is no question of revelling in pain or suffering for its own sake. It is a matter of taking that which seems to work inexorably against us and making it work for us; taking a negative and making it positive.

The aid that a book of this kind can give is invaluable, yet many fail to appreciate this. Books which talk of suffering and evil are considered as "too sad"; it is thought that spiritual authors ought to write only about "nice" things. But this is to take the guts out of religion, making it pale and lifeless. Surely the greatest service a Christian author can render to the world is not to avoid the darkness but to show us how to confront it and turn it into light. That is what the book is doing.

We are being invited here to embark on a journey, a journey into the mystery of God. This journey involves the whole of ourselves: our minds, bodies, feeling, imagination, hopes, aspirations, triumphs, failures, joys and sorrows. This is a flesh and blood book, because it is born from flesh and blood experience. The author has lived what she writes and can share with us her experience of the journey. Therefore she makes no attempt to separate off the dark element from the rest of life in order to study it under laboratory conditions, as it were. Darkness can only be understood in relation to

light and joy; the part can only be understood in relation
to the whole. So this is not simply a book about the dark,
but on the whole of human life and experience, and how the
dark fits into that. This is in itself a very great achievement
and gives the book a certain bracing and invigorating quality.
The whole problem with darkness is that it tries to draw too
much attention to itself, to make us become obsessed with
it, so that we either succumb to it in despair or flee from it in
terror. The moment we see it as a part in a greater whole, a
detail in a larger overall picture, it loses much of its power.
Therefore, this is not a "heavy" book; it is not hard labour
but refreshment and encouragement.

It is also animated throughout by a great love of God
as manifested in Christ. This means that it is the Christian
believer, sharing that faith and that love, who will be able
to make the best use of it. The journey it describes can
only really be undertaken by those who believe in Christ
and are ready to follow his traces, like a hunter pursuing
his quarry. They also need his grace and power to take them
where human strength cannot go. To all who desire to give
shape and direction to their lives by following Christ through
death to resurrection, through darkness to light, this book
will prove a powerful aid.

Cyprian Smith OSB
Ampleforth, 1992

Why This Book? Why Me?

This is a book about life, love, sunshine and energy – and God as the source and goal of it all! The fact is that I value and treasure life. To be alive for me is glorious. To be in love is important to me, and always has been. I can't separate love and life. I want to share that experience with others, even though I am not sufficiently in love yet with some aspects of life. That is my problem, because I do not let God's light shine and illumine those aspects of His vision of love.

At eighteen, quite unexpectedly, Christ as Love won my heart. I was planning to go to university and have a good time. Dating had been fun – for a while. Tennis, as a love, lasted longer. Golf with my dad, in a happy, silent companionship, confirmed a growing feel that life was more, much more than sunshine events and abounding energy. Even success revealed its impermanence. Then God said, as Ezekiel so well puts it: 'I saw you as I was passing. Your time had come, the time for love. I made a covenant with you . . . and you became mine' (Ez 16:8–9).

I know the day, date and hour when, in the midst of my classmates, I heard deep in my heart: 'I am the Love that you are seeking.' At the end of an hour, I knew without any doubt that indeed I had met Him who 'set me like a seal on his heart' (Song 8:6). I did not need to consult anyone. He had spoken too clearly. My heart responded with joy. I made arrangements immediately and was accepted as an aspirant in the Institute of St Louis. My disbelieving friends gave me a farewell party and allowed me three weeks to 'come to my senses' when we could have a proper party! Despite a lot of pain, and my frequent infidelities, His everlasting love has been strong enough to overcome all.

Prayer, or special time alone with him, became my lifeline. Despite a good home where prayer was part of every day, I knew I had a lot to learn. He continues to this day to teach me through people, events, joys and sorrows. This teaching and learning is a 'presence of God' in my life which I find stimulating. It keeps me on the *qui vive*. I can indeed be angry, hurt, irritable and impatient, but never bored, unless I let 'darkness' creep in. I would find it impossible, I think, to be half-alive. It's all or nothing. I enjoy growing older, despite inconvenient aches! The savour of life becomes more special.

In this book, I want to share with others a little of what I've been taught by God through so many of the encounters in my life. Of course all is not sunshine, but the potential of God's presence and light is always there, if we are childlike enough to believe, to trust and to let God be God. Darkness too is a reality in our lives, a darkness that can hurt, can diminish the precious gift of our humanity, a darkness that can even destroy. The choice is ours. He who is Light, Life and Love passionately desires to transform all that is not of Him into his saving presence of love.

Light became important to me about fifteen years ago when I was threatened with blindness. Eye surgery was not as successful as had been hoped. The prognosis was for two more years of sight. This event resulted in my leaving school administration, where I had enjoyed working with a first-rate staff, dealing with the challenge of seven hundred teenagers in Ireland. I went to the United States to study. The prayer of God's people, however, worked wonders. Now, fifteen years later, despite medical forebodings, my eyes continue to serve me quite well, with minimal vacation time!

Through this event, I was again taught much. I learnt to value the 'inner light' within myself and others much more. I can take so much of God's goodness for granted. Now I savour in ministry the light of God's presence in another as darkness is overcome, or as the 'inner light' becomes more luminous.

Light and the gift of our humanity were the initial grace of creation for us. As God continues to re-create us in his unchanging love, we have the option of growing fully as human beings, living in the light of His presence, rejoicing His heart as we allow Him to spread light in us and through us as we grow into His likeness.

Come, join us, and let your riches bless us all, God's own beloved people.

Light out of Darkness

Light out of Darkness is a totally revised and updated version of the original book, *A Way of Life*, which, during the five years since its publication in 1987, has been extensively used by groups led by trained leaders. Requests for a book from individuals who desired something of the transformation of lives which they had witnessed in our prayer-life groups coincided with the end of the second reprint. A new book was needed.

Light out of Darkness preserves some of the original material used in groups but goes far beyond that. The new approach, with its contemplative thrust, reflects the gains of five years of retreat work. The many and varied chapters attest more strongly than ever that appreciation of our human identity as the work of God's hands leads unerringly to a spirituality that is in touch with reality. This journey from the unreal to the real, from darkness to light, is rooted in Christ who is love, in the Spirit who lives within us, to the glory of the Father.

Human as we are, and indeed sinners, repentance can open us to the power of God working in us which 'can do infinitely more than we can ask or imagine' (Ep 3:20).

This is not only a journey into 'light out of darkness' but a continuous growth into freedom. We are never alone as we journey. 'I am always with you,' Christ promised, and support comes also through our membership of the body of Christ.

How does this book *Light out of Darkness* help to effect this growth into freedom? It shows us how to integrate the human and the spiritual, prayer and life. Thus a 'separation', not intended by God, becomes a greater wholeness. 'Let your behaviour change modelled by your new mind. This is the only way to discover the will of God and know what is good, what it is that God wants, what is the perfect thing to do' (Rom 12:2). Through discernment, we learn to recognise the movements of the Spirit within our being, attracting, challenging, enlightening and alerting us to spirits that are not of God. Through the healing power of the Spirit of love acting within us, we become healed and reconciled with God and with other people. We begin to share the vision of Christ, in whose unchanging love we are brothers and sisters, dearly loved children of His Father. As a result of being healed and reconciled, we begin to change our values and attitudes, and in growing more like Christ we reveal him more. Thus by the quality of our lives, by who we are in Christ, we become true evangelisers.

I hear today the same cry as moved me to do the research in 1980 which resulted in *A Way of Life*. That book has been experienced by laity, priests and religious as a positive answer to the cry expressed to me of many needs:

the need to know not just a Sunday God but one who cares for all His people and all their affairs;
the need to know that we have something worthwhile to offer despite an often poor and humiliating self-image. 'Keeping up a front' can become depressing, killing the joy of life;
the need to experience support from others, from people who share perhaps similar dreams and hopes, people who know the same God.

In answer to the spiritual hunger which is increasingly evident, *Light out of Darkness* emphasises continuous 'listening to the Spirit'. Moreover by highlighting 'incarnational reality today', the way is more clearly opened to experience more fully the Pauline: '*I live now not with my own life but with the life of Christ who lives in me*' (Ga 2:20).

We who are sinners and frail, need hope. We are only too aware of the corruption of sin all around us, within ourselves, within others and in the environment. Corruption is rooted in injustice today as it was when our ancestors rebelled in the garden of Eden. The enemy tempted them successfully to rebel against the One who created them in love and to reject his rightful sovereignty over them. Pride – with its many faces – leads now, as then, to the corruption of sin.

Where then is our hope? If love is the 'one thing necessary' which God desires *from* us, so *for* us, love is our way back to God, and we experience love through the Holy Spirit, who is the mutual love of the Father and the Son.

In John, chapters 14 and 16, Jesus passionately comforts his mourning disciples. He will not leave them alone: 'I shall ask the Father, and he will give you another Advocate to be with you forever, the Spirit of truth' (14:16). In receiving the Spirit, they are not losing Jesus: 'I will not leave you orphans; I will come back to you . . . You will see me because I live and you will live. On that day you will understand that I am in my Father and you in me and I in you . . . and anybody who loves me will be loved by my Father . . . and we shall come to him and make our home with him' (Jn 14:18–20, 21,23).

This Advocate will teach them everything and remind them of all Jesus has said to them. It is for their good that he, Jesus, leaves them for a while: 'When he [the Advocate] comes he will show the world how wrong it was, about sin, and about who was in the right, and about judgement: about sin: proved by their refusal to believe in me; about who was in the right: proved by my going to the Father . . . about judgement proved by the prince of this world being already condemned' (Jn 16:8–11).

What was true for 'His own' then, continues to be true for us today. Jesus prayed not only for them but also for all of us who believe. Jesus is always faithful. He honours His promises. His love for His own, for all His people, is everlasting. It is our responsibility to listen to the Advocate, to the Spirit whom Jesus has given us to guide and teach us. He lives within each of us, His Temple. In His power, *pride* must be overcome by humility, if the corruption of sin is to be destroyed. We need to get reality into perspective in our lives. We human beings are totally dependent on God, on the power of the Spirit for everything. Without Him, we cannot even say 'Abba Father'. We cannot overrate the importance of our being the temple of the Holy Spirit. We need to value that reality. The Spirit who leads and guides us, who brings us into light out of darkness, lives within us.

As members of the body of Christ, alive with his Spirit, we must follow the example of Christ with whom there was no distinction of persons, neither Jew nor Greek. 'Saul, why are you persecuting me?' 'Who are you, Lord?' 'I am Jesus, and you are persecuting me' (Acts 9:4–5). Jesus takes as done to himself whatever we do to our neighbour, be it a form of persecution, or the blessing of a cup of water.

In our frailty and weakness we certainly need the power and the prayer of the Holy Spirit who has been given to us by the risen Jesus. This Spirit never ceases to pray for us in our weakness, 'expressing our needs in a way that God perfectly understands' (Rm 8:26). In true humility, it is essential to be taught and reminded by the Spirit, that we need to have the heart of a child, because 'it is to such as these that the kingdom of God belongs' (Mk 10:14).

We are just little people, children who are dearly beloved by the Father. We don't have to do great deeds, nor be great people. Only one thing is required of us: to learn to listen to the Spirit of God and to be obedient to what God asks of us. The more we surrender in love to God, the more we hand over our lives, even daily details to Him, the more quickly we grow into His likeness. *Light out of Darkness* aims to foster this process.

As children we learn that we cannot achieve anything apart from God. All growth is the gift of God. It cannot be won by our striving. St John of the Cross says: 'Put love where there is no love and you will find love.' It is in finding love in the ordinary, daily routine, that we find the power of the Holy Spirit transforming darkness into light. When we are faithful in little things, the light that is Christ shines more brightly. Then we learn that even darkness can become a blessing when we allow God to exercise victory and transform darkness into the light of His Kingdom. This is surrender.

Some comments from people who have attended our retreats

'My wife has become so much like the girl I married that I want to experience some of that change too. May I come along?'

'I found it so difficult at the beginning to set aside even fifteen minutes for daily prayer. But the example of others in the group helped me and I tried to be faithful to giving the time. Now prayer is no longer a duty. It has become necessary, something I would greatly miss. It gives, somehow, a direction and a meaning to the day.'

'My life changed when I became aware of my arrogance and pride. That was a shock. I know now that talking things over first with God, then looking at the pros and cons of decisions, has made me a more contented person.'

'I used to avoid leadership roles in church – too much trouble! Now, I'm out there, trying to give a little of what I have received.'

'*A Way of Life* was a joy for its ecumenical reality . . . It was amazing how barriers went down, even from the first day of the retreat.'

'It was in fact the most important eight days of my life, and an event which has given me a totally new direction and calling.'

'Our marriage was on the rocks. Then we followed *A Way of Life*. We were in separate groups, so did not know what was happening to the partner. We faithfully observed the contemplative silence – and I think that was what worked! Gradually God revealed me to myself – at least parts of me – and I was taken aback. I saw for the first time that I was transferring to my partner unhealed hurts, angers, feelings of revenge since childhood. The healing service during the retreat gave me the first inkling; after that every word seemed to bring greater clarity. I now know how greatly I value my partner who put up with me and, yes, even kept on loving me.'

'I was accepted as I was and my acknowledgement of former prejudices only seemed to win me more love. I am still stunned.'

'I cannot put into words the impact of the retreat, but I know the impact by the fact that all is retained within me. I remember thinking during the teaching sessions: how I wish that this was being taped so I could listen to it again and not lose a word, but the Holy Spirit has proved to be my own personal recorder . . . I am so thankful to God for the gift of myself.'

**Yahweh, you yourself are my lamp,
my God lights up my darkness. (Ps 18:28).**

STAGE ONE

FIRST STEPS

Part One: First Steps – Exploring

Introduction

Exploring consists in laying a sure base for future human-spiritual growth. I begin with:

Looking at the wonder of being human
The material in this section opens up for us the value of our humanity and the spiritual truth that the Spirit of God lives within us. The wonder of being human involves looking at some of the gifts closely associated with our human-spiritual growth. Too often their value is underprized and their potential undeveloped.

I emphasise the value of our *personal experience*, which involves the gifts of *awareness*, *reflecting*, *listening*, *feeling*, *discerning*, and *breathing*. Proper use of these gifts brings an increase of light to our lives, which lessens our darkness.

Exploring consists also in facing the reality of frailty in our lives. I continue with:

Looking at light and darkness in our lives
This transformation of darkness into light is the meaning of salvation. It is the saving action of God's love in our lives. This process of growth and transformation of darkness is treated throughout the *three stages* in this book

in ever-increasing depth. The common themes are: *Light and Darkness*, the *Sower*, *Prayer* and *Freedom*.

Light and Darkness: In this stage, Part One, we look at 'darkness', as it masquerades under the 'unreal'. The process of growth and transformation is seen in the movement from the *unreal into the real*.

Fears, masks, unrealities of different kinds are aired. When darkness is faced, recognised, claimed and shared, the road to healing, wholeness and light is opened. Each step of the journey is supported by the light of God's presence, especially when the way is rough and dark.

The Sower: This parable is another theme which is repeated throughout the three stages in increasing depth. It urges us to look at our own life story as we become aware of the darkness and our desire to move into greater light.

Prayer: This constant, necessary relationship with God steadies our waywardness, helps us to glimpse new ways, taste new life, dream dreams again that become more rooted, however, in Christ. Prayer needs to be supported by a sound discipline – especially in the early stages of coming to know God.

Freedom: The goal of 'prisoners' and the gift of God. Freedom is given by God to those who leave the darkness of the selfish ego to live in the light of truth which sets the children of God free.

We come eventually to *First Steps*, when we have completed Part One. The steps are basic. They give us footholds which are carved from the material which we have been discussing above. These steps are measured to each person's size. They are the first steps in this important journey of seeking God and finding Him in the details of our daily life.

1 The wonder of the human being – the Temple of the Holy Spirit

I remember well the day that Psalm 139 made an impression on me. It spoke about the wonder of my being. I was in

Ireland and a sea breeze fanned my cheek. I thought, I can feel that breeze, I can enjoy it. That is part of the gift of being human. Then I was led deeper into this experience. I am now sharing something with Jesus, I thought. He too could feel a breeze. He too could experience the wonder of His being, the wonder of being human. I stayed for a long time with this realisation. Jesus was truly human, like you, like me, sin alone excepted. Jesus could be lonely. He could weep. He could be tempted. He could hurt. He could love. He had dreams. In Nazareth He was a quiet man, but fire burnt inside Him. He was the kind of person whom people loved or hated. One could not be indifferent to Jesus.

The lesson of the humanity of Jesus became deeper for me when I was first introduced to the concept of contemplative eating! I had scoffed at the idea of being able to eat contemplatively – for example, contemplating the love of God coming to me through the food I am eating, from the seed in the ground through all the human hands preparing it for my enjoyment. But I was challenged to try it. I did. It was in a large dining room for students under the Rocky Mountains. I began with a roll of bread and soup. Soon I found it quite difficult to continue eating. The reality of the Eucharist was brought home to me. Jesus, too, in His humanity had taken bread. Bread, so simple, so easily accessible as food to His people. He had blessed it and it became His body and blood.

That experience opened up a new chapter for me on the wonder, the marvel, of being human. I began to revere the gift of humanity that God had given us. I looked at my hands. I could touch, I could feel. I had ears and could hear, eyes and could see, a tongue that could taste and speak. I had feet that could walk: the marvel of the human body. Jesus incarnate, the Son of God, knew the same gifts of humanity. Out of His own experience He learnt the marvel of touching wood, of looking at birds soaring or resting. In His body He experienced weariness. Early in the morning He walked to the mountain. In this solitary experience His Spirit was lifted high. He listened. He felt. He discerned His Father's will. He breathed and marvelled at the breath of God, the

Spirit of God. Jesus developed His gift of awareness, and of reflecting on that awareness.

Jesus of Nazareth truly shared our humanity. He became human so that He could share with us His divinity. We are the temples of His Spirit, the Spirit of Jesus. Our humanity is wonderful in itself. It is wonderful in that the gifts we have received are to help us to come to know God better. Our humanity is more wonderful still in that, in this moment, the Spirit of God lives within us!

The forgotten Paraclete or Holy Spirit

St Paul says, 'Your body, you know, is the temple of the Holy Spirit, who is in you since you received him from God' (1 Cor 6:19). In Ephesians 2:22 he says 'you too, in him, are being built into a house where God lives, in the Spirit'. Yet for so long we have ignored the reality of the Spirit in our lives and have not called on His love and power. We have forgotten Him.

It is quite impossible, I think, for us to become mature Christians unless we are open and eager to live by the Spirit, to be led by the Spirit and to be guided by the Spirit. Jesus in His humanity was guided by the Spirit. We hear of the Spirit leading Jesus out into the desert, to be tempted by the enemy. Jesus of course conquers the enemy as He always has conquered, is conquering and will complete the conquest. Then we will be restored to our Father in Heaven, through the power of the Holy Spirit of Jesus.

We need to listen to Jesus in the last discourse, to begin to grasp the meaning of the Holy Spirit today in our lives, as Jesus intended. Jesus is nearing the end of the journey of His human existence. He loves His disciples. He is pouring out His heart to them. He is suffering their pain of separation and we, too, are in His mind. Let us hear Him with open hearts. Jesus says, 'I shall ask the Father and He will give you another Advocate to be with you for ever, that Spirit of truth whom the world can never receive, since it neither sees nor knows Him; but you know Him, because He is with you, He is in you. I will not leave you orphans; I will come back to you. In a short time the world will no longer see me; but you will see me, because I live, you will live' (Jn 14:16–20).

And then again Jesus continues, 'the Advocate, the Holy Spirit, whom the Father will send in my name, will teach you everything and remind you of all that I have said to you' (v. 26). These words pour out from the heart of Jesus, who knows the enemy and who knows the need of His followers to have a Spirit of truth who will not let them be deceived. He knows that we can't be left alone and He will not leave us orphans. He knows the world that will not receive Him, since, as He says, it neither sees nor knows Him.

From our own experience we, too, can see that unfortunately we can often belong to that world, can forget the Spirit, can try to go it alone independently even of God! When Jesus tells us that the Spirit will teach us everything and remind us of all the things that He said, we still don't seem to recognise our need for the Holy Spirit. What a sadness for us. It was a sadness for Jesus, too, who recognised that His own disciples were troubled. To them He said, 'You are sad at heart because I have told you I am going' and then adds, 'still I must tell you the truth; it is for your own good that I am going because unless I go, the Advocate will not come to you; but if I do go, I will send Him to you' (Jn 16). Have we grasped in our own lives the vital importance of what Jesus is saying to us here? While He remained on earth in His human incarnation He could exhort His apostles but He could not live in them, and in us, for ever. In and through the gift of His Spirit, however, He can live within us. 'I live now not with my own life but with the life of Christ who lives in me' (Ga 2:20).

One can sense the pain of Jesus who knows that what He has taught His disciples cannot be retained by them on their own. He knows that He has still so many things to say, but they are too much for His people at that time. His hope is, as He says, 'When the Spirit of truth comes He will lead you to the complete truth' (Jn 16:13). Is the Spirit of Jesus a living reality in my life, in your life, in the life of your friends and the life of the world? If not, why not? In Jesus' humanity the enemy was attacking Him in the flesh.

Today the warfare is spiritual warfare. It is the warfare of
the Spirit of Jesus against the spirits of the enemy. It is in
and through the Holy Spirit that Jesus is with us. It is in
and through the Spirit that we are going to be saved and
brought back to the Father by Jesus, who died to achieve
just that.

In my ministry I sometimes hear people say they fear
that if they pray to the Spirit they might be forsaking Jesus
or forsaking the Father! This is quite impossible. This is
confusion. This is error. The Spirit cannot be separated
from the Father and the Son. The Holy Spirit is the personal
expression of the mutual love of the Father and the Son for
one another. St Paul says: 'God's love has been poured into
our hearts through the Holy Spirit which has been given us'
(Rm 5:5).

People who are intellectually well-informed on the doctrine of the Holy Spirit still tell me that He can remain
almost unreal to them, that there seems to be little personal
relationship between themselves and the Spirit! Perhaps they
need to realise that the Spirit can only be experienced from
within. The action of the Spirit always proceeds from our
interior, and it is from the interior that we recognise Him.
'You know Him because He dwells in you' (Jn 14:17).

To others the Spirit seems to be more mysterious than
either the Father or Jesus. 'We do not know from whence
He comes or whence He goes' (c.f. Jn 3:8). Yet, by the gift
of God, the mystery of the Spirit is closely connected with
the mystery of our own being. When we have developed the
gift of awareness, of sensitivity, of feeling, of discernment, of
reflecting and of listening, then we can discern the movement
of the Spirit within us. We *experience* the call of the Spirit
and the action of the Spirit.

Other people are apprehensive about the Spirit on the
emotional level. They are afraid of confusing what is
spiritual and what is purely emotional – they fear illusion.
The authenticity of the Spirit must of course always be
discerned. However, if we have allowed the gift of the
Spirit given to us by Jesus to become ignored or forgotten
in our lives that is our personal responsibility before God.

Jesus, who is truth, has taught us our absolute need of the Spirit.

Jesus who is truth, will guard us against illusion when we trust Him with all our heart.

2 Personal experience, awareness, reflection

We have seen something of the wonder of being human, and the importance of the Holy Spirit in our lives. Let us now consider some of the ways in which we can come to know the Spirit. As we have seen, God's gifts to us which we often neglect are: our personal experience, awareness, reflecting, feeling, listening, discerning, breathing.

Our *personal experience* is a most precious gift. It is unique. It is me, yet much more than me. It is God in me, with me, acting through me. I need to focus on God and let it happen. Jesus used all His humanity, His mind, His heart, His will, His senses, everything, to know Himself and to know His Father. Through these gifts He experienced life. Do I?

Awareness and *reflection on awareness* are vital, if my experience is to become a living reality of salvation for me. God's Spirit is living in me, empowering me to become aware of the value of my personal experience. It is God's Spirit who is helping me to become *aware*, to *reflect*, to *listen*, later we will hear how He helps me to be in touch with my *feelings*, to *discern* where He is, and to crown all with His *breath*.

Let me give a simple example of how I can develop my gift of *awareness* through my personal experience. To see a beautiful sunset does not necessarily mean that I become aware of it. It is a deeper experience when I become aware.

Do a simple experiment with yourself. Next time you see a lovely sunset or something beautiful that speaks to you, *pause*. Become aware of it. Just stand and gaze and look and see and let all your senses enter into your experience. Let the stillness, the silence, the gazing, draw you into an awareness of the Spirit who is alive within you. Reflect on the new awareness that you are now enjoying. In the Spirit, it may well be that you will discover that you are sharing your human experience with Jesus. You live in His Spirit, let His Spirit guide you as it guided Him. He will teach you in every moment of your personal experience whatever you need to know.

To become aware moves me deeper into the mysterious humanity that is God's gift to me and the Spirit within me. When we develop our sensitivity, to become aware is like opening a door of an inner room, where everything takes on a richer, deeper hue.

For someone else, however, an experiment may lead them into the area of their feelings. This happened to me once. It was in Denver. As is usual on a thirty-day retreat, one has a repose day. Such a day does not disrupt the retreat but creates a kind of watershed where one can reflect more deeply. At that time I was seeing the beauty in everyone else but could not see it in myself. In a Natural History Museum in Denver I stood before a case of shells. I caught my breath when I saw a beautiful queen conch shell, cut right down the middle. The exquisite pattern on that shell was breath-taking. More than that, the colouring moved me deeply. It stretched from cream to all shades of delicate pink. I was moved to say, in the Spirit, 'Lord what beauty. You are beautiful and wonderful. This is the work of your hands.' I was enraptured! Then, within my temple I heard the words, 'Yes, that is the work of my hands. You, too, are my work of art. You, too, are beautiful but you will not believe it.' I was startled and stunned!

In due time, I hurried back to college. By now I was walking on air. I believed and I accepted. I praised the Lord for His great glory. Ten days later, on the next repose day, I hastened back to the same museum, to my queen conch shell. My director was wise. When I had told her of my plans, she said nothing but let me be taught by the Spirit through my mistake. One cannot possess God, or possess even a gift of

God. I was doing just that! When I stood in front of that case again, I looked impatiently for my shell. I had brought my camera. I had made plans how to keep closely united to God through this picture I was going to take.

My shell had gone. I could not see it. In its place stood an *ordinary* queen conch. The delicate workmanship was excellent, yes, but the wonderful colour that had entranced me was gone. This shell seemed lifeless.

Impatiently I turned to an attendant and queried sharply, 'Sir, ten days ago a queen conch shell was here. Where has it gone?' To cut a long story short, I was assured by two frustrated attendants that nothing had been changed in the case. I looked again. The light, the delicacy of colouring that I had seen and which had attracted me, was no longer visible. This could not be the same shell. I felt deserted, broken, almost betrayed. The tears flowed. In near despair, I turned to God within me. Then I heard in my heart: 'Why are you weeping? I have more gifts to give you than just one. I am giving you a precious gift now.' Through my tears I cried: 'You have taken my gift. I don't see what You are giving me.' The silence between us was long. I stayed there waiting. I reflected on the whole experience. Gradually the heaviness within me began to lift. Then, at last, I knew! I was being taught by the Spirit a second important lesson: 'Do not cling. Live in the present. God is in the present moment. If you cling to the past and are living there, you are missing Jesus who is passing your way in this present moment.'

This experience taught me the vital importance of each one's personal experience. It must be reflected on, however, otherwise we are in danger of letting Jesus, who labours for us all the time, labour in vain. It is through His Spirit that He is teaching us the things we need to know for our salvation. Moreover, through what He teaches us, He will later use us so that we share with other people. St Paul talks about that in 2 Cor 1:3,4: 'Blessed be the God and Father of our Lord Jesus Christ, a gentle Father and the God of all consolation, who comforts us in all our sorrows, so that we can offer others, in their sorrows, the consolation that we have received from God ourselves.'

Out of my reflection on my experience, I now can find the Holy Spirit more truly within me, as I pray Psalm 139: 'It was you who created my inmost self, and put me together in my mother's womb; for all these mysteries I thank you: for the wonder of myself, for the wonder of your works' (Ps 139:13,14). To which, in the power of the Spirit, I am now able to respond in heartfelt praise to His glory, 'Amen'.

Your personal experience of life is unique. It is yours. The lives of others may impinge on yours, as yours on theirs. Yet, your personal experience is distinct and different from theirs – even if you watch the same sunset!

Such is your value before God. He fashioned your uniqueness. He loves it. He finds his image there – in embryo. He wants you to co-operate with Him in growing into the fullness of life. This is your destiny.

If I asked darkness to cover me,
and light to become night around me,
that darkness would not be dark to you,
night would be as light as day (Ps 139:11).

3 Listening

Let us look at the experience I shared of reflecting on a beautiful sunset. Awareness, reflection and the breath of God – the Holy Spirit – transformed what could have been an ordinary human experience, namely, watching a sunset, into a Gospel experience. A Gospel experience is a coming of the kingdom, now. It is the transformation of the seemingly ordinary into a Christian reality, and then into the experience of Christ being present with us.

The second experience I shared was the queen conch shell episode. In addition to personal experience, awareness and reflection, there was a *listening* to one's own mixed feelings. There was *discernment* of God's presence and call, an awareness of personal resistance combined with attraction to His presence. These vital elements are fundamentally interrelated. The development of one – for example, awareness – leads to a keener listening and surer discernment, because in and through them all, the Spirit of God is working. The breath of God, the Holy Spirit, becomes the Healer and Teacher. In this section I wish to discuss the gift of listening at greater length.

The prophet Isaiah says, 'Listen to me. Pay attention to me; listen, and your soul will live' (55:2,3). Perhaps we ask ourselves why is it so important to listen? Why is it so important to listen to God? Isaiah has answered that for us. 'Listen and your soul will live.' In the same chapter he says, 'For my thoughts are not your thoughts, my ways not your ways – it is Yahweh who speaks' (v.8).

This makes it clear. If we wish to live, if we want to ensure that our thoughts are indeed God's thoughts and that our ways are His ways, then once again let us hear, 'pay attention, come to me: listen and your soul will live'.

To confirm what Isaiah has said let us listen to St John. 'Do you know why you cannot take in what I say? It is because you are unable to understand my language,' says Jesus (Jn 8:43). He continues, 'I speak the truth and for that very reason, you do not believe me. Can one of you convict me of sin? If I speak the truth, why do you not believe me?' (8:45). These are very important truths that we need to listen to and to hear. Jesus continues, 'A child of God listens to the words of God; if you refuse to listen, it is because you are not God's children' (8:47).

We need to allow the Lord Yahweh to open our ears and to learn the secret of being true listeners: Each morning he wakes me to hear, to listen like a disciple. The Lord Yahweh has opened my ear. (Is 50:4) We *hear*, when we listen with the Spirit of God which is a gift of the Lord Yahweh to us. In addition we recall the line from the psalmist: 'If only you will listen to him today, do not harden your hearts' (Ps 95:7,8).

To be able to listen and to hear, therefore, as God would

have us do, we need to allow the Spirit of God to open our ear and to ensure that we listen with a heart of flesh, not with a heart of stone. This is what we mean when we say 'the art of listening with the heart'. When we listen with the heart, we do more than merely listen to content. That is listening with the head. The head is of course necessary and has its role in listening. Listening with the head ensures that we are listening to facts, that in a measure we assess them and that we do not let our feelings run away with us. But fully recognising our God-given intellect, we need a balance between listening with the head and listening with the heart. Listening with the head only is not helpful in building relationships. Those who listen with the head only tend to erect barriers between themselves and others. They do not seem to be in touch with their own feelings or the feelings of other people. They appear to be selfish as if they are interested only in what appertains to their interests, their concerns, their precepts or their intellectual prowess. They need a measure of heart!

Body language

When the heart is well balanced with the head, the listener tends to listen as a whole person to the whole person of the other. Body language therefore is important. It speaks volumes. The listener with the heart notices the hunched shoulders of the other, the shaking hands, the eyes that dare not look into one's own, the expression on the face, the tension that is communicated.

The listener needs to be aware of his or her own body language. The listener's body language is often more clearly heard by the other than the words spoken. It helps the one who is in distress or who needs a listening ear when the listener is quiet, still, at ease. The attitude of the listener communicates itself clearly through the body, through unspoken words, especially through the eyes and most especially through the quality of the listener's awareness of the presence of God.

It is important to know why I listen. Am I a willing listener? Do I consider it a job, a duty or a privilege? When listening is understood as a privilege, then there is nothing more important than being fully present to the other. With that sense of privilege, the listener is fully aware, in the Spirit of God, that there is no need to solve problems, to do anything, to say the right thing or even the wise thing. That can be entrusted to the wisdom of God. The listener's main role is to be there in empathy with the one who is speaking, or weeping, or being angry, crying or whatever. The heart attitude of 'empathy' is necessary.

What is empathy?

Empathy needs to be distinguished from *sympathy*. Both are qualities of the heart. Empathy, however, goes deeper. One could say it has a greater dimension of intimacy.

Sympathy, at its best, is a genuine experience of sadness, of compassion for the plight of another, a genuine desire that it could be otherwise. Sympathy may lead one to take appropriate action, at great cost to oneself, to alleviate the burden of the other.

Empathy involves all the above, and more. It is the power of entering into another's personality and imaginatively experiencing the actual experience of the other. Empathy may mean participation in the pain of another at personal cost. Empathy, therefore, is an ability to appreciate more fully what the actual experience of another may be.

Empathy is a quality of the heart. It is given to those who are willing to be emptied of self and to transcend their ego. To let go of the ego is, of course, a life-long process. It is a gift of the Spirit and depends on our openness to it. It means that, with confidence, we learn to hand over every event to God. We entrust it to His safe keeping. Knowing that of ourselves we are nothing, we wait on the power and the love of God. We receive from Him a listening heart and words for the wearied. Then empathy makes us life-givers to others.

Empathy, therefore, requires us to walk in the moccasins of the other person. This is a difficult thing to do. If we are not empty of self, how can we care for others? If we do not understand or know ourselves how can we enter into the deep feelings of others? We can only try. The Lord is our fortress and we can trust in Him.

Empathy requires that in a particular situation, we are there not as a judge, not as a sentimentalist, not as one blind or deaf. We may clearly see the dark side of the one who is speaking. We may see the faults, the failures, the weaknesses that are obviously there. But the genuine listener is there in the Spirit of Christ. What is He teaching us? He condemns the sin but He loves the sinner. That is what we mean by saying that empathy requires us to be accepting of the other, wherever that other may be in life at this moment.

Empathy means that in this acceptance of the other we become a measure of hope to the other. By our non-judgemental attitude, we are opening the way to a new direction, to a possible change of approach, for the other. That results in a measure of faith and hope for them. Empathy is the humble recognition that the listener too is wounded, frail, a pilgrim in the unknown territory of another person. Therefore, one not only walks in the moccasins of the other, but more importantly takes off one's own sandals in the presence of a burning bush. This 'other' is the one with whom Jesus always identifies, as He reminded Saul on the road to Damascus: 'Why do you persecute me?' (Acts 9:4).

Empathy is the humble acknowledgment that the Spirit of God alone can plumb the depths of another, can know the truth, the reality, the desires and the hopes of the other person.

Empathy is being for the other, as Jesus was, irrespective of the degree of darkness in the situation. The listener is there to be a life-giver and a bringer of light into the darkness. For this the listener is totally dependent on the gift of the Holy Spirit. Such a listener is filled with a sense of privilege. She listens, therefore, not from an elevated position of personal strength or power. She listens humbly, aware of her own total dependence on the Spirit. She is aware of her own darkness. She does not let that intimidate her. Rather she focuses on the Light that transforms darkness, making it become light.

When a listener approaches such a situation, it needs to be from prayer and from much listening to the Spirit beforehand. The results of this kind of listening are over-whelming. Frequently, as the listener hears a story of pain that pierces the heart, or hears the anguish of one caught in spiritual warfare, the end result often surprises. Healing and liberation come not only to the one suffering but to the listener! In the power of the Spirit, mutual growth and healing take place. Isaiah says, 'Listen, listen to me, and you will have good things to eat and rich food to enjoy. Pay attention, come to me; listen, and your soul will live' (55:2,3).

A listening experience

When I began to write about 'listening' I felt urged in prayer to go out among the people and listen. I went into a fish-and-chip shop. The space was very limited. It was a bitterly cold day. Perhaps the cold made us a pretty soulless group of people. I was trying to listen. There seemed to be little communication between us. I smiled at a little girl who was splashing vinegar on her chips. For a moment, her mother half looked and half smiled at me. We were there seemingly for one purpose only, to get our food, to get home and be comfortable. I felt depressed as I listened.

Suddenly I became aware of a change in the atmosphere. I continued to listen. I looked around. I saw space where there had been none behind me. Then I understood why. A traveller of the road stood now in that deserted area. Those around, perhaps unconsciously, had drawn closer together, leaving space around the stranger.

My interior listening became more acute. Silently, out of nowhere, an authority figure replaced a young attendant. It was all so polite! Yet the travelling man dominated the scene in a strange way. His presence made people uncomfortable. A certain freedom emanated from him. His needs were simple, a cup of coffee. He had money for that. He was cheerfully independent of us all. His belongings were under his right arm; his coffee he lifted with the left hand. I opened the door. Our eyes met. I saw a flicker of surprise, then a half smile of amusement. For me, things changed quickly and radically. I was the one taken off my feet by the God of surprises. As I met that glance, the eyes that met me were those that Peter had seen: 'And the Lord turning looked at Peter.' I managed to close the door.

In a flash my life passed before me. Innumerable incidents came to mind where I had not listened as I ought. Too late now, I saw how often Jesus of Nazareth had passed my way, had looked at me, but I had not recognised him.

In that moment, standing at that closed door, I became vulnerable to Jesus. In my heart I heard the words of the Gospel narrative: 'And Peter went out and wept bitterly.'

Perhaps like me, you too have tears to shed? Tears for past experiences of darkness? The most subtle darkness is that which we will not see. Only God can help us. Job says, 'God robs the depths of their darkness, brings deep shadow to the light' (Job 12:22). He is the God who said: 'Let there be light shining out of darkness' (2 Cor 4:6).

To summarise, the art of listening with the heart involves more than listening to words. It means being present humbly to another, to oneself, to each event, to life's circumstances. Such listening involves a resting in the Spirit, a being filled and used in each situation by the Spirit, to the glory of God.

**'Believe in the light
and you will become sons of light'** (Jn 12:36).

4 Feelings

There is an interdependence between listening, awareness and reflecting. In this human-spiritual growth process the one leads to the other. For example, the more we become aware and reflect on that awareness, the keener becomes our listening. When, on the other hand, we begin with listening, this inevitably leads to a keener awareness and a deeper reflection.

Listening and *feelings* go hand in hand. They support one another. They enlighten one another. Together they enrich our personal experience. They are special gifts of the Spirit of God in our human-spiritual growth process. They are invaluable. Continually they help us grow into our true image, the likeness of God.

Unfortunately, due to background, culture, education, social customs, too often people are not in touch with their feelings. Consequently they do not recognise them and do not know how to handle them. In fact, many seem to fear emotions. They fear they will be sucked into a vortex without knowing how to cope.

Those who are free in themselves are able to cope with their own feelings and to understand and enter into the feelings of others. It is unfortunate that in the area of feelings, restrictions were placed on so many since childhood. Men, for example, were not supposed to cry, to show tender feelings, to participate in the rearing of the children. They were expected to be very macho. Their *anima* was neglected while the *animus* was overstressed. On the whole, that is changing, but not quickly enough, nor far enough yet.

Women, on the other hand, often felt that they were second-class citizens. Their intelligence didn't seem to matter. In their homes and families they were taken for granted. Their qualities of loving, of nurturing, of giving life began to turn sour. All of this is regrettable and we need to learn from that unfortunate experience now. Feelings play a vital role in our development as a human being.

To be a listener of the heart, we need to be in touch with our feelings. To be compassionate with our neighbour we need to be 'feeling' people. To be followers of Christ, we need to recognise that it is in the area of our feelings that the Spirit of the Risen Christ moves.

We all have both positive and negative feelings. It is reasonably easy to get in touch with our positive feelings.

We are happy to claim any of the following: are you cheerful, happy, sanguine, contented, generous, kind, considerate, loving, tender, compassionate, open, playful? The list is infinite. It adds zest to living when we begin to recognise our own positive feelings.

Discover from your own experience, not just from wishful thinking, what these feelings are. In listening to yourself become aware of how you are feeling at this moment. Be honest. Are you, for example, tender hearted? If that is real, then be grateful. Reflect on it for a little while, because it is difficult to get to know our real selves. Ask yourself, 'am I tender hearted, kind, compassionate to *everyone*? Or am I selective?' You are selective in your tenderness, in your compassion, if you discover there is an ulterior motive in your manifesting compassion or tenderness to someone. Again you are selective if you find you are compassionate to some but not to everybody. The learning here is that even a 'good' feeling can have its dark spots. The discovery of that is a gift of the Spirit. We know then what to pray for and where we have to be careful.

Negative feelings are not so easy to claim. They can be recognised all right. I am angry, I am envious, I am jealous, I am hard hearted. This is my darker side, but I need to befriend my feelings so as to know my truth. So often today, particularly in the ministry of healing, grown adults are seen to be suffering still from the pain inflicted on them in childhood. Children can often experience much injustice, abuse of various kinds from parents and from significant people in their lives. The result frequently is severe emotional disorder. Consequently, many who have been damaged are laden with fear. And we must never forget that it takes perfect love to cast out fear. Emotional disorder is also experienced by those who have witnessed or participated in such abuse. The abused often themselves become the abusers.

As I have already said, people who are free are at ease with their feelings. They do not fear to be in touch with them. They do not fear to probe deeper. They do not even fear to make mistakes. For them it is a learning experience.

Yet to become free is in itself a slow, life-long process. It comes from within.

It was in America at a time when I was only beginning to understand the importance of feelings in human-spiritual growth. Fifty of us from all over the world were following a course on leadership. At Christmas time, at my request, my community generously invited an Australian to visit them, as she was far from home.

Easter came. I turned down two invitations with families to have, instead, a meal with the Australian lady. However, when she received an invitation which pleased her more, she had no compunction about turning me down without even saying so! My Easter Sunday dinner was spent on the campus, with squirrels as companions, and two beef sandwiches to console me. An Agatha Christie book held upside down alerted me to the turmoil of my feelings. The ingratitude and the rejection incensed me. Suddenly loneliness hit me. I panicked. I dashed to the telephone, just to talk, to share my wrath. All my human contacts, however, were avoiding calls as they celebrated Easter.

Alone in my small bedroom, I began to tremble. I felt powerless, out of control and caught in a welter of emotions. I didn't understand myself. Usually I could cope! I just sat and sat. Eventually, I became more quiet, less distraught. Then, somewhere in my being, I heard what I have never forgotten: 'You are hurt. You are angry. Stop running. Look. Reflect. Enter more deeply into the eye of the hurricane. I am there, waiting to heal you.'

It took me about two hours of reflection before I could let the Spirit move me to recognise and claim every feeling I had experienced. I understood later that this was how I entered more deeply into the eye of the hurricane. I could not be healed until I had claimed my feelings. When I did, the action of the Healer was instantaneous. I was both healed and transformed. A shame-faced returned Australian wanderer, full of excuses, became silent in the presence of the joy and peace I experienced.

I had been taught something of inestimable value. To be healed I had first to recognise my feelings, claim them, acknowledge my powerlessness, and listen to the guidance of the Spirit. Then I could be healed! The dark feelings which we all experience at times are deprived of much of their power when we rest in God and trust Him. 'Yahweh, my light and my salvation, whom need I fear?' (Ps 27:1).

Yahweh, you yourself are my lamp,
my God lights up my darkness;
With you I storm the barbican,
with my God I leap the rampart (Ps 18:28–9).

5 Discerning

Discernment is one of the vital elements of our personal experience, linking in with awareness, listening, reflecting, feeling and, of course, the presence of the Holy Spirit.

Discernment is a growing ability to listen to *movements* within one's being. Movements are interior attractions *to* God or *away* from Him.

Discernment involves a willingness to wait on God's revealing word or action which confirms that it is truly His Spirit that is moving me.

Discernment involves an openness and a willingness to be obedient to God's call to us to take necessary decisions, and in it we must be aware, to the best of our ability, of all the facts that are relevant to the issue being discerned. We listen with all our being to what the Spirit is saying to us. We get in touch with our feelings and reflect on the whole process.

Movements
The movements within one's being are a reality. Sometimes these movements draw us to God, at other times unfortunately they draw us away and towards our own satisfaction.

When we follow the attraction to God, we experience a feeling of peace, or joy, or love, or some other positive response.

When, on the other hand, we yield to selfish interests and reject the attraction to God, we are left with a negative feeling. This may be something like irritation, anger, frustration, restlessness, a sense of disharmony within ourselves and with other people.

These interior movements, as we call them, alert us to the necessity of discerning the various spirits, good and bad spirits about which St Paul speaks in Galatians 5: 'Since self-indulgence is the opposite of the Spirit, the Spirit is totally against such a thing, and it is precisely because the two are so opposed that you do not always carry out your good intentions. If you are led by the Spirit, no law can touch you. When self-indulgence is at work the results are obvious: fornication, gross indecency and sexual irresponsibility; idolatry and sorcery; feuds and wrangling, jealousy, bad temper and quarrels; disagreements, factions, envy; drunkenness, orgies and similar things' (vv. 16–20). 'What the Spirit brings is very different: love, joy, peace, patience, kindness, goodness, trustfulness, gentleness and self-control' (v. 22). 'Since the Spirit is our life, let us be directed by the Spirit. We must stop being conceited, provocative and envious' (v. 26).

We need to discern the action and the results of the spirits that are active. Look therefore to their *direction*, their forward movement. If they are leading us into peace, joy, love, etc. then this is confirmation that the spirit is of God. If, on the contrary, we are being led into confusion, into anger, irritation, deceit, animosity towards the neighbour, self-centred activity and attitudes, the spirit that is active is not of God. We must turn to God humbly, implore His help, repent of our sinfulness, trust Him, and begin again.

Discernment and prayer

If one wants to become a discerning person, it is necessary to take daily prayer seriously and to be committed to integrating prayer and action, so that our insights in prayer result in sound Christian behaviour. It is by good fruit, i.e. sound Christian behaviour, that one recognises that the Spirit is confirming that insights in prayer genuinely come from the good Spirit. To suit his own purpose, the enemy can at times give good thoughts with the intent of misleading us later. Hence the need for discernment! Through discerning, one becomes therefore more obedient to the voice of God. One listens with the intent of hearing and doing.

A deepening of our prayer relationship with God helps the growth of discernment. The awareness, reflection, listening, feeling, that take place in prayer and in life helps us develop a greater sensitivity to the presence of the Spirit within us. Through this prayer relationship, we become more at home with Him who makes His home in us. Likewise we become more eager to recognise His ways in our life and to feel His touch in our hearts.

This deeper sensitivity brings our mind, our heart, our emotions, our whole being into harmony. This growing harmony within ourselves and between God and us, reaches out also to a better understanding and acceptance of our neighbour.

Prayer likewise helps to make us more aware of our resistance to the Spirit. We recognise our efforts to escape from reality and to hide behind masks. We discern our folly more easily!

Discernment leads to reality

Discernment helps us to become aware of psychological blocks or imbalances which tend to distort both our view of ourself and our view of God. An imbalance tends to focus us on 'self' rather than on God. It clouds discernment. Through prayer and reflection we become more discerning, therefore more real. We more easily 'sense' or discover the real God, and the real us.

The 'caricature' God, the result perhaps of poor teaching, is revealed to us through discernment when we are open and listening. We can be quite disconcerted by discovering our 'false god'. It can shock us to discover how we respond to this false image. We treat God as if he were a sadist, a tyrant or a taskmaster. Rarely does genuine love enter in. How can it? We are transferring images from past experiences in the history of our wounded self on to God. We do not know a real God, a loving God!

At other times, our caricature of God is that of a 'soft God', who can be cajoled, manipulated, made manageable. This is an effort to control our God as we learnt in the past to control parents or significant adults. There is great need here for genuine prayer and true discernment, for they help us to come to know our real selves. The darkness of blindness is transformed into seeing more clearly. Ultimately we come to know a much deeper truth about ourselves and about God.

There is nothing magical about discernment. It is the action of the Spirit. But discernment is based on certain facts as we know them in our limited knowledge. If new factors come to light, then a new discernment is necessary. We are frail, therefore we may misinterpret or hear incorrectly. Consequently we say that discernment is limited and temporary by reason of the limitations of our human experience.

Confirmation of the discernment made is always necessary to ensure that the discernment is of God. Confirmation may take the form of quiet peace, of peace even when things are difficult, of surrender to God. In short an experience of, 'My peace I give to you'.

Confirmation may also come from outside, whether from people or from circumstances. This kind of confirmation is less open to self-deception and therefore more convincing and reassuring. A letter or a suggestion which comes from an experienced and wise person on the same lines as one's own discernment is strengthening, particularly when that person is not aware that one is currently involved in a discernment.

There will be more on discernment later as we begin *Prepare the Way*.

**'Yahweh, you yourself are my lamp,
my God lights up my darkness'** (2 Sam 22:29).

6 Breathing

We can all breathe. We take it for granted. We rarely think of thanking God for it. Still more rarely do we praise Him and glorify Him for it!

Rarely are we aware of the fact that we are breathing, until perhaps we suffer from asthma or a heavy cold. Then we begin to appreciate our breathing when it flows in and out more easily again. Our breathing can remind us of the breath of God, namely, the Holy Spirit. Just as we breathe naturally and are unaware of it, we can unfortunately do the same with the breath of God within us. We remain unaware and unreflective. Let us begin to remedy that now.

Experience reflective breathing

Breathe deeply. Focus quietly on the Holy Spirit within you. Take it slowly. Rest in awareness. Focus on that still presence. The Spirit is unobtrusive. He waits patiently until we become aware, listen, get in touch with our feelings, and reflect. Perhaps then we discern the presence of the living God within us through the power of the Spirit.

Breathe in deeply. Breathe in the power of God who is present in your breath. Become aware of our independence. We can be so independent of God. Yet we are more dependent for a share in God's life than we are for natural life or natural breath. Sinners though we are, we can be so arrogant. Yet God loves us. No matter what we do or are, He longs to give us light and abundance of life.

You have become distracted perhaps or are disturbed? You lack peace. Focus again on your breathing. As you breathe, focus on the still presence within. Now, consciously focused on the Spirit as you are, draw in a deep breath. Let the Spirit of God flow into your mind. Recall Yahweh's words – 'Your thoughts are not my thoughts.' Let the Spirit of God, through the breath of God, cleanse your thoughts. Hand over your mind to be filled with God.

Your emotions may be disturbed. Hand over your emotions to God, drawing in the breath of God, the Holy Spirit. Let the Holy Spirit enter into every nook and cranny of your emotions. Thank Him, praise and glorify Him. As you breathe out, empty yourself of all your pain, your sorrow, your anguish.

Your senses can be distracting. They can lead you to God or from God. Hand over your senses one by one to the care of God. Hand over your eyes, then your ears, your sense of touch and taste, your sense of smell. Let the breath of God, which, in a spirit of faith, you have drawn in, refresh your senses. Let each of your senses be cleansed. Then let each of them be filled with the presence of God.

Breathe for others
You can go still further. What you have done for yourself, you can do for other people. Begin with your immediate family. Then extend it to whomsoever you will, be it at home, in the underground, on the farm, in the streets, on the football pitch – everywhere.

This simple exercise of breathing naturally and finding the breath of God in it, through the power of the Spirit, can help you 'sense' God's presence wherever you are. If you are at a bus stop or walking on the street, doing housework, climbing a hill, taking care of children, whatever, breathe deeply. Focus on God. You can use that breathing to ask for the gift of becoming more aware. Include others always in your prayer for yourself. If you are unreflective, let your breathing be a prayer for that grace. The same holds for the gift of listening and for the gift of being in touch with your feelings, and the same for the gift of discernment. Always go beyond your own needs to include those of other people, the people of God.

You recall that we use many gifts when coping with our personal experience, like awareness, reflecting, listening, getting in touch with feelings and discerning. I want to adapt a beautiful saying of St Paul to encompass these gifts.

St Paul advised the Colossians to put on love 'over all the clothes' of compassion, kindness, humility, gentleness and patience (Col 3:14). I suggest, that we, too, put on love, over the gifts of listening, discerning, feeling, reflecting and being aware. In this way, our breathing will be a reminder of God's love which is manifest in all His gifts. Likewise the use of all these gifts will remind us of the love and the presence of God's Spirit. Let us breathe in love, breathe out love and fill God's world with His own gift of love.

Yahweh is my light and my salvation (Ps 27:1).

7 Light and Darkness – The real and the unreal

God is the only absolute reality. All else is relative. If we wish to live in the light of God's presence, we need to discern the real and the unreal. Choosing what is real increases the light. The unreal holds us in the dark.

Take a simple example from the experience of a child. Parents or a favourite adult appear perfect and wonderful to a child. Eventually experience reveals their clay feet. Disillusion hurts! The hurting, however, facilitates the letting go of unreality. The real goodness in the same adults eventually shines through and strengthens the relationship between them. The relationship is now more real. Darkness has been transformed!

Fear
Like illusion, fear can hold many of us in the dark. When someone says to me, 'I am afraid of nothing and nobody', I know that I question that statement! It may be true. It

may be a reality for this person. I still am aware that I question it.

There may perhaps be an area within such a person, or a past experience, which 'fear' does not allow to be explored. It may be that such a person has not yet encountered within himself any manifestation of the dark; any encounter with the unknown, any experience of being out of control, of being powerless to take control.

Perhaps such a person has not yet been tested by God: 'it is a terrible thing to fall into the hands of Almighty God' (Ex 34:10). Perhaps this over-confident person who protests that he fears nothing and nobody, has never been engaged in the struggle 'against the sovereignties and the powers' against whom St Paul warns us to 'put God's armour on so as to be able to resist the devil's tactics' (Ep 6:11–12).

It has been said that more people die as a result of fear than from killing or from war. I cannot vouch for that. I have, however, learnt in my own life and ministry, that fear is the pernicious reality which underlies many of the frailties of our human nature.

For example, underlying much psychosomatic illness is a layer of fear. We may know a person who cannot or will not walk, or who cannot or will not speak. This may be directly attributable to an unconscious and paralysing fear of someone, something, some memory, some failure that grips.

Why is it that so often I find it difficult to trust God? Is it not partly my fear of the unknown field out there? Am I afraid of this unknown God who may ask more of me than I can give? Am I afraid of trusting too much and running the risk of being deceived?

Why is there so much mediocrity in the world? Is it perhaps fear of what others may say or think about us? Is it fear that I may be overstretching my actual ability? Yet as a teacher, I used to marvel at the achievements of determined pupils who intellectually were but middle grade. Their work lacked the sparkle of genius, yet it was more than adequate. It was good. They did not know, or acknowledge or accept that enemy called 'fear', which others would call 'their limitations'.

Human frailties

I will group human frailties under the categories of 'external', 'psychological' and 'natural characteristics'. This is a very rough division. There is nothing scientific about it. It is meant to stimulate awareness about one's own reality or unreality, awareness of one's own experience, awareness of the dark that needs transformation into light.

'External' fear may be fear of dark, lonely places, of fierce or not-so-fierce animals, of violence, failure, rejection, poverty, loneliness, homelessness, isolation, being unsuccessful, unable to provide adequately for self or dependants . . .

'Psychological' fear underlies a poor self-image: not sufficiently capable, not dependable, friendless, broken relationships, anxieties, make-believe, mask-wearing, over-spending, loud and aggressive behaviour, inward shrinking, overly dependent, insufficiently independent, ill-health, psychosomatic symptoms, living fearfully in the future, clinging to the past, avoiding the present, exaggeration – in speech, behaviour, gestures, claims.

Fear is present, too, in 'natural characteristics': untruthful, wilful, destructive, unreliable, untrustworthy, deceitful, sharp, mean, cold, unloving . . . Do we not see here fear of consequences, fear of others, fear of becoming a 'nobody'?

Masks

Our response to this darkness of fear is often to wear masks. Do we not do it in some measure some of the time? This wearing of masks is closely associated with 'fear' of 'the real and the unreal' in life. Do we have a visitor's face, an at home face, a Sunday go-to-church face, a playing prank face or a disapproving face?

This is a form of our darkness in the sense that we are not yet fully free to be our *real* self. As we mature and become more free, mask-wearing becomes less necessary. It can be an accepted defence mechanism for those who are extremely vulnerable and are trying to cope with life. But it is well to help people recognise the pretence or the unreality behind mask-wearing. By facing the unreality, it helps us to let the masks gradually go. Thus we move into greater reality.

Growing from the unreal into the real is a part of our process of growth. It is part of our personal experience. The growth process is strengthened with our turning to God. By handing a situation over to God, by imploring the Holy Spirit to bring us to light out of darkness, the 'real' is already taking over!

Frequent use, therefore, of God's gifts of awareness, reflecting, listening, getting in touch with feeling, and discerning what is happening, becomes our support. It is a day of relief and of growing freedom when eventually I discover and accept that this is who I am. I am anything but perfect. I am growing. I am not always my real self. I am, however, discerning more easily the unreal that impinges. Then I am able to accept that the struggle still goes on. I am not now living in a fantasy world. I recognise what is happening. I experience God within me, helping me. In recognising the measure of unwholeness that is within me I am accepting that for now the light is shining more clearly than before, but the process of transformation still goes on: 'Let there be light shining out of darkness' (2 Cor 4:6).

The process of the real

The more we allow God, the only absolute reality, to enter into our present experience, the more real we become. I need to become aware of my own particular areas of darkness. I need to claim them. I need to hand them over to God who will heal me.

To 'recognise' my frailty or darkness is not enough. It is a first step in the process. I must now 'claim' that this alloy of light and darkness is in me. Is me. This claiming is a movement of self-surrender within me. Claiming is a statement. I am led to say unequivocally:

I am now ready to move forward.
I reject this darkness, this frailty.
I cannot heal myself.

> I surrender with trust to the Light.
> The Healer, who is light, who reads my heart,
>   knows that now I am ready to be stripped.
> I recognise that this same process must continue.

The transformation of the darkness of our human frailties, by the light of Christ, into greater wholeness, is a gradual process. It can happen in this present moment if I am responsive. It continues throughout the whole of our lives.

The healing experience of light which is now transforming a darkness, is, at the same time, illuminating that same darkness. In the healing of what is unwhole, I actually see its unwholeness more clearly. Thus my awareness of the subtlety of darkness, of the deceit of the prince of darkness becomes more real.

Though Satan is conquered, he never gives up. When great gain is impossible for him, because of one's fidelity to the Light of Christ, he is content if even for one moment he can gain a resting place within our being. But our strength is in the Lord, the Invincible One. What have we to fear? 'With God on our side who can be against us'? (Rm 8:31). Our God hears our cry and stoops to us. Of him, we can say joyfully:

> He has pulled me out of the horrible pit,
> Out of the slough of the marsh,
> has settled my feet on a rock
> and steadied my steps . . .
> He has put a new song in my mouth,
>   a song of praise to our God (Ps 40:2,3)

**Walk while you have the light,
or the dark will overtake you** (Jn 12:35).

8 The Sower – Mark 4:13–18

The parable of the *Sower* is familiar to all of us. You know how the seed fell on the path: some fell on rocky ground, some on thorny ground and some on good ground.

Christ explained the meaning of the whole parable to his disciples. In this section, I refer only to St Mark 4:13–17. In this passage Jesus said to them, 'Do you not understand this parable? Then how will you understand any of the parables? What the sower is sowing is the word. Those on the edge of the path where the word is sown are people who have no sooner heard it than Satan comes and carries away the word that was sown in them. Similarly those who receive the seed on patches of rock are people who, when first they hear the word, welcome it at once with joy. But they have no root in them, and they do not last; should some trial come, or some persecution on account of the word, they fall away at once.'

The sower, who is God, is every moment of our lives sowing a word, a seed or something that is meant to be life-giving to us. Here again we discover the importance of the gifts of awareness, listening, reflecting, feeling, discerning, and breathing. Without these gifts we are in danger of being like the people who receive the seed on the edge of the path. No sooner is it there than Satan comes and carries away the word that was sown. That can happen to us too if we are shallow and do not listen. We need to keep asking God to help us, through the Spirit. God's word to us can be lost if we do not pause and reflect on it, and if we do not apply it to our daily ordinary lives. A word or an experience that was meant to be life-giving for us dies, because we can be heedless or thoughtless.

You become aware, for example, of an elderly person who wants to cross the road. You do not reflect on what you have seen because something that panders to your own self-interest distracts you. The opportunity is lost! You might have joined a group of young people who are doing good works. Some were painting homes for the elderly, formed play groups to allow parents to have necessary leisure time for themselves. At first you were enthusiastic, but because there was no root, no reflection, you did not persevere. Perhaps you did not allow yourself to get in touch with your feelings. You did not give yourself time to recognise that selfish feelings were taking over. The Holy Spirit had sown seed in your life, but it did not last. His labour, unfortunately, was in vain.

Do we want to be responsible for letting God's word be spoken to us in vain? Do we want to have ears which do not hear, hearts that remain closed? If not, we need to take time to be still, to listen, to reflect. We are called to apply the teaching of the Spirit to our lives now. We must then go and do what we have discerned as His will for us.

**The Word was the true light
that enlightens all men** (1 Jn 1:9).

9 Prayer – what is it?

It is evident throughout the book that I consider as important to our human-spiritual growth process the gifts of awareness, reflecting, listening, feeling, discerning and breathing. These gifts are as important when we pray as when we communicate with another human being. It helps us to know that when we listen to another, reflect on what they say, reflect on how we speak to them, learn by reflection how our relationship is growing, or deteriorating because we are not using these gifts well, that our own prayer life is being affected. We use the same gifts whether we communicate with God or with one another. We are the same person, with the same heart, the same desires and the same blind spots.

By using these gifts in the power of the Spirit of God, it happens eventually that life itself helps our prayer, in fact can become prayer. If I am doing a business deal, breathing the gift of the Spirit of peace and love upon the person, aware of kingdom values and of the Spirit within us, then my reflection on that encounter will draw me to my special prayer time to listen to God about my day. There will be less talk about being too busy to pray.

What is prayer? Prayer is whatever unites us with God, brings us to an awareness of God, to a love of God, to a longing for God, to surrender to God. That is prayer. Whatever makes us aware of how far we are from God is also a form of prayer. It is real. For example, you are angry with God. You feel alienated with regard to all things spiritual. Yet, somehow, somewhere within your being, you are still seeking God. In this whole process there is a movement of prayer.

Prayer is building a relationship with God. We build it whenever we are in touch with who we are before God. We want to be real. We want to know the real 'God. We question the truth and the sincerity of our longings. We are willing to take steps to develop that relationship no matter what the cost. We are in earnest therefore about trying to build that relationship with God. This is prayer.

When we say that relationship with God is paralleled with relationship with one another, what does that really mean? We are the same people, the work of God's hands, gifted with the same qualities, the same mind and heart and senses, the same desires. From the way we relate to human beings we can learn how we are relating to God. For example, if you were to say, 'I don't know how I am relating to God', then I would ask, 'Do you know how you relate to other people? Are you open with them? Are you trusting? Are you genuinely concerned about them and their interests and ready to help them by putting yourself on the line?' The same questions apply to your relationship with God. You will find that the answers to both questions are similar.

Whether we are building a relationship with God or with human beings, a few things are necessary. We must be real. We must be open and generous. We must give time. We must share who we really are, sharing the weak as well as the strong side. We must be willing to listen as well as to speak. We must be willing to hear what is really being said, even if it disturbs us.

In prayer I find that too many people are afraid to be their real selves. They feel they have to show a good side to God. I have heard people say, 'If God really knew me the way I am, He would have no more to do with me. I have to get my act in order first.' What kind of a relationship is that? Could that person's prayer be fruitful? It is based on unreality. It seems to imply that God does not know us through and through. Do we not accept that God knows areas of darkness in us that He has not yet revealed even to us? Have we not yet learnt that no matter what darkness is within us, nothing will ever change the degree or the quality of God's love for us? He loves us with an unchanging, everlasting love. Of course it is true that God wants to draw us from darkness to light. He wants to give us abundance of life. Therefore in our conversations together, which is prayer, He will call me to renounce my dark self and move into His light. But His love never lessens, never changes.

The old catechism definition of prayer is: 'Prayer is a raising of the mind and the heart to God.' I like that. The raising of the mind and the heart says to me that already in the very act of praying we are being lifted up out of the murkiness of our dark selves into the light of love that is God. It says more than that. The mind and the heart are both involved in this reality of prayer. I find this integration of head and heart important. This implies that a good thought which is given remains only a thought, until we allow our feelings to refresh it, as it were. This refreshment is the power of the Spirit which involves the whole of our being and draws us into action, which is the fruit of the thought.

Lately I saw this definition which made me smile: 'It is impossible to lose your footing on your knees.' There is genuine humility there. There is also a being rooted in reality.

If my prayer is a reaching up and into God, while remaining rooted in the reality of my God-given circumstances, then that prayer is sound. My circumstances at the moment may be clothed in darkness, in turmoil, in trouble. Nevertheless, the prayer that is rooted in humility allows the light of God's saving presence to conquer the darkness, to strengthen my frailty and eventually to clothe me with light.

Gandhi's definition of prayer as 'the key of the morning and the latch of the evening' has a desirable contemplative note. It stresses the continuity of prayer throughout the day; the presence of God in all things; and the ability to rest in Him. That definition delights me.

For me prayer has also a trinitarian dimension. It is the overshadowing of each one of us by the Spirit. Through the Spirit Christ comes to life in our ordinary daily life experience, our Bethlehem. This is all the work and the gift of the Spirit, to the praise and glory of the Father.

Prayer, understood in this way, happens not only in formal prayer times but at every moment of the day, whether we eat, drink or whatever we do. The essence of prayer is the recognition that it is all the work of the Spirit. The result of such prayer is our ongoing growth into Christ, through the action of the Spirit.

This kind of prayer requires the simple heart of a child. Jesus says, 'of such is the Kingdom'. He seems to favour those who have a trusting heart, an open childlike heart, a heart that focuses on Him in love, a heart that through dependence on Him, is saying without words 'I love you'. This kind of prayer is a matter of God's choice. It is not reserved for 'special' people, as is sometimes erroneously thought. Rather it requires above all an uncomplicated openness of being, a childlike attitude of heart and mind.

The deepest picture of the prayer experience that I can imagine is when the Father looks at His Son Jesus and sees a beloved child cradled in the heart of Jesus. As the psalmist says: 'like a child in its mother's arms, as content as a child that has been weaned' (Ps 131:2). None of this can happen through our striving. It is God's gift. It is given and it is achieved solely in the power of love, which is the Spirit.

Though we cannot of ourselves attain to this kind of prayer, we can desire it. We can, through fidelity, through sincerity, and through surrender to God in our daily living, prepare ourselves to receive it, if such is God's plan for us.

The base line in prayer must always be humility. For us sinners to be able to come before God at all in prayer, is privilege. When we come to prayer, it helps to praise, glorify and thank God for whatever kind of prayer He is planning to give us today. We are willing therefore to pray as is given to us. If our prayer is dry, we look first to see if we are responsible for that dryness. Then we ask God to help us do what we should do. But always we praise Him, even for the dryness which is teaching us something, and for the opportunity of surrendering to Him.

Sometimes my prayer will be filled with distraction. I will talk to Him about those distractions, as a troubled child would with a trusted parent. I will ask Him to teach me how to avoid those distractions. I will listen and I will try to be obedient to His voice.

One thing is very clear. If I am genuinely eager to build a relationship of prayer with God, then I need a daily discipline of prayer in my life.

A discipline of prayer

When people want to excel as artists, painters, writers, sculptors, musicians, in sport, in anything, what do they do? We know that they devote hours to being taught, to learning, to training, to disciplining themselves. They have the desire to excel, and they have the will power to use the necessary means. Can we say the same about ourselves with regard to prayer? Only God Himself, through the Spirit, can teach us the art of speaking to Him, of listening to Him, of being able to be with Him without words. Only He can strengthen our will to persevere when it becomes difficult. We must always be mindful of our fallen state and of our frailty. If we are to grow into mature children of God, we need a daily prayer diet. Fidelity to daily prayer gives us the necessary moral fibre to keep our focus on God and His plan for us, namely to grow into His image and likeness.

Fifteen minutes daily is a foundation for beginners. For those who are in earnest it needs to increase gradually to thirty minutes daily. An hour is necessary for those who are more proficient in prayer.

We need to decide the specific hour at which we are going to pray each day.

We need to decide the place in which we are going to pray. We need a place where we can be quiet. It helps if we create an atmosphere in that place, such as an icon or a candle or whatever helps the individual. If it is necessary, we need to arrange to be left undisturbed.

We also need to know how long we are going to spend in prayer, whether it is the fifteen minutes for beginners, half an hour, or an hour. We need to be faithful to the length of time.

Remote preparation

It helps if, about ten minutes before the scheduled time, we begin to become relaxed and to wind down. To do this, we begin to move more slowly, to become more quiet. It helps if we begin to look forward to our meeting with Almighty God. It also helps to know if we are going to use a book, the Scriptures, or if we are going to talk to God about the circumstances of our daily life. None of this can be left to chance. So far we are clear about the length of time which we are giving to prayer, the hour at which we are going to pray, the place in which we are going to pray and the material for our prayer.

Consider also posture. Are we going to pray while we kneel, sit, lie on the floor? It is well to avoid changing position so that stillness is not disturbed.

Immediate preparation

I find that the most important part of the prayer period is the beginning, when we take time to become still. Too many rush into the book or the Scriptures, or perhaps a prayer that appeals to them. To do this without letting the Spirit lead us is folly.

Just let your body be quiet before God. Let your mind

become still. Hand your mind over to the Spirit of God to be cleansed of all that is not of Him.

Do the same with your emotions, your feelings, your senses. Hand each of them over to God, reverently, one by one.

Ask Him to cleanse them and fill them with His Spirit so that they are channels of light in your prayer.

Hand your whole being over to God so that His Spirit takes possession of you. When you are utterly still, rest in the Spirit who is within you. Rest in His love, like a child on its mother's breast. Do not move even to reading Scripture, until the Spirit within you urges you to the next move. Then follow the movement of the Spirit.

Let us suppose therefore that you want to talk to God either about a human relationship that is disturbing you, or about your relationship with God himself. Speak to Him about your present awareness, like a child to its beloved parent, or as friend to friend. Be present to God within you. Do what is right, natural, and fitting for you in those circumstances. Let us suppose therefore that you have talked to God and spent some time in silence with Him. You will gradually learn how to listen to Him. He will usually speak to you through the movements within you. Become aware of those attractions. Thank Him for them. Become aware also if you have resistances within you to what He is saying to you. Talk to Him about those resistances. He will teach you through them.

Thank Him for allowing you to be with Him. Thank Him for the good things He has given you in your life. Thank Him most especially for challenging you! He is telling you that you are growing; that your weaknesses are changing into more of His strength; that His grace is sufficient for you.

How you behave in prayer will depend upon the movement of the Spirit within you, and your own willingness to co-operate. If you are filled with remorse or regret, tell Him that. If you are aware of any kind of bondage in which you are held, you need to talk to Him about that above all. Take time with the question of bondage.

Remember always to be real, to be open, to be sincere,

and all will be well. God is able to bring good out of any evil. He is the light of the world. He shines in darkness. He always conquers the darkness. It does not matter if you are nervous, or courageous, or willing to risk, or unable to trust God. Tell Him what is real for you. Remember He is already reading the depths of your heart. He wants you to be open and trusting with Him. You are only beginning to know the depths of your own heart! God reveals gradually in prayer, what is always an open book to Him, namely your real self. St Paul reminds us that the grace of God is always sufficient for whatever He reveals to us, or calls us to do.

It is also an act of trust in God to thank Him not only for what He has done and is doing for you, but for what He is going to complete in you. God always completes what He has begun. It is an act of trust and love to recognise that you can trust His love to care not only for your past, for your present, but also for your future: 'Lord, you are great, you are glorious, wonderfully strong, unconquerable' (Judith 16:16).

You may wish to intercede for other people who are burdened in various ways. It pleases God when we pray for others, for the other members of His body. Thank Him, not only for the help He is giving you but for the help He is giving to other people.

In prayer, perhaps something will have moved you. Something will have struck you. That is what is called an insight in prayer. You must reflect on that. The Spirit of God is urging you to put that insight into action this day, every day, until it becomes part of you.

For example, it may be that in prayer you recognise that you are irritable with your family, not easy to get on with. The obvious grace that you need is to ask God to give you a gentle and kind heart. During that day try to be gentle and kind. Try also to guard your tongue.

It may be that in prayer you get an insight into how selfish you can be. Try this day to concentrate on being selfless and on being concerned about other people. This is what we call the integration of prayer and life. It gives meaning to our prayer as we see how it can affect the quality of our living.

The process of saying our prayers and then trying to be better people is vastly different from totally integrating our prayer and our living. In this process of integration there is an ongoing, daily dynamic operating. We are all in danger of artificially separating what the secular world calls 'reality' from the spiritual. In prayer we focus on the Spirit of God who points out through 'movements in our being' the insight which is His special word for us today. We may be attracted or resistant to this.

The Spirit is continuously the focus throughout the day as one tries to put into practice in daily life the specific insight received in prayer. Even if one fails and fails again, a great deal is gained. A golden thread runs through the day from the gift of the prayer period. One tries to call on the Spirit to help. Perhaps that cry resounds in our hearts a few times. That is progress! At the nightly reflection time, one is again united with God. One learns even from the failure to call on the Spirit. The important point is that strength gradually comes from a clear focus – here it is on the action of the Spirit who is giving an insight in prayer. The focus continues through the day and as the effect is looked at in the nightly reflection, one becomes aware of the beneficial effect.

Gradually, through fidelity, this pattern of prayer transforming life becomes second nature.

As you advance in prayer, ask God to help you remember Him more frequently throughout the day. If you genuinely desire it, this is certainly a grace that He will give to you. This is when life becomes prayer. When that happens, you will discover that you are as concerned about other people as you are about yourself; even more so. You are not separating life from prayer and you are not setting yourself apart from all of God's people. Then you become more real. Life becomes real. God becomes real.

Hopefully you will find that fifteen minutes is indeed too short even for a simple way of daily prayer, like this. Hopefully, too, you will discover that this daily discipline of prayer has made you not only someone committed to prayer but someone who is growing as a fully alive human person.

In later sections we will deal with prayer at a deeper level.

I am the light of the world;
anyone who follows me will not be walking in the dark;
he will have the light of life (Jn 8:12).

10 Freedom – liberation from bondage

Interior *freedom* is the deep desire of every mature Christian. It is not something for which one can strive. The very striving prevents the freedom. It is more the result of the process of growth which is happening. Freedom is the crowning point when the Christian, led and sustained by the Spirit, has done one's best in the struggle against the ego. Freedom is never captured once and for all. It is a continual growing process. It is an experience of liberation from darkness and an entering into a measure of light. It is always a liberation from the self or from attack by the enemy. It is always Jesus through His Spirit continuing to save His people.

Freedom must never be confused with licence. St Paul makes it very clear. He says, 'You were called as you know to liberty but be careful or this liberty will provide an opening for self-indulgence. Serve one another rather in works of love since the whole of the law is summarised in a single command: *love your neighbour as yourself*. If you go snapping at each other and tearing each other to pieces, you had better watch or you will destroy the whole community.

'Let me put it like this: if you are guided by the Spirit you will be in no danger of yielding to self-indulgence, since self-indulgence is the opposite of the Spirit, the Spirit is totally against such a thing, and it is precisely because the two are so opposed that you do not always carry out your good intentions' (Ga 5:13–18).

St Paul goes on in the same chapter to show that bondage, the lack of true freedom, is the result of yielding to the spirits of darkness. By contrast he gives the influence of the good Spirit: 'What the Spirit brings is very different: love, joy, peace, patience, kindness, goodness, trustfulness, gentleness and self control . . . You cannot belong to Christ Jesus unless you crucify all self-indulgent passions and desires. Since the Spirit is our life, let us be directed by the Spirit' (Ga 5:22–6).

Freedom or liberation – understood in this sense of interior freedom – is an essential part of the gospel of salvation. Jesus came to set people free. As St Luke says, Jesus came to 'proclaim liberty to captives and to set the downtrodden free' (4:18).

Faith in Christ, however, is necessary to make this freedom possible.

Let's look for a moment at the two disciples on the way to Emmaus. They were not enjoying the freedom of the children of God as they travelled on their way from Jerusalem to Emmaus. Their lack of faith held them in bondage. Their idea of liberty had political connotations. It had very little to do with the interior spirit. They said, 'our own hope had been that Jesus would be the one to set Israel free' (Lk 24:21). It is this kind of bondage, this kind of blindness, which always remains when we are seeking our self-interest. That was the experience of those two disciples before their conversion. When Jesus set them free on the road to Emmaus, however, they then began to think of other people. They wanted to spread the good news of their freedom, to tell others about Jesus. They returned to Jerusalem. They found that Jesus had been there before them and had set their brethren free.

Spiritual warfare
Christian freedom results from the victorious death and resurrection of Jesus. In this way Satan was conquered. No

wonder that there will always be spiritual warfare between Christians who are genuinely following Jesus, and Satan, the enemy. St Paul says, 'this is what God has done; he has taken us out of the power of darkness and created a place for us in the Kingdom of the Son that He loves, and in Him we gain our freedom, the forgiveness of our sins.' (Col 1:13,14).

Here it is clearly stated that freedom results from the forgiveness of our sins. Such forgiveness is the work of the Spirit, 'where the Spirit of the Lord is, there is freedom' (2 Cor 3:17). The following verses give a description of freedom that moves the heart. 'And we, with our unveiled faces reflecting like mirrors the brightness of the Lord, all grow brighter and brighter as we are turned into the image that we reflect' (2 Cor 3:18). This ends in a triumphant cry of victory, 'this is the work of the Lord who is Spirit'.

Christ's first call is for us to repent of our sins. Confession of our sins to one another and to God is a liberating experience which can heal us of a variety of spiritual, mental and physical diseases. When we discover that we are in bondage of any kind the first step to liberation is forgiveness of sin. Hence the need for reconciliation. The role of purification is central to this liberation process from the bondage of sin. The result is true freedom. Christ himself taught that if we want to follow Him we must take up our cross daily. As we move out of our self-centredness we grow into greater freedom. We begin to concern ourselves more truly with our neighbour. We are all oppressed at times by the spirit of self-centredness, but to set our neighbour free is very pleasing to God.

Isaiah says that lying on sackcloth and ashes is not a form of fasting that Yahweh finds acceptable. He then continues: 'Is not this the sort of fast that pleases me' – it is the Lord Yahweh who speaks – 'to break unjust fetters, to undo the thongs of the yoke, to let the oppressed go free, and break every yoke, to share your bread with the hungry, and shelter the homeless poor, to clothe the man you see to be naked and not turn from your own kin? Then will your light shine like the dawn and your wound be quickly healed over . . . If you give your bread to the hungry, and relief to the oppressed, your light will rise in the darkness, and your shadows become like noon. Yahweh will always guide you, giving you relief in desert places' (Is 58:6,7,8,10,11).

Loving our neighbours and setting them free is a sure manifestation that we are already enjoying a measure of freedom: 'We have passed out of death and into life, and of this we can be sure because we love our brothers. If you refuse to love, you must remain dead' (1 Jn 3:14,15).

St John goes on to describe a rich man whose heart was closed to his neighbour. How could the love of God be living in him, he asks: 'My children, our love is not to be just words or mere talk, but something real and active; only by this can we be certain that we are children of the truth' (1 Jn 3:17–19).

And it is the same St John who in his gospel says of truth, 'You will learn the truth and the truth will make you free . . . So if the Son makes you free, you will be free indeed' (8:32,36).

The sign of confidence

Another sign of the action of the Spirit on us is that Christians who are free are filled with bold confidence. That means they have the freedom to say everything. They become fearless and keep the focus on Christ. Such a free Christian is led by the Spirit to act as a child of God: 'Let us be confident then in approaching the throne of grace, that we shall have mercy from Him and find grace when we are in need of help' (Heb 4:16).

This finding of grace is when we never let go of the faith that we have professed.

St John puts it in another way: 'Live in Christ, then, my children, so that if he appears, we may have full confidence, and not turn from him in shame at his coming.' (1 Jn 2:28).

We are filled with tremendous courage when we read the apostle John's call:

My dear people, if we cannot be condemned by our own conscience, we need not be afraid in God's presence, and whatever we ask him, we shall receive, because we keep his commandments and live the kind of life that he wants. His commandments are these: that we believe in the name of the Son Jesus Christ and that we love one another as He told us to. Whoever keeps his commandments lives in God and God lives in him. We know that He lives in us by the Spirit that He has given us (1 Jn 3:21–24).

The free man no longer lives by the spirit of a slave but by the spirit of an adopted son. He can proclaim with Paul:

All I want is to know Christ and the power of His resurrection and to share His sufferings by reproducing the pattern of His death. That is the way I can hope to take my place in the resurrection of the dead. Not that I have become perfect yet: I have not yet won, but I am still running, trying to capture the prize for which Christ Jesus captured me (Ph 3:10–12).

The ideal of the free person is to speak thus and to be able to proclaim proudly with St Paul, 'for me to live is Christ' (Ph 1:21). This is total commitment, total surrender..

In the area of freedom we need especially to use the gifts which have been frequently mentioned. *Discernment* is the gift that embraces all the others. Through reflecting on our awareness, through listening to our feelings and to the movements of the various spirits within and around us, through constant turning to the Spirit, the breath of God, we discern the traps of bondage and the presence of God in the truth that sets us free. Then as St John says: 'So if the Son sets you free you will indeed be free' (Jn 8:36).

You were darkness once, but now you are light in the Lord; be like children of light, for the effects of the light are seen in complete goodness and right living and truth (Ep 5:8,9).

Part Two: First Steps – Stepping out in Faith

Introduction

These programmes can be followed by *individuals* or *groups*.

Each section has simple instructions to follow.

We always begin by handing the whole experience over to God. We beg for His Spirit to enter into us and bless us.

We say together the Glory be to the Father prayer.

Each section has a special theme.

Questions are asked to help us reflect, speak to God and discover more about ourselves.

The *Nightly Reflection* is a very important part of First Steps. It is clearly explained in each section.

We always end by saying the Glory be to the Father prayer, either as an individual or together as a group.

The following is a summary, in table form, of the eight sections to First Steps – Stepping out in Faith.

1. Getting to know myself better.
2. Using my memory.

3. Entering into deeper water with regard to feelings.
4. The mystery of my being.
5. Finding God in myself, in others, in the circumstances of my life.
6. Finding God in the Scriptures.
7. Finding God in our particular walk of life.
8. A Quiet Day for reflection.

In the previous sections you read about being a human being. Then you discovered that you have feelings. You can listen. You can reflect. Now we move on to a new stage: 'Stepping out in Faith'. In the first section there is an opportunity for you to learn through your own experience.

You are not moving into this new event, of reading, discovering and becoming aware, on your own. The Holy Spirit is with you. The more conscious you become of that the better. The more at ease you are in turning frequently to the Holy Spirit, the more real you become. Consequently His influence will spread over all your day. This is how we fill the ordinary events of every day with the presence of God. This is how we recognise who we are, temples of the Holy Spirit.

It is a good thing, when you intend to listen to music, or to read a book, for example, to become aware of what you are about to do. Then hand that event to God. Speak to Him about it.

For example: 'God, thank you for the opportunity of having this time in which to reflect on who I am. I offer that to you and I thank you and praise you and glorify you. I will try to begin and end always with the prayer, "Glory be to the Father" ':

Glory be to the Father and to the Son, and to the Holy Spirit. As it was in the beginning, is now and ever shall be, world without end, Amen.

1 Getting to know myself better

How did you feel when you began to recognise the difference between reading a page of a book without thinking of God, and handing it over to Him first, thus bringing God into your experience? As we move into 'First Steps', get in touch with how you felt. Perhaps you felt delighted. Perhaps encouraged. Maybe a bit ashamed that you had forgotten God for so long. The important thing is to become aware of your feeling and to claim it. Talk to God about it. That makes all the difference. So become aware, then reflect and claim.

If you want to grow as a human being you need to become more sensitive to your own feelings. Develop awareness of your feelings. Too many people deny their feelings as if they were ashamed of them. In the previous pages we have seen how that attitude blocks out reality. It denies what is true and prevents your maturing.

When next you meet up with some people, become aware of your feelings towards them. If you have a friend, and can share what you are discovering about your growth as a person, your conversation will be worthwhile. It will be a richer experience than talking about the weather! You are sharing what you have received.

Let us look now at the way we use our gift of listening. It may help you to look back at the earlier section on listening. We are not all good listeners. At least not all the time. Did you, for example, really listen to what you read about feelings? Did you hear it or did you block out whatever you didn't want to hear?

Next time that you are speaking to somebody become aware of how you are listening to that person. You may be anxious for the other to stop talking so that you can get in with your word! Try instead to listen with all your being, not just to the words the person is saying, but to their whole body language. Are you at ease in their presence? If not, why not? Maybe it is because *they* are not at ease. Listen with your heart, and you will begin to understand them. You will be concerned for them. That is listening with the heart.

Listening with the heart means that you are listening to what lies underneath the spoken words. You hear the shyness, or the nerves or the frustration of the speaker. Thus you become a better listener.

What can you learn for example if someone is speaking and you notice the shaking hands, or the hunched shoulders. What are they saying? Maybe they are saying, 'please keep out, I'm afraid, I'm nervous . . . but don't go away.' What about your own body language? Is your language such that you are inviting the other to continue speaking? Do you listen to your own body language? Do you let it tell you that you are open to hearing one colleague, one neighbour, but you have shut out another one?

Ask yourself if this is true of you, if this is your experience. Ask yourself: 'What has struck me most in what I have read so far? How does it apply to my life? How do I feel about it all?' Pause.

Reflect on the quality of your listening to others, always remembering that Jesus says, 'whatever you do to one of these my least brethren, you do to me.' It helps in this pause to talk to Jesus about anything that strikes you.

You may have taken a risk in recognising how you were feeling, in recognising how you listen or don't listen. Maybe you are confused. Maybe you are angry. Maybe you are happy. Whatever it is, reflect on that and talk to God about it.

Maybe you have a good feel about what's going on. You are becoming more alive. Maybe you have a feeling of excitement, maybe a feeling of eagerness? You are getting to know yourself better as a human being. As you get to know yourself better, you are getting to know other human beings better too. That is something to look forward to. That is building up another person, another member of Christ's body.

Whatever your feeling, claim that feeling as *real* for you.

That word 'real'. Let it stay with you. The more real you become the more easily you get in touch with the real Christ. That's important for you to hear and practise. Claim any feeling that is real to you and say, yes, that is how I feel, that's me. Your feeling may be negative not positive. That does not matter. Claim it!

Without forcing the pace, you may, by claiming a feeling, be able to go deeper into the experience. Remaining quietly with the sense of eagerness, or whatever it is, keep an open heart. When you do, wonderful things can happen to you. A closed heart shuts us off from neighbours and unfortunately it shuts us off too often from God as well.

Soon you will easily be able to discover your own feelings. You will also recognise what they are telling you. You may, for example, discover that under the eagerness, and at a deeper level, you have a longing to grow both as a human being and as God's child. You may have a longing to discover new truths about yourself and even a desire to risk. That is a great desire. Such a desire leads to new life. You may want to risk letting go of old ways. On the other hand you may experience boredom or confusion or resistance of some kind to what we are about. The important thing is to recognise it, claim it and learn from it. Underneath that boredom or confusion or resistance is perhaps a fear, an irritation, or disillusionment. Even to discover that means new growth. Pause and talk to Jesus about it all. Listen to what He has to say to you.

Nightly reflection

I would like to talk now about what is called *nightly reflection*. This is a simple prayer that you can do at the end of the day.

Look back on the day. Look back on this experience of your new discoveries. Reflect on how comfortable or uncomfortable you are with learning more about yourself. It can be exciting when you realise that you are taking personal responsibility for your own growth. In itself that is a good thing.

Maybe, at first, you are anxious. If you are, that's a feeling. Recognise it and claim it. As a result of claiming it, the fear lessens. Fear lessens still more, if you are fortunate enough to be able to share any of this with a friend or with a group. Try it.

In your nightly reflection you can also learn about yourself as a *listener*. You can practise that listening at home. Listen to your family, to your friends. In your workplace, how do you listen there? If you are a poor listener, try to discover why that is so. You can reflect quietly tonight too about your honesty with yourself. Are you holding back anything? Are you afraid to make discoveries? Are you giving all you can to this new way of growing and becoming more aware of yourself?

Reflect on the quality of your *awareness*. Are you aware of your feelings when someone to whom you are talking keeps looking over your shoulder at something else or at someone else? What are your feelings? Name them.

Are you aware of the discomfort of another when you look over their shoulder instead of looking at them?

What are the feelings which you find easier to claim than others? What about compassion, sympathy, love, gratitude, delight? Do you claim those easily? On the other hand, do you tend, perhaps, to repress feelings of anger, irritation, envy, jealousy, fear? Why do you repress certain feelings?

Are you aware that you claim some feelings and not others? Perhaps you can talk this over with a good friend, or share with a group.

Talk to Jesus Christ about it. He will listen. He always does, and He honours our trusting Him.

Look seriously at the question of *reflection*. Without reflecting, a day is scarcely worth living. Without reflection it means that God has been labouring for us all the time and we have missed meeting Him. A reflective person tends to live at a deeper level than a non-reflective person. To reflect deeply is a good way to deepen our whole personality. Check out your day. Have you reflected today? Much? Some? Not at all?

End by saying the 'Glory be to the Father', as an individual, or together as a group.

2 Using my memory

Once again before starting this section on using memory, hand the whole experience over to God. Ask for the power of His Spirit to help you so that you can come to know yourself better, as the work of His hands. Thus you will be able to praise, honour and glorify Him as your Creator.

Now as usual let us say the 'Glory be to the Father', slowly and reverently, bringing before God all those people for whom we want to pray.

Glory be to the Father, and to the Son, and to the Holy Spirit. As it was in the beginning, is now and ever shall be, world without end, Amen.

In this section on using memory we are referring to a human gift that we have. We are at this time not specifically drawing God into it! This is to show how valuable our humanity is in itself as a gift of God. We forget too often that God is the Creator of all that is. God is *our* Creator. We need to learn that in all of creation God is present, and we need to grow in awareness of Him, whether we mention Him specifically or not.

Would you like now to use your memory? Recall an incident that happened yesterday, a year ago, ten years ago, an incident which you now know on reflection was important to your growth. What feelings have you about it now? What greater awareness have you about it? The following is an example.

A friend of mine was coming out of the Underground one day and heard beautiful music. She approached the sound, as she loved music. Then she saw that the musician had mere stumps for legs and arms. My friend was taken aback until she looked at his face, at his expression. Then she let the music flow over her. She was deeply moved. So much so that, to this day, she cannot recall precisely how he was managing to play. She also regrets that what she gave that musician was money. Now she longs to have given him a word of appreciation, a word that would have said how much the music had meant to her. In this way there would have been real communication between two human beings. She received delight from his music. Her few coins were a meagre return.

What about you? Perhaps you would like to pause now and recall an experience which is important to you. The musician was a significant person for my friend because he made her become aware and reflect. What were your feelings at the time of the incident you now recall? Was there a significant person involved there? Was the incident a moment of truth for you? Perhaps you now regret the way you then acted? Perhaps you weren't sufficiently sensitive to the other person. Are there things which you would like to be more conscious of and about which you would like to reflect more deeply? Would you like to be able to say those things to that person? Perhaps he or she is absent or dead? Yet in the power of the Lord to whom all time is present, you can now say to that person that which you would like to have said, in the past. We can learn a lesson from that. Live fully in the present moment. Do now the most loving thing that you can. Have no regrets when that special moment is past.

Use your gift of memory now again with regard to what you have learnt or experienced more deeply since you began reading this book. What have you learnt about yourself as a listener? As a person who reflects? As a person who feels? What have you learnt about others? Have you been able to share anything that you have learnt with another person? How do you feel about that? To help others to discover more about the proper use of God's gifts to them is of great value.

Have you discovered for yourself that recognising your feelings, reflecting on them, being a good listener, affects relationships? Look back on the past. If you were a good listener I am sure that you found it easy to build relationships with other people. Try it out for yourself. Recall someone to whom perhaps last week you were not exactly a life-giver, a joy-giver, a consoler! You can easily make up for that. Next time you meet that friend, that person, accept her exactly as she is and not as you want her to be. Avoid judging her. Begin to try to understand her. Notice her body language. Does it say that she is happy or unhappy, comfortable or uncomfortable in your presence? You have a lot to think about there. You can be a life-giver to that person. Perhaps you have already recognised that you find it harder to be kind and understanding to those who seem to have frailties like your own! Is it that they mirror you back to yourself? That you find that uncomfortable? Are you therefore willing to be a life-giver to another but unwilling to accept the same service yourself? Reflect!

Nightly reflection

Let us turn to our nightly reflection again. First, hand it over to God. That means that you are asking God to help you, to be with you in this action. It expresses your trust in His loving care.

Reflect on how you have taken personal responsibility for your growth today. One proof of that would be the degree to which you are willing to use help from others, especially if it is close to the bone.

We also grow to the extent that we give other people space and freedom to be themselves. People must develop at their own pace, not at the pace we want for them. Do I let this happen? If not, why not?

Are you in touch with your feelings now? Were you in touch today at the actual time that something untoward happened? That would be progress. What are your feelings telling you? How comfortable are you with that knowledge?

Before you finish your nightly reflection thank God for

the gift of a lovely day. Thank Him for all He has taught you. Thank Him for all the people who crossed your path this day. Ask Him to bless each person. Ask Him to help you begin to see people as He sees them, to love them as He loves them.

End by saying the 'Glory be to the Father', as an individual, or together as a group.

3 Entering into deeper water with regard to feelings

Once again, as we begin 'something new' it is right and fitting to hand it over to God to be blessed by His Spirit. Rest in His Spirit. Let yourself be guided by His Spirit. Beg to move into this new stage filled with the love of His Spirit.

Let us gather into our hearts the people we have met today, the people we are going to meet tomorrow. In their name let us say together, the Glory be to the Father, slowly and reverently.

Glory be to the Father, and to the Son, and to the Holy Spirit. As it was in the beginning is now and ever shall be, world without end, Amen.

We are going to use our memory again to get to a deeper level of feeling. First, however, let us relax. One way to relax is through our breathing. I mean deep breathing, not shallow breathing just from the chest. Breathe deeply. Breathe slowly. Keep breathing, in, out. As you breathe in, envisage your being empowered through the Spirit to breathe in the peace of God, the calm of God. As you breathe out, let go anxieties, tensions, edginess, disturbances, whatever disturbs you. Keep breathing in and out until you feel that you are calm.

In that experience of calm, look again and see if anything is disturbing you, any fear, any anxiety, any frustration. Whatever it may be, let it surface, recognise it, claim it. Choose now to let it go, at least for the present. Choose to hand it over to God and to ask Him to take care of it for you. Let it go willingly. Keep calm. Pause to say a word of thanks and to praise the glory of the Lord.

Once again recall an incident. First, as usual, hand over your memory to the Holy Spirit. Consecrate your memory to Him. Ask the Spirit to guide you in this recalling of memory and in all that follows. You are not therefore alone.

I suggest that when you recall the incident, you will immediately try to be more deeply aware of any feelings connected with it. In this incident, are you aware of anything that is unreal for you? You must always be on the alert to discover what is unreal. Anything that is not quite you. Something that you are a little uneasy about because you can't claim it as true, as genuine, or real for you.

Pause here for a moment. Talk to God about your feelings, about your discovery, about what seems to be real or unreal for you. Give it to Him as a sign of your trust in Him. Relax, take God's pace. Don't rush the Spirit. Don't try to grasp anything. Be ready to wait on God. And be at peace with what is happening.

Recall the incident again. Don't analyse it too much. You are becoming more experienced now in feelings. Get in touch instead with your *initial feeling*. Do you think that that initial feeling was deep or just surface level? Is there more feeling underneath? If you are not quite sure, ask God to help you to know. Wait on Him.

Are you easier now about claiming initial feelings and about being willing to go deeper? What are you learning about yourself from all this which should encourage you? What are you learning about your eagerness, your willingness to learn, your obedience to God who made your human nature? Great things can happen to you if you just go slowly, step by step, and keep talking to God about it.

Let us take this a step further. Stay with the initial feeling whatever it was. You now hope to get right into that past incident. How can that be done?

All time is present to the eternal God. He holds the past as well as the present in His being. If the incident happened when you were a child, be that child now. Enter into that incident, as the Spirit guides you. He makes it present to you now. Become aware of what happens to the initial feeling that you had, as you first recalled the incident. Become aware of what is going on within you now as you recall the incident. Look at the people. See them. Reflect on your feelings. Are you at peace, excited, content, surprised, having a feeling of expectancy? What is your real feeling? Perhaps in fact you are irritated, frustrated, disappointed, bored? That's all right too. Get to the root cause of why you are feeling as you do. Do you want to do anything about it? Would you like, perhaps, to share with a good friend, or with a group of friends? Most certainly share with your best friend, God.

To reflect on a personal experience, or on an incident as above, helps you discover a little more about your humanity. You get in touch with both positive and negative feelings. Having these feelings is one thing. To be aware that you have them, that you are comfortable in claiming them is a further step. Hopefully you are growing more as a result!

You will see from the next section that in all of these incidents, as we claim our feelings, our awareness, and our reflection, we can find God. It doesn't have to be something great. God loves the widow's mite, the hair of our head, little things, little ones. So let us find God.

Are you truly beginning to experience that being in touch with your feelings helps you to know more about yourself? Do you see that your feelings play an important role in your growing into the fullness of being human? This is all part of the wonder of your being, as the psalmist says in Psalm 139. Growing in awareness of whatever is happening, is also important for growth. It helps in building better relationships with other people. It makes us more sensitive. We become less self-centred and more God-centred and that is growth. All of this is bringing you to greater wholeness and harmony within yourself. Rejoice and give thanks and praise to Almighty God.

Nightly reflection
Reflect each night on the material presented in the section. Reflect also on the action that you need to take so as to become more real, more whole, more sensitive to others, so that they grow at their own pace.

End by bringing to prayer all those people who have nobody to pray for them. In their name let us say: *Glory be to the Father, and to the Son, and to the Holy Spirit. As it was in the beginning is now and ever shall be, world without end, Amen.*

4 The mystery of my being

You are probably quite accustomed now to handing over every new event to the Holy Spirit. Rest with him. Listen to Him. Discover how much He loves you. Believe that. Ask Him to guide you and to stay with you.

Are you beginning to discover that you are more alive? That all this is making a difference, not only while you are experiencing it here as you read, but as you meet with other people? Above all, be careful with other people that you do not judge them. Instead, open up to them. Let them be who they are. Be grateful for whatever you receive from them. Do not lay your expectations on them.

We are going to move now much more consciously into the mystery of our being. We hope to discover that Almighty God, the God of love, is present in all our experiences, in our actions, our sharing, our reflections and our decisions. We have learnt how to find God in our feelings. We have learnt to value them, to see that they are part of us. We know that God is aware of our feelings, so we don't have to repress them as a way of escaping from facing ourselves and from facing God. Some people feel that if they are angry, they should try to hide that from God. How foolish. God knows much more deeply than you or I do both the cause of our anger and the reality of our anger. He longs to help us get to the root of our anger and to understand it. Do not hide your feelings. At this stage we are only touching on them, getting to know that we have them. Let us praise God for them.

Let us now recall a new incident or one that you have reflected on already. It may be that you were not aware of God's presence in it at the time. You may have been so engrossed with what was happening to you that you completely forgot God. You may not have responded to him as sincerely or as gratefully as you may now choose to do. It is possible to make up for that. How?

We know that Jesus Christ is the same yesterday, today, and for ever. God is eternal and He holds all time in His eternal now. We can be as truly present to Him, to the same Jesus, at this moment, as when the incident first occurred! Be in His presence. Let your heart speak to Him in your own words. Have the simple heart of a child. You know God loves you and accepts you as you are. Trust Him. *Pause* for a few moments to reflect on that great truth that God loves you. Praise and glorify and thank God with all your heart.

In that incident in the past which you are now recalling, Jesus of Nazareth was passing by in your neighbour and you were unaware of Him! He comes in so many disguises. Sometimes it is hard to recognise Him. He may be a musician with stumps for limbs. People, events, joys, sorrows, can all be channels of God's presence to us. We need to be aware and alert.

Be present to Him now, if you are able. If you find that difficult, be real and honest and tell Him what the difficulty is. There should be no make-believe. Begin where you are, admitting to Jesus that indeed you are one who is blind or deaf and without music for Him. This is all part of the wonder of your being. Even the discovery that you were not aware of Him can be the beginning of a new life, because you turn to Him now in trust. Take a little time with that thought. Let your heart be warmed. Jesus is with you. You are never alone. He never forsakes you.

Let us think how close Jesus is to us. Just think of your breath. It is very close to you, yet Jesus, through the breath of the Spirit, is closer to you than your own breath. He is so close that the risen Jesus, through His Holy Spirit, lives within you. 'Make your home in me, as I make mine in you' (Jn 15:4). This is surely mystery.

Have you grasped yet that God longs for you, and for me, and for all of us, more than we can ever long for him? He is reading our hearts. He knows our frailties, but he also knows our longing. Begin with your longing. Tell him that, because that is real. That is reality. The real God is waiting for you with love. Do not rush. Be quiet, be still. Pause. Reflect.

In the stillness, listen to Jesus. He will move you to good thoughts, good desires, good decisions. That is how Jesus answers you, how He speaks to you. You can have a rich dialogue with your God, if you will. That is what it is to be a human being! That is the mystery of your being.

Each day try at different times to pause and to be aware of God present in the slightest incident. Take time to reflect. While you are at breakfast or doing the housework, the gardening, driving the car, in your office or whatever, God is present! If you reflect, you will discover Him.

Wherever you find God in prayer, in events, in upsets, in people, just spend time with Him. It might only be for a moment. I wonder if you could 'pepper' your day with brief thoughts of Jesus. You see the sun. Instead of saying, 'oh, how lovely!', let it bring you into His presence. Praise and glorify Him for the gift of sunshine. See how often you can find Him like that. Listen to Him. Stay with Him. Become quiet and get in touch with your feelings. Tell Him how you feel about His being with you and your being with Him. How you feel about His longing to be with you and how you long to be with Him.

How long will you stay with Him? As long as Jesus holds you there. His Spirit will let you know when it is time to go. He will move you on. What is Jesus asking you to do while you stay with Him? Are you learning how to let go and to let your God be the one who is ruling and guiding your life. This is important. This is how you come to greater wholeness.

Nightly reflection

At this time ask yourself perhaps, if you are trusting more each day in God's constant love for you. That gives strength. How do you show your trust? Are you beginning to forget yourself and to focus more on God and on the needs of others? Reflect on what you discover. Have you begun to share with a friend or friends? Perhaps you have a prayer group and you could all do this together. End by saying the *Glory be to the Father* . . . as an individual, or together as a group.

5 Finding God in myself, in others, in the circumstances of my life

Once again, hand this new event, namely reading this section, over to the Lord. Entrust it to His Spirit in great confidence. He loves you. You love Him. You want to find Him in all things.

Gather into your prayer all who are seeking God as you are, as I am. Let us say together the *Glory be to the Father* with a great sense of privilege. *Glory be to the Father, and to the Son, and to the Holy Spirit. As it was in the beginning, is now and ever shall be, world without end, Amen.*

First we try to find God in ourselves. We have been discovering who we are, in our feelings, in our ability to reflect, in our ability to listen, to discern, to breathe the breath of God. You might like to read Psalm 139 very slowly and prayerfully. This is a Psalm which tells us about God's continuous presence with us. He never leaves us. We are never alone. Here the psalmist talks of 'the wonder of my being'. Is that really how I feel about myself? Do I give wholehearted assent to that truth? What is that truth? That the wonder of God is present within me and revealed in all that is me – my mind and heart, my body and senses, my spirit and feelings? ALL.

Yes, it is true that God made each of us beautiful and found us good. Yet as soon as we say or hear that, we think of our sins and get upset! Of course we are fallen sinners. Of course we need forgiveness. But let us claim our sins and sinfulness and repent! None of that destroys the fact that God made us good, with His goodness. God made us in His image and likeness, Alleluiah!

What do you really value about who you are? For example, what would reduce the quality of life for you? If you were deprived of some of the things that you take for granted like your eyes, ears, health, tongue, mind, ability to move, how would you feel? If you lost family, friends, had no music, no birdsong . . . If you lost your inner peace or your fellowship with other people. Or if you lost gifts like courage, honesty or desire for God. How would it be for you if you lost the very desire to know God, or to be with him? What would it do to you?

Pause and think.

Have you grasped the fact that God has given all these wonderful things to *you*? He is the Giver. Without these gifts your life would be so much the poorer. In these gifts, God has also given Himself. God is really present in all that He gives. Thank Him.

Even when you are unfaithful and stray from God, He is still with you, close as ever. Yes, without doubt you can find God within you if you desire to find Him. Not in your own striving or power, but in God's gift of the Spirit. You must, however, be honest, open and sincere. There is a lot of thinking to be done here. A lot of honesty.

Pause. Reflect.

Listen to God. What are the answers He is giving you *in your mind*, through your coming to know the things you must do? What are the answers he is giving you *in your feelings*, through your recognising whether you feel happy about what's going on, or at least feel the first movement of desire. Hand over your mind and your heart to God and let Him purify them. We are only at the first steps to finding God. But they are real.

Let us look at how we can find God in other people. It is wonderful to recognise how truly God comes to us, speaks to us, supports us, calls us, and challenges us through the mystery of another person. Unless we are willing to listen to others, we will not experience that! We will miss what God is saying. We resist the presence of God in another, because we see only their frailty! Yet none of us is perfect. We are all sinners. We, however, seem to have very keen eyes to pick out the negative qualities in others rather than their good and positive qualities. We tend to listen more readily to our friends! Why? We need to look at our motivation. Sometimes there is a lot of self-interest in our relationship even with 'friends'. I'll listen to them, if, in their turn, they heed me! At other times an act done by a friend is acceptable to me; yet the same act of generosity or humility or honesty can become distorted in my eyes when it is done by a 'non-friend'. We need to know our 'real' self!

Pause. Reflect. Am I genuinely seeking God in others? Or am I seeking myself and my best interests?

The good God loves each one and sees the truth of the heart. He is waiting now in your heart to see if you are going to open wide the door to receive Him. He is present in others irrespective of whether they are your friends or not. He is present irrespective of whether what they say comforts you, strengthens you, or challenges you! The truth is often in the challenge. The psalmist says, 'hidden in the storm I answered you' (Ps 81:7).

We can therefore find God in ourselves and in others. What about the daily circumstances of life? The little things? It is relatively easy to find God when life pleases me and goes my way. Even here I need to be alert, to become aware. Is it God I am finding in these pleasant circumstances, or my own natural satisfaction? I will know whether I am finding God or myself by the 'fruit', by the result – 'by their fruit you shall know them.'

I find God and not myself when the focus of my attention

stays on God or my neighbour and not on my self-interest. To find God when He challenges me, especially through others, is more difficult. These are not pleasant circumstances! Yet the reward is great.

And so in the nightly reflection, seek Him by asking yourself these questions.

Nightly reflection
Whom did I find today, God or myself? Where? Was it in life's circumstances that I found God or in a neighbour that challenged me? What was the result? Having found God, did I stay with him? Did I let His grace pour over me and did I know that no matter what He asked I could do it in His strength, in His power? Or did I fail lamentably? Did I then bring that to God? Did I ask His help? Then, thanks be to God, I found Him even when I failed Him. Let us end now with the *Glory be*, and bring in my heart all those who have been the instrument of God in my life today. Let us say: *Glory be to the Father, and to the Son, and to the Holy Spirit. As it was in the beginning, is now and ever shall be, world without end, Amen.*

6 Finding God in the Scriptures

Up until now we have been finding God in ourselves, in others, in the circumstances of our lives. Now we are going to try to find God in the Scriptures, the sacred word of God.

We will begin with the Psalms. This is not, however, a *study* of the Psalms. That would be a head exercise. These 150 Psalms were prayers which were familiar to Jesus. He constantly referred to them in His preaching. On the cross Psalm 22 came from the depths of His heart: 'My God, my God, why have you deserted me?'

We have been talking about feelings. The Psalms are full of feeling. Read and hear the cries of the psalmists. The

Psalms are full of love, despair, anger, hope, trust, longing. Using them for prayer helps us get in touch with our own feelings. We are now more free to own our feelings. Pause when you are moved by the Spirit of God. He will speak through a word or a phrase. Something will speak uniquely and directly to each one of us.

When we are moved or struck by a word, a phrase, we pause. We speak to God or listen to Him so as to be taught by Him. 'Each morning He wakes me with the ear of a disciple.' A disciple is one who is taught.

Here is a simple example of how we can pray with any piece of Scripture, but particularly with the Psalms which we now choose. Begin by handing over this prayer experience to the Holy Spirit in love. Then say the *Glory be to the Father, and to the Son, and to the Holy Spirit. As it was in the beginning, is now and ever shall be, world without end, Amen.* It is good to use the breathing exercise that we did earlier. Be still. As you read or listen to a psalm – Psalm 3, for example – one verse might spring to life for you. That happens through the action of the Spirit. Through His power, that word or phrase spoke His message to you. It is as if your name at this moment were written on that verse for you.

Be in touch with your interior being. Which verse, which word moved you? What is the feeling it evoked? Was it positive or negative? Whatever it is, own it, stay with it. Speak to God or listen to God and be still. Don't strive over eagerly with your head, with anxiety, to find out the word or the phrase. It will come. If you read a letter from a dear friend, a word will strike you, will have meaning for you, will have reference to your life now, will spark off a special feeling in you. It is the same with Scripture. This is how God speaks to you. Listen to Him.

Having heard your special word, thank God for the privilege of receiving His message. No matter what the content, even if it is a challenge, be grateful and reverent. Praise and glorify Almighty God who is speaking to you through the Spirit within you. Be quiet and still so as to reflect on the meaning of that message for your life and your behaviour.

For example, if in Psalm 3, the line 'Yahweh, my encircling shield' spoke to you and moved you, how does that speak to your life at the moment? This is important for you as God's word used in prayer is meant to change your life. Look at that line again. 'Yahweh, my encircling shield.' How is it speaking to you? Your feelings will let you know how you are being led. You will recognise a feeling that God wants you to act differently.

For example, one person who is moved by this line 'Yahweh, my encircling shield' may recognise that life frightens her and that she has not trusted in God to help her. She feels so alone. Therefore this line brings to her an awareness that she needs to pray for trust. If she trusts her neighbour more, she will also learn to trust God more, remember, if we want to know how we relate to God, look at how we relate to our neighbour.

On the other hand, another person may be called by the same line to remember God's protection in the past. Such a person is moved with great hope, and can let God enter now more deeply into his affairs. He lets go so that God can hold all things in His care. Such a person may feel called to hand over all to God at the beginning of every new work, new event.

A third person may have been struck by the opening lines in Psalm 3 about people turning against her. She is perhaps moved by the Spirit to look honestly at her own part in relationships. Up to this she has been blaming other people. Now she is being moved to recognise that there are two sides to every story. She, too, has a share in these broken relationships. So she asks herself, what changes God is asking her to make in her attitudes? Where is she taking personal responsibility for improving relationships?

You can try that approach with any of the Psalms, particularly those that reveal deep feeling.

Nightly reflection
In praying, it is important to ask for the light and wisdom which we need. How can we expect to have light and wisdom unless we beg God for it? Listen to the Spirit moving you,

touching your mind with thoughts, or your heart with feeling. If you experience resistance within your being, do not run from it. Stay there, and pray to God for help. Believe that it will come, in God's time. It certainly will, but not necessarily in your time! You may therefore have to stay in prayer a little longer. Keep asking for light and help. Remain filled with faith and hope.

Finally, always give thanks to God. Praise Him and glorify Him for caring for you as He does. Once again end with the *Glory be to the Father*, including all the people for whom you want to pray. *Glory be to the Father, and to the Son, and to the Holy Spirit. As it was in the beginning, is now and ever shall be, world without end, Amen.*

7 Finding God in my particular walk of life

The story of Emmaus is one of my favourite Scripture passages. This story describes clearly how we can find God, no matter where we are, or how we are feeling. He is to be found in our ordinary daily routine of life. It doesn't matter what the circumstances are, we can always find God. He is in the present moment. He is with us there. Finding Him depends more on Him than on us. In fact when we desire to find God it means that already He is with us. He has found us, as He always does, but we also are finding Him through our very desire to find Him.

Look at the story in St Luke 24 about the two disciples on the road to Emmaus. The two disciples – I like to think of them as husband and wife – chose to leave the other disciples who were in Jerusalem. These two disciples were angry. They were frustrated, they were disillusioned. They were disappointed, they had lost hope. Yes, indeed, they were depressed and downhearted as we so often are. Notice all their negative feelings! Their world was black indeed and they were escaping from too much pain. Do you ever experience that? Yet it is in this very dark experience for them that they meet Jesus. They are powerless to help themselves. This is when Jesus loves to come to our help. We must be open to receive it. In the disguise of a questioning stranger, Jesus comes to rescue the two disciples and to give them renewed hope.

When we are likewise lost, we can watch for the coming of Jesus. Indeed if our hearts are open He is already on the way to meet us. He needs to see that we want to meet Him. Pause to reflect on that truth and on the circumstances of your own life. Are you lost? Do you want to find Jesus?

Jesus understands the dark side of pain. It is salutary to reflect and discover what is happening to us. He accepts the disciples where they are, just as he will accept us. We must cease playing games with Jesus, cease wearing masks. We must be our real selves. Notice that this stranger, Jesus in disguise, helps the disciples, through His questioning, to express their feelings. Sometimes those questions were not welcome to them. Often the interruptions or the questionings of strangers or of neighbours are not welcome to us! Jesus helps them by His questions to express their feelings. He almost provokes them to become exasperated with Him. Surely everyone should know what was happening in Jerusalem! Jesus was patient with them and His timing was perfect. He did not start explaining Scripture when He first met them. Why not? They were not ready. They were not in touch with their human selves. They were not in touch with their feelings. We must recognise our feelings. We must own them, if we want to hear Jesus.

Jesus waited. He healed their bruised spirits by helping them get in touch with their feelings and to express what was burning them up. Only then, chiding gently, did He use Scripture to banish pain and confusion and to enlighten their darkness.

When the disciples listened to Jesus, they experienced a longing for His company. They began to sense vaguely that He was a life-giver. They begged Him to stay with them. They claimed their need of His presence and they expressed that to Him. Their hearts became open to Him. His response then, as now, is always the same. He gave more generously to them even than before. He gave them Himself. *Reflect*.

Then, as He so often does, He left them. He leaves us too at times, so that we can take personal responsibility for our actions. The disciples reflected. They discovered that their hearts were burning within them when He was with them. Being in touch with their feelings helped them make a decision. It was the correct one. They returned to their brethren in Jerusalem so as to share with them their experience of Jesus. And they listened with joy to the experience of the other disciples who had also met Jesus. This is what we call *faith sharing*. You will hear more about that later.

Nightly reflection
We all have an Emmaus story. Reflect on your own story and how Jesus found you when you were wandering or perhaps seeking him. Recall how he offered you new life and an abundance of it. Does it surprise you to know that you, yourself, can be a 'good news' story? That in fact your gospel story is being written each day. The scribe is the Holy Spirit of God. The events of your daily life provide the material.

Let us glorify him and all those who have helped us today as we say together, *Glory be to the Father, and to the Son, and to the Holy Spirit. As it was in the beginning is now and ever shall be, world without end, Amen.*

8 A quiet day for reflection

As we begin this new section, let us hand it all over to God as usual. Let us gather into our prayer of praise all those who do not know Him, who reject Him, who probably never knew the real God. Let our prayer be a prayer of intercession for all God's children, as we say together, *Glory be to the Father, and to the Son, and to the Holy Spirit. As it was in the beginning is now and ever shall be, world without end, Amen.*

We have talked a lot about *reflection*. The closer we come to God the more we need time for reflection. This is to give us time to treasure all that God is teaching us. He labours for us. Without reflection, however, we can forget so much. We tend to stay at a shallow depth instead of listening more keenly to Him in the power of the Spirit.

Today is going to be a different kind of day! I'd like to suggest that today you arrange to have a long reflective period, a quiet day, or even a few quiet hours. Some might like to spend this time quietly in church or before the Blessed Sacrament. Do whatever is right for you according to your faith and the custom of your church. The purpose of this quiet time is to let things come together for us through the power of God's Spirit. There is always need for consolidation. We need also to check out whether we are taking personal responsibility for our actions and for our attitudes to God and to people.

Here are some points which may help you. *Reflect on them.*

You, a human being, have discovered that you have received many gifts which too often you took for granted without expressing thanks. If that is not true for you, then rejoice and give thanks to God.

Bring now a past incident into the present and thank all those who were good and kind to you. Ask God to bless them now for all the goodness you received from them. Praise and glorify God who was and is present in all the goodness and kindness that you received. That could take you quite a long time this day.

Reflect on the importance of expressing 'thanks'. Hopefully, in the future expressing thanks in your heart will be a constant response, not just in retrospect, but at the time. This is how we grow as God's dear children.

Look now at the gift of *feeling*. Become aware of the gift of feeling, given you by God. Without this gift, your experience would not be so rich. In the past perhaps you too often denied or repressed your feelings.

Glorify God by claiming them now. Thank Him. Praise Him for having taught you so much about your feelings. Pray that you may never again deny them or repress them. Pray that you use this gift always for His Glory. Use your feelings for His Kingdom and for the benefit of others.

The most precious of all gifts is Christ Himself who is present in each gift. He is present in His sacrifice at Calvary, in the sacraments, in everything that is. St Paul says it all with striking and simple clarity. 'There is only Christ. He is everything. He is in everything!'

Pause on that statement of Paul's. Let it speak to you.

Glorify Him by resting, full of trust, in Christ our Saviour.

He is all, and without him we are nothing. He is teaching us now as we read, pray and reflect on our feelings. Always we move in Him, through Him and with Him. Of ourselves we are nothing: that's what we have to learn by experience.

The sad story is that too often we have acted as if the roles were reversed, as if we own the gifts. Think about that. Reflect. That really is what sin is about: acting independently of the God of love who has given us all. Now let us act appropriately as is fitting for us, the work of His hands, creatures, sinners, yet loved. Let us repent of our pride and give Him our wholehearted love. Wherever you feel that the Spirit is speaking to you, drawing you to be silent, to pause, to reflect, do that. Listen to Him. Rest quietly in Him. Let Him open wide your heart. Respond, not out of your head, but from the heart, a response of love. Hear what the Spirit is calling you to do. Do that. Then it will indeed be fruitful. And the Lord will be glorified.

Get in touch with the feelings that arise in you now. As a result of all of these past weeks of praying, what do you notice about your *awareness*? Do you feel you have grown? That you have received some of the abundance of life which He promised? If so, claim that joyfully, and to His glory. To Him be the glory. Let us willingly recognise the truth, whatever that may be. Thank Him.

You may ask yourself what you can give Him in return. One thing He really wants is your open heart. Are you ready to give Him that? Perhaps you are not yet quite ready. Be honest, and real. If you are not yet ready, tell Him that and listen to Him. Let this be a deep conversation between you and Christ. A conversation that is honest, open and real. That is what sets you free.

Nightly reflection
In the nightly reflection, look again at what happened during this day. Did you give God glory? Were you centred on Him? What are your responses and desires now? Above all, is your focus moving gradually each day from you to God? From you to your neighbour? Are you no longer the centre of your world? No longer so egocentric but hopefully more God-centred? That is growth. What do your actions, your attitudes, the quality of your heart-response, and your desires reveal?

We end now by coming before the Lord, with a humble and grateful heart. We gather into our prayers all those out there in this world with nobody to help them. In their name we give voice to the glory of the Lord, as we say *Glory be to the Father, and to the Son, and to the Holy Spirit. As it was in the beginning is now and ever shall be, world without end, Amen.*

STAGE TWO

PREPARE THE WAY

Part One: Prepare the Way – Laying the Foundation

Introduction

As we move into this next stage of our journey, we need to ask what 'Prepare the Way' means. For whom are we preparing? What is the goal we keep in mind?

In *First Steps*, we became familiar with the importance of our humanity and with a growing desire to know Christ better, to have a more real relationship with Him. On that strong base, we begin to lay a foundation for future building of our life in Christ by taking a good look at some dark areas in our relationships. We receive the strength to do this by recalling that we are the temple of the Holy Spirit. Now, before looking at darkness, we steep ourselves in the truth that we are 'members of the body of Christ'. We are never alone. Christ is always with us. Moreover we have the privilege of giving life to one another and of receiving life. Again the choice is ours. Unfortunately, as we know to our cost, darkness can enter into all our relationships.

We take up again the same four themes: *Light and Darkness, the Sower, Prayer* and *Freedom*.

Light and Darkness

In Stage One we considered our unrealities, our mask-wearing under this heading. We move now into the deeper area, not only of personal sin and sinfulness, but also of corporate responsibility. We pray to be as honest as we can and as real. This requires courage. Yet such courage is graced by repentance and new life.

The Sower
These verses deal particularly with the picture of this world and the way that neighbour exploits neighbour. They speak strongly about the aspect of corporate responsibility for the sin of the world. The lure of riches is all around us and we need to be alert and on our guard.

Prayer
To combat the greater danger of the enemy, we hear about listening to God's word in Scripture. God's own word strengthens our personal reflections and gifts us with its special unction and strength. Likewise the prayer of faith-sharing is when the body of Christ shares with other members their healing experience of Christ moving in their lives, in the power of the Spirit.

Once again, we see how the gift of prayer is the presence and support of God revealing darkness so as to let it be conquered in the love of Christ.

Freedom
It is encouraging to note the same movement happening here as in the last section when we came to the theme of *freedom*. Prayer begins the healing process and the forward movement into freedom. This is the movement from darkness into light. The necessity of our recognising and claiming our darkness is the necessary basic step which leads to *repentance*. With genuine repentance comes a breath of freedom, which heralds Christ's victory once again over darkness.

Part Two: *Prepare the Way* follows the above reflections. By commitment to prayer and its influence on our daily living, conversion of heart begins to take place. In this turning of our hearts over to God, the way is prepared by the removal of obstacles for the eventual deeper following of Christ, which is the building of the Temple.

1 Building the body of Christ

'I have discovered that my destiny is to build the body of Christ. I began to grasp that fact as I prayed through the First Steps.' So spoke one of those people whom I have seen transformed. The experience of this person and many others is described below, in my words.

'In First Steps, I was essentially concentrating on who I am. I was reflecting on my personal experience. I was interested in the "real" me, the "reality" that this unique person, this me, experienced. On the human level, it became exciting, even breath-taking to discover how my God-given gifts were mine to help me grow, expand my consciousness, *become*!

'Well-known statements like: "We are God's work of art" (Ep 2:10) or "there is a new creation; the old creation has gone, and now the new one is here" (2 Cor 5:17) began to ring with the confirmation of my own personal experience. "It is all God's work" no longer sounded as a cold statement divorced from my reality, but almost a shout of personal joy. "Eureka" was touching my real and personal experience of Scripture!

'This truth of the "wonder of my being" was no longer coming at me from outside, from the words of other people. I had heard, experienced, reflected, listened and discovered. I was ready to "believe" more truly in the reality of the *spiritual* me, because I had seen, and touched and discovered the new growth of the *human* dimension of me. Moreover, I had observed the same kind of new life happening in others, but in each person's unique way.

'I was ready – from personal experience reflected upon – to discover my new reality: I belong to the body of Christ. I was ready to reflect more deeply on the meaning of being created in the image of God. I became more ready to confess to the power of the Spirit within me; more ready to believe that without the Spirit, this wonderful "human me" became an empty shell. I discovered that my destiny, in the power of the Spirit, is to build the body of Christ.'

The experience described above can happen to you, an individual reader, whose heart is open to the other members of the same body, the body of Christ. It happens especially when *Light out of Darkness* is experienced in a group. Through personal experience you discover yourself alive with a strength beyond mere human effort. You discover yourself nurturing and being nurtured in ways that draw on your 'reality', but go beyond it. You discover a presence. In the light and truth of that presence, you see your darkness and frailty at first dimly, and gradually with ever growing clarity.

As defences come down, as the light increases, one longs for greater reality, deeper truth. In the gift of presence in other people, especially in group members, you are both strengthened and challenged. Growth in others strengthens and challenges. Blindness in others reveals the reality of darkness. It evokes compassion and understanding. Seen at a remove, it is seen more clearly. You experience your own weakness and helplessness. You are moved to cry out to God from the depths of your being: 'Lord, be merciful to me, a sinner.'

Through mutual pain and support in the group, you venture to risk. You desire to know, to claim weakness, to open up, to receive help from the Source of all strength. You wait, powerless, helpless to rescue yourself.

> In the waiting, trust grows,
> as do wisdom and patience and surrender . . .
>   gradually.
> In God's time, weakness is transformed into
>   His strength:
> His strength, limited indeed by reality, yet
>   His becoming yours.
> A long journey from weakness to strength!
> From nothingness to Infinity.
> Yet in Him all things are possible,

If we but know our place!

The mystery of redemption

The transformation of our weakness – the sad reality of being a sinner – into the strength of Christ depends on two other realities:

The mystery of redemption – objective and subjective; and the mystery of free will – through it I can refuse to co-operate, and so die, or, I can see, recognise, acknowledge and claim my personal responsibility as a sinner. I can respond in love with the act of my will, to the will of God, and live.

What is objective redemption?

I am a sinner. No one can 'stand in the gap' (Ez 22:30) for me before God, except the Only Begotten Son, Jesus Christ, who did, who continues to do so today and who will, until the end of time. Jesus Christ bought us back from the evil power of Satan – at the price of his own suffering, and through surrender to the will of His Father, to the very last drop of His blood.

Thus Jesus Christ has redeemed us. This is because of His obedience to the will of His Father, because of His love for His Father, and because of His and His Father's love for us. This is what we mean by saying that Jesus Christ 'became sin' for us. This is *objective redemption*.

By objective redemption we mean that reconciliation with God has been achieved objectively. The gates are wide open – objectively – for those who, seeing what they must do, enter in. Each member of Christ's body has a personal responsibility, however, to apply to himself the fruits of objective redemption, thus making the process of redemption *subjective*.

Subjective redemption depends on the power of the Holy Spirit living within each one of us, His temple. Without the Holy Spirit, we cannot say 'Abba, Father'. Still less can we so live, that our personal redemption becomes a lived reality. Subjective redemption depends also on my free and loving co-operation with the power of the Holy Spirit.

Redemption, therefore, is linked to the reality of my being the 'temple of the Holy Spirit'. It is also linked to my being a member of the body of Christ. It is in the power of the Spirit alone that I can grow as a member of the body of Christ.

This growth has an individual and a corporate reality.

A chain is only as strong as its weakest link. The strength of a group, of the body, is affected by the generous giving or the refusal of effort, by each member, weak or strong.

I have therefore a personal responsibility for my own growth in Christ and a corporate responsibility for the body. I must recognise that I either build up the whole body or drag it down by the quality of my response to the action of the Spirit within me. In this sense we bear the burden of one another, the burden of responsibility.

There is another side to this same coin, a positive side! In Christ, as members of His body, we are brothers and sisters. The Spirit of the risen Christ animates us, calls us to be filled with the love of Christ, individually and as a body. Each one of us receives 'his own share of grace, given as Christ allotted it' (Ep 4:7). Moreover, His grace is always sufficient for each one (2 Cor 12:9). Nevertheless, when I am faithless or weak, I am supported by the goodness and strength of the whole body! This is the privilege of responsibility!

Christ of course intercedes for each one of us. Nevertheless, His final plea for those who, hearing about Him, believe, must have a special efficacy. 'I pray not only for these, but for those also who through their words will believe in me:

May they all be one.
Father, may they be one in us,
as you are in me and I am in you,
so that the world may believe it was you who
    sent me'

(Jn 17:21).

Here is the corporate witness to Christ that goes beyond the strength of the individual members of the one body.

The ideal to which we aspire will, of course, be accomplished only in the power of the Spirit. St Paul's words are inspirational:

> You are God's chosen race, his saints; he loves you, and you should be clothed in sincere compassion, in kindness and humility, gentleness and patience. Bear with one another; forgive each other as soon as a quarrel begins. The Lord had forgiven you; now you must do the same. Over all these clothes to keep them together and complete them, put on love. And may the peace of Christ reign in your hearts, because it is for this that you were called together as parts of one body. Always be thankful. Let the message of Christ, in all its richness, find a home with you. Teach each other, and advise each other, in all wisdom (Col 3:12–16).

Light out of darkness

One way to live in the Spirit, to grow together as members of Christ's body, concerned about one another, supporting and supported by the others, is through this book *Light out of Darkness*. An individual who endeavours to follow the introductory material in each stage of this book and then follows the practical steps in *First Steps*, *Prepare the Way* and *Building the Temple*, will become more spiritually sensitive. Almost unconsciously he or she will become more aware of other people, of their value, of where they are, and how they respond. Gradually his or her personal life will become richer and more real by this reaching out and becoming interrelated. Thus the Spirit lives within us and binds us together.

A *group*, led by a trained leader in a parish, or by a director in a retreat, can experience an overwhelming encounter with the Spirit, and become alive in the body of Christ. When that initial group experience – finding Christ alive in His Spirit in all that is – becomes one's daily life experience, then one knows what it is to be fully alive. Then even the darkness of one's frailty becomes 'a way in' to the light that transforms the face of the earth.

Prepare the way

The second stage of this book, *Prepare the Way*, is the foundation to the future building of life in Christ. Our progress must be rooted in the Spirit of Christ. It must also be rooted in the painful reality of our sin and sinfulness, which is always against the background of God's love, experienced through the power of His Spirit. Eventually this power moves us into the Pauline approach: 'So shall I be very happy to make my weaknesses my special boast so that the power of Christ may stay over me' (2 Cor 12:9).

Throughout both *Prepare the Way* and *Building the Temple*, we remain aware of the necessary integration of the human and the spiritual in our lives.

Integration

When we recognise the frailty of our humanity we are led into a deeper awareness of sin and of our need for forgiveness. By integrating prayer and living we are helped to discover the tenderness of God towards us as sinners. As we pray, openly and honestly in the presence of the Lord, we are given an insight into our darker side. We then claim that specific prayer-insight. We take personal responsibility, in the power of the Spirit, for taking appropriate action immediately, this day, to put right what is wrong.

It needs to be recognised that this dynamic of listening in prayer, of discerning where I fail, of reflecting on what I must do, of letting that prayer-insight change my way of living, *is the most constant and powerful factor of transformation and growth in the whole programme outlined in this book*.

Besides being an instrument of *integration*, *Light out of Darkness* is also an instrument of *discernment*, of *healing* and of *evangelisation*.

Discernment

Throughout the three stages of this programme, I need to keep discerning. Apart from discerning the various spirits which I have mentioned before, I need to keep in touch with my reaction or my response as I pray. This is where the gift of feeling is helpful. When I wish to use an insight received in prayer so as to change my daily approach to life, I need to be discerning. This involves discerning how I'm feeling about my neighbour, be that in the home, on the street, wherever. I need to discern the rights of others so that I discover what is appropriate in my behaviour to them. I must beware lest I should be tempted, unwarily, to impose my good intentions on unsuspecting and unprepared neighbours! I must wait for the necessary 'confirmation' of a discernment to ensure that the movement comes from the Spirit of God. (See pages 22–26.) This, in its simplest form, is a sense of peace which flows from genuine consideration for my neighbour, especially if I *decrease* in the process!

I need to discern whether my moods, attitudes and emotions are helping or hindering me in my pilgrimage with Christ. My anger, fear, guilt and anxiety, and the roots of these, will, if not dealt with, inhibit or prevent my spiritual growth and healing.

Healing

As we progress we will discover that healing is an integral part of *Light out of Darkness*. Healing is the process of salvation – it is a basic activity of God. It is the process of moving from darkness to light. As we accept the authority and rule of God over our lives we receive equilibrium in place of imbalance, peace in place of disturbance and wholeness in place of brokenness. By integrating the ministry of healing into *Prepare the Way*, we find that participants experience a deepening sense of wholeness and well-being.

In our meetings, parishes, and homes we can all benefit from being set free from the disease, the lack of wholeness, which is a negative and disintegrating element in our lifes, alienating us from the world and from God. We can rediscover that, as part of the body of Christ, we are called to be healed and to be instruments of healing.

Evangelisation

Experiencing integration within oneself between prayer and living; continuously discerning the power and presence of the Spirit; being healed and reconciled as a result of claiming and repenting of one's frailties, inevitably result in our putting on the mind and the heart of Christ. Is this not the foundation stone of genuine evangelisation?

When others experience the presence of Christ in a person, that person is an evangeliser without any other word being spoken. Such an evangeliser has indeed become the very 'word' of God, through which he was initially created.

The change that *Light out of Darkness* has worked on those who have prayerfully 'listened' to the Spirit and been transformed, has been quite remarkable. Family, friends, co-workers benefit from the wiser, more genuine approach to life that becomes apparent in such a person. There comes a new awareness, a deeper concern for others, a more generous attitude, a down-to-earth approach that yet seems rooted in a deeper interiority. This attracts. It speaks of things unseen yet desired. The result often is that others want something of what they have seen and heard and witnessed, without fully understanding, as yet, what they are seeking. News that comes by word of mouth is good. Growth, human and spiritual, as a member of Christ's body, speaks more powerfully still! The visible leads back to the invisible:

'Christ is the image of the unseen God . . . in him were created, all things in heaven and on earth: everything visible and everything invisible . . . Before anything was created, he existed, and he holds all things in unity. Now the Church is his body, he is its head' (Col 1:15–18).

Anyone who loves his brother is living in the light and need not be afraid of stumbling (1 Jn 2:10).

2 Relationships

The theme of 'relationships' is central to *Prepare the Way*. Relationships with myself, with others and with God are vital to the laying of a sound foundation. They are also vital to the soundness of the new building, the new creation which replaces what had become unsound.

My darkness
Excavations for the foundation deal with recognising the dark side of my being which can contaminate even the good, unless it is uprooted and replaced. The sinner that I am, the sinfulness that contaminates, is central to me and to all that I touch. Where that is wilful, it must be eradicated through repentance and the saving grace of Christ.

Some of my darkness is human frailty. In itself, this is not sinful, but it can become contaminated, and therefore must be looked at and brought to wholeness.

My neighbour
My neighbour can help me to enter within myself and recognise my darkness. Almighty God, in His wisdom, gave me my neighbour as a touchstone of my integrity. He gave us two commandments: to love the Lord, my God and to serve Him alone; to love my neighbour as myself. Thus my behaviour to my God and my behaviour to my neighbour will convict me or sanctify me!

Even more pertinent, in view of the fact that 'neighbours' build the body of Christ together, is that Jesus binds the commandment to love our neighbour, indissolubly, to the command to love our God (Mt 22:34–40): 'On these two commandments hang the whole Law, and the Prophets also' (Mt 22:40).

Jesus' understanding of *neighbour* is universal. In Matthew 5:43–48, Jesus goes beyond the Old Testament command 'You must love your neighbour' – with seemingly less obligation to love our enemy. He emphasises His new command by the solemnity of its introduction: 'I say this to you: love your enemies and pray for those who persecute you' (Mt 5:44). Here our behaviour and heart attitude to our neighbour is clearly linked with His view of our morality: 'In this way you will be sons of your Father in heaven . . . If you love those who love you, what right have you to claim any credit? . . . Even the pagans do as much, do they not? You must therefore be perfect just as your heavenly Father is perfect' (Mt 5:45–8).

Finally, lest we don't yet understand, Jesus gives us the parable of the Good Samaritan (Lk 10:25–37). We have here a practical application of the command to love our neighbour. It is clear that it is not for me to decide who my neighbour is. My neighbour is the one, the traveller, whom God puts across my path. Why? Because Jesus identifies with everyone, as He told Saul: 'Why do you persecute Me?'

I deliberately stress this question of God's command to love my neighbour. We need to see that our love of God can only be a form of 'cupboard love', a form of necessary 'insurance policy', if our behaviour to our neighbour is filled with much that is contrary to God's law. Love of neighbour is the test.

Let us look at our world today. Look at the sins of injustice, greed, murder, violence, denial of legitimate rights, stealing, corruption in manifold ways, abuse of power, abuse of the powerless, abuse of God's gifts. The list goes on, the sad list which describes our society today. And many of these perpetrators of sins against our neighbour will not miss worshipping God in church on Sundays! Will God accept this kind of worship, which cloaks defilement of his image in our neighbour?

On this matter of abuse of the neighbour, Isaiah could have been speaking to our society and to our relationships with one another:

> Fasting like yours today will never make your voice heard on high . . . Is not this the sort of fast that pleases me – it is the Lord Yahweh who speaks – to break unjust fetters and undo the thongs of the yoke, to let the oppressed go free, and break every yoke, to share your bread with the hungry, and shelter the homeless poor, to clothe the man you see to be naked and not turn from your own kin? Then will your light shine like the dawn and your wound be quickly healed over . . . your light will rise in the darkness, and your shadows become like noon.

Yahweh will always guide you, giving you relief in desert places. . . . You will rebuild the ancient ruins, build up on the old foundations. You will be called 'Breach-mender', 'Restorer of ruined houses' (Is 58:4–12).

We may be inclined to say: 'Yes, that is true of our society and it is terrible. But what has it to do with me?' We dare not leave it there! We ourselves are part of those ruins. We too must be restored. The Lord addresses those words of Isaiah to each of us: 'Fasting like yours today will never make your voice heard on high.' Here and now we need to recognise that our sin against our neighbour is a sin against God. We must recognise, claim and repent of it. In a later section, we will deal with personal and corporate responsibility for sin.

Fortunately, as a help to our recognising more clearly and more realistically the nature of our sinning and the roots of some of it, we are blessed with the *healing ministry*.

Healing
One of my former prejudices was directed against the healing ministry. This, in fact, is one instance of where God draws good out of all things. Because of my own former negative feelings about healing ministry, I find myself now in a good place! I understand that same attitude in others. I understand some of the blocks. I am now fully convinced of the gift of this powerful ministry. The fruits which I have seen and experienced convince and convict me. The humility and prayer which I have witnessed in God's instruments of healing fill me with wonder and joy. Consequently I now praise God continually for this ministry, which has brought healing and new life to me and to so many others.

A healing ministry forms an integral part of *Prepare the Way*, as I have already mentioned. This is more than praying with people for a specific healing which they recognise that they need. It is deeper than that. It is part of the excavation process, so necessary when preparing a sound foundation. It is necessary to dig deep, uprooting much that has been long buried and forgotten.

The particular form of this ministry that I use on the

retreats I lead is a group experience of the 'Life Prayer'.*
The process of this Life Prayer moves from the healing
of ancestral influences, through every stage of life, from
conception to the present moment. Through the use of the
sword of the Spirit, pernicious ancestral influences are cut off
and handed over to Christ, the Healer. Praise and thanks are
given to Christ and to those ancestors for whatever beneficial
influence we have received from them.

As we move together in prayer as a group, from conception, through the period in the womb, from the time of our
birth, through our childhood, adolescence and adulthood,
we offer each precious moment and year to the Lord with
thanksgiving. We lay each period of life before Christ,
the Healer and Saviour. We wait upon Him silently and
reverently, listening to what He has to say and offering our
prayers of petition, praise, thanksgiving and surrender. We
recognise the presence of Christ at every stage in our life,
in every situation. Participants stay in prayer with Christ
when they recognise a time in their life during which they
were hurt or damaged. It is better to remain humbly still
at that point, patiently allowing the Lord to deal with the
particular memory which He has identified. Frequently we
will be led to give and receive forgiveness in the name of
Jesus, and similarly to give and receive love in His name.
Because Jesus is the same yesterday, today and for ever He
is not limited by time in His ability to bring total healing.
Therefore we can be reconciled with those who have died.
We can confidently leave the pains of the past in the loving
care of God.

The actual healing experience moves through the same
steps for the whole group, irrespective of the specific life
period in which the damage occurred.

We move into deep silence and stillness.

We come in faith and hope and love before Christ, Healer
and Saviour.

We recognise that healing is not curing. It is salvific,

*Fuller details may be obtained from the Maranatha Community,
Westway, Western Road, Flixton, Manchester M31 3LE.

a saving experience. Often the healing of psychological hurts, obstacles and blindnesses can lead to a curing of an illness, even of a cancer, where the roots of the illness lie in psychological or spiritual wounding.

Christ was actually present through His Spirit at each incident when damage was done. He wept with you weeping or hurting. His love was with you, then, as it has been surrounding you ever since. It is that same love that has brought you now to this experience of release.

Because of the gift of 'free will' which God has entrusted to each one of us, Christ had to suffer, with you, the abuse of that gift of free will in the past. Now, because of your proper use of the gift of free will, you are freeing Christ, in this present moment of time, to heal you. This healing must be the result of your free will inviting Christ the Healer to heal. Invite Him now into this situation. Beg Him to heal you. You who have been wounded, freely, allow Jesus to lead you again into that situation of the past where you were wounded and damaged. Freely, you let Him bring into this situation that person or persons who were responsible for your wounding. This responsibility is culpable in some cases. In other cases, for example, at birth, a mother is not maliciously responsible for the experience of separation from the womb which brought with it certain traumatic associations. Nevertheless, the 'birthing' may have resulted in an experience which affected the child's attitudes later. One such birthing resulted in a woman seeking, in many future relationships, a surrogate mother, instead of enjoying the normal relationships which were her right.

After the healing ministry, and the forgiveness extended to all involved in that birthing experience, the woman's immediate family enjoyed a rich and happy life experience together.

Freely, in a spirit of prayer, you face the persons involved in that earlier experience. You have prayed for this hour. You have prayed for love and forgiveness. Freely now, you let Jesus lead you closer. You may be able to reach out and touch. Even reach out and embrace – depending on the past situation.

Freely you may be able to say, and mean, 'Yes, I forgive you with all my heart. I love you.' (The situation may still be painful however. What is real for you may be to say: 'Yes, I wish to be able to say: I love you and I forgive you. At the moment, I say with truth: I forgive you as Christ forgives you. I love you as Christ loves you. I hope soon to be able to say that from the depths of my own heart.')

You may be aware and able to accept that there are usually two sides to any situation. You may be able to say: 'I ask you for your forgiveness for whatever I may have done, then or since, to have hurt you. I ask you to love me!'

There remains an important stage to this healing ministry. *It must be handed over to Christ, Healer and Saviour.* Personally, I like, at this stage, to direct attention to Christ's wound of love for us, namely His wounded heart. I invite the person or people to move towards Christ, to look with love and gratitude at His wounded heart which loves us with unchanging love. Then, in humble gratitude I invite them to hand over to Christ the wound that has been healed. Ask Him to place it in His heart and to keep it there safely. Thus our wound becomes part of His own wound, becomes part of *healing for the world*.

Healing must continue. This is our responsibility. Each will know how complete or incomplete has been his own healing. One may have to continue praying for some time, offering the past, offering those who inflicted these wounds, to God. One must beware, however, of clinging to the past. The present is here. New life awaits us.

For some, as for myself, the healing experience may result in a healing from prejudice against the healing ministry. This is a great release. This initial healing can result in further healings related to prejudices, without any further ministry. It just happens! One never knows the plans of the Lord. I did not believe that I was being called into the healing ministry. The initial basic healing releases one into the care of the Lord and His plans.

In my experience many people declare after praying the Life Prayer: 'I had no idea that I needed any healing.' Reconciliation with God and with men and women in this way becomes a mighty influence on the way we think and act. It penetrates our inner being. It enriches our experience of sacrament. It builds up our faith.

When people have been healed, if they are faithful to praying and living with more love, and more wholeness, their lives become charged with meaning. Frequently they themselves become 'wounded healers'. The forgiveness which they freely gave, the reconciliation which was effected, becomes a stepping stone for growth. They no longer feel as if they were alone, hugging wounds or a poor self-image. They feel bonded with the Body of Christ. Their healed wound is held in the heart of Christ. Giving up their wounded state, freely, has resulted in healing for the whole Body, through this individual healing.

Relationships are important. Our relationship with God is vital. We are invited to enter into a new and living relationship with God and a right relationship with men and women. This is wholeness.

**Anyone who claims to be in the light
but hates his brother
is still in the dark** (1 Jn 2:9).

3 Light and darkness – sin and sinfulness

In First Steps, we dealt with a basic form of this theme of Light and Darkness, namely, the real and the unreal.

Here, in *Prepare the Way*, we expressly want to look honestly at the reality of sin and sinfulness in our lives. We have already seen in the preceding section the baleful influence of sin in the world today. Warfare is shamelessly declared on our neighbour. We swallow this neighbour alive in our determination to procure what is best for ourselves. We cannot do this to God, we dare not. We do the next worst thing: we punish our brothers and sisters, the image of God. Still worse, we seem to have lost the sense of our sin.

This necessitates our looking deeply at original sin and at its implications for us today.

The sin of Adam was an act of exterior rebellion. A human being consciously opposed God by violating one of His precepts (Gn 3:3).

Prior to the exterior act of disobedience, however, there was an interior act resulting from the subtle suggestion of the serpent. Adam and Eve wished to substitute themselves for God in deciding between good and evil. This was a desire to be independent of Him who created them. Thus they perverted the very relationship which united them to God.

The relationship with His creatures, as intended by God, was essentially one of friendship. The necessary dependence on God was to ensure the safety of those He loved, whom he had created. The God of the Bible had refused nothing to His creatures, who were 'created in His image and likeness' (Gn 1:26f).

This God reserved nothing for Himself, not even life, for: 'God did make man imperishable, He made him in the image of His own nature; it was the devil's envy that brought death into the world, as those who are his partners will discover' (Ws 2:23,24).

The wily enemy suggested to Adam and Eve that the precept given them by God was in fact a device to safeguard His privileges! To which the father of lies, Satan, added that God's threat was a lie! 'No! You will not die! But God knows in fact that on the day you eat it your eyes will be opened and you will be like gods, knowing good and evil' (Gn 3:4,5).

The very notion of God was perverted. God who is in Himself supremely perfect and lacks nothing was presented as One who is centred on preserving His own rights, thus protecting Himself against the creatures to whom He had given all!

This perverted notion continues to this day.

These human beings in the Garden of Eden, destined to

live for ever, to be one with God in whose image they were made, were first subtly corrupted in spirit before they were finally perverted and lured to an act of disobedience.

The dire consequences of sin, depicted above, began immediately for them. These two human beings began to 'hide themselves from the face of God' (Gn 3:8).

The threat proved to be no lie. Banished from the Garden of Paradise, access to the tree of life was impossible (Gn 3:22–4). Only death was left. From then on followed a rupture in relationship between God and human beings; a rupture in relationship between Adam and 'bone of his bone and flesh of his flesh' (Gn 2:23); a rupture likewise to this present day between members of human society. Disharmony, acrimony, loss of love became prevalent. "'Who told you that you were naked?", God asked. "Have you been eating of the tree I forbade you to eat?" The man replied, "It was the woman you put with me; she gave me the fruit, and I ate it." Then Yahweh God asked the woman, "What is this you have done?" The woman replied, "The serpent tempted me and I ate"' (Gn 3:11–13).

Later there followed the murder of Abel and the wild song of Lamech, evidence of the increasing ferocity of Cain's descendants: 'Lamech said to his wives: "Adah and Zillah, hear my voice, Lamech's wives, listen to what I say: I killed a man for wounding me, a boy for striking me. Sevenfold vengeance is taken for Cain, but seventy-sevenfold for Lamech"' (Gn 4:23,24).

The corruption of humankind continued. 'Yahweh saw that the wickedness of man was great on the earth, and that the thoughts in his heart fashioned nothing but wickedness all day long. Yahweh regretted having made man on earth, and his heart grieved. "I will rid the earth's face of man, my own creation . . . and of animals also, reptiles too, and the birds of heaven; for I regret having made them". But Noah had found favour with Yahweh' (Gn 6:5–8).

Once sin entered the world, it proliferated. It increased in malice and in destruction of one's neighbour. Yet the goodness of God appeared from time to time in people like Noah and his sons. Such people found favour with

God, like Abraham, Jacob, and many others through the centuries. God spoke in various ways to His people, through the prophets and finally through His Son, Jesus Christ.

The story has always been the same. God favours His people, and is repaid with ingratitude and infidelity. God's people Israel, like so many of us today, preferred a god within reach: 'They gathered round Aaron and said to him, "come, make us a god to go at the head of us"' (Ex 32:1). Israel was a 'stiff-necked' people – refusing to obey: 'Remember; never forget how you provoked Yahweh your God in the wilderness. From the day you came out of the land of Egypt *you have been rebels against Yahweh*' (Dt 9:7,8 italics mine).

This is something of the mystery of sin. It is rooted in independence of God, the Creator; rooted in self-love and unbridled passions; rooted in blindness and darkness, especially the darkness of pride. That is not all. The mystery of sin goes beyond our human world. The tempter, the instigator of this tragedy of separation, the father of lies, exacerbates the situation continuously by intervening between God and us, wherever, through self-love, we give him a shred of a toe-hold. This is the evil that is darkness. The darkness that must be banished. The darkness that can be mercifully transformed by the Light that is Christ.

We, however, have our part to play. We must discover our own darkness; be willing to reject it and hand it over to Christ. Then even darkness becomes light in the power of God's Holy Spirit. 'The people that walked in darkness have seen a great light; on those who live in a land of deep shadow a light has shone' (Is 9:1).

The enemy of Christ, Satan, is not creative. He can only imitate. We can learn from the above history of sin how he beguiles and fools us humans. He moves into our self-love. We are unique, so the area of our self-love is unique to you, to me. We learn where we are most easily entrapped by looking to our personal experience. Become *aware* of where, when, how we deviate even slightly from God's path for us. *Reflect* on that in prayer. *Listen* to how my behaviour in that area of self-love affects me, affects others, and affects God's plan for

His kingdom. We use the gift of *feelings* and of *discernment* and, of course, above all else, we hand the whole situation over to the Holy Spirit before even looking to awareness. Through breathing, through turning to the Spirit, we clothe all our efforts in the love and power of the Spirit.

We deepen our awareness of darkness in our life, even at its inception, if we are faithful to our *nightly reflection*. This puts us in tune at once with where we were walking with God during the day, for which we thank and glorify Him. But it also makes us keenly aware, day by day, of our danger, of our sinfulness. In this nightly reflection we are seeking to learn how we are putting ourselves, and the beguiling importance of our affairs, before our God!

It helps greatly to become very familiar, as I have said before, with the passage in Galatians 5:16–26. We see there how the Spirit of Christ brings peace, joy, self-control, and so on, into our lives, while the presence of the enemy is signalled by anger, feuds and quarrels. We need to reflect frequently on this passage. Where do I let the enemy have a toe-hold in my life?

In addition to all this, I think we need to be alert to a particular trap of this wily enemy. Often, coming as a deceptive 'angel of light', he entraps us into doing too much work, becoming over-busy, working apparently with good intent for God. We are so busy that we neglect to discern! Is this truly the work and the degree of involvement that God is asking from me? Or is my self-love, fear of failure, ambition, etc. blinding me to the truth? Whose kingdom am I actually building? God's or my own?

Again over-involvement and crowded schedules tend to blind me to what is happening in my *prayer*. Even if I manage to be faithful to my allotted prayer time, for example, am I aware of how I am short-changing God? My attention to His presence is less; my preparation for His coming gets shortened; my humble waiting on Him becomes tainted with impatience. I need to pray for *awareness*! The 'spirit' of my relationship with God will be under attack first. Then it becomes easier to lure me to acts of disobedience. Such acts become all the more possible through my many rationalisations. Adam and Eve taught me that! I can also cover up my own intent by cowering behind what 'others' do – these are often 'pillars of the church'. Adam even put the blame on God! 'The woman you put with me gave me the fruit.' All Adam did was to eat it!

We have to be careful, too, that we do not act like the pagans. Their idols have eyes but never see and ears that never hear. But, warns the psalmist, 'Their makers will end up like them, and so will anyone who relies on them' (115:8).

Blindness, deafness, hardness of heart are a sure way of falling into sin. We have received the gifts of our senses to lead us *to* God. How often we have abused our senses, and let them lead us far *from* our God!

Personal and corporate responsibility

We have seen earlier how we have a personal and corporate responsibility to build up the body of Christ. Unfortunately, we have to accept that we have likewise a personal and corporate responsibility in adding to the darkness of sin that fills the world.

We are not personally responsible for the robberies, rapes, murders, injustices that are perpetrated. But we do share a corporate responsibility. Every time that I am, to any degree, violent in word, action, attitude, I add to the degree of violence in the world. My personal sin, therefore, adds to the totality of darkness in the world. Instead of giving life and light to the world, my sinful behaviour gives the enemy easier access to the frailties of humanity.

To be more precise: I add to the violence in the world to the degree that I show anger, irritation, violent body language, or other manifestations of darkness. I add to the injustice in the world, if, in any way, I have shown injustice to another.

Have I put others down? Have I refused anyone a just wage? Have I rash-judged someone? Have I spread that by talking, or by cleverly writing a character reference that serves me, but is an injustice to the other? Have I been unjust by not taking my full workload, or by not carrying the full responsibility of my job? Have I always given as generous a contribution to the needy as my means allowed? Have I as keen an eye for injustices perpetrated against others as for those that target me?

One last pointer to my corporate responsibility. Do I accept that all is relative? There is only one absolute – God. All else is relative. As I look at television and the world scene of degradation, violence, destruction which is offered, what is my reaction? Christ condemns the *sin* but not the *sinner*. For us, this is a hard lesson to learn. The culprit is as much a victim as a wrongdoer. His background may not be good, much less ideal. Do I see my corporate responsibility for the existence of such social conditions? Have I remained an armchair observer? Have I let my voice be heard and my vote count? Or is my sin that of self-love which places my own interests always first? If that is my reality, then I must recognise it and own it. At least, let me spare others my 'word-offerings', however eloquent. My *action* may appear to be less serious than that of others. But how does God see it, relative to all my opportunities? When we grasp that the darkness of the world is part of the passion of Christ, our responsibility, as well as our personal pain increases. We are called to 'fill up in our lives what is wanting to the passion of Christ' (Col 1:24).

At least, let us begin by taking our personal sin more seriously and pray that our commitment to the body of Christ may further awaken our sense of corporate sin.

The way of the wicked is as dark as night,
they cannot tell what it is they stumble over (Pr 4:19).

4 The Sower – Mark 4:18–20

When I spoke about the sower in *First Steps*, I used Mark 4: 13–18 to illustrate what can happen to 'beginners' in prayer. I used them especially with reference to the devotees at the altar of this world. They rejoice at the good news, then become enthusiastic, but they lack root. They fall away easily, especially when any form of persecution or trial crosses their path. They have not learnt how to make the soil of their being more receptive. They do not call upon the power of the Spirit, nor grow in awareness and reflection.

Such people would certainly fall away before they came to this stage of cleansing and purification in *Prepare the Way*.

We come now to three verses in the passage which are relevant to what we spoke of earlier about relationships. These verses deal especially with the picture of this world and the way that neighbour exploits neighbour. 'Then there are others who receive the seed in thorns. These have heard the word, but the worries of this world, the lure of riches and all the other passions come in to choke the word, and so it produces nothing' (vv 18–20).

These verses say more about corporate responsibility for the evil of this world than I could say. Succinctly it is stated that, yes, the word has been preached to them. It even seems to imply that they believed, at least for a time. But self-love became an idol, an all consuming, devouring idol. It began with worries of the world which were not brought to Christ, worries that ate into their very soul, until rationalisation took over. 'I have to do this,' they say, 'competition is so keen . . . I have a family to support . . . a father to bury.' In short, *I am so very busy*. Here is the first step of the malaise of Christian spirituality which we see all around us. We must not 'wash our hands' like Pilate! This 'over-busy' syndrome loses more red-blood members to the body of Christ than many another trap. It weakens the morale more than it weakens the physical body.

The Gospel puts Jesus at the very centre of our lives, the ground of our being. Our God is a jealous God and He demands the totality of our being. He is the most important truth in our life or He is nothing. If we say we have no time in our lives, we are in danger of totally rejecting Him.

That word 'nothing' falls on our hearts with a hollow sound! It comes too close to 'nothingness' for comfort. It is exactly what happens to those who have not learnt the salutary lesson 'Without God I am nothing'; nor have their hearts been lifted by the promise that 'With God all things are possible'.

When the possibility of riches casts its lure around us, we are already on the downward path, ready to fall for the wiles of Satan, prince of darkness. Once riches have caught us, then the neighbour is the next target. Greed, lust for power, injustice follow in easy succession, 'and all the other passions come in to choke the word'. The harvest is not just poor. The harvest for God is 'nothing'.

Fortunately for those of us who fall for this ploy of the enemy, there remain a few steadfast planks of salvation. The love of the Lord is everlasting. Within us the image of God still is, even though its potential for revival seems to be in question. We need more help. That help is there in the body of Christ. We seem too weak to help ourselves. But other stalwart followers of Christ are mindful of the enemy on the prowl like a 'roaring lion'. For love of their Lord, these 'vigilantes' are likewise praying, loving to intercede, with lamps burning, for His Glory. This is our hope. Darkness can always be transformed into light. Fidelity in little things is saving the sin-torn world. Especially dear to the Lord is the widow's mite, the cruse of oil, the sparrows, the hairs of our head, the present moment . . . the little things. If some are faithful to the little things, then the Lord will speak: 'Well done, good and faithful servant; you have shown you can be faithful in small things, I will trust you with greater' (Mt 25:21).

What can be a greater thing, than participation with Christ, with other members of His body in saving even *one* soul. This soul is made in His image. This soul was signed with the seal of His Spirit. Our 'little' act of self-denial can be transformed into saving power, the power of Almighty God. This is the Light that transforms darkness.

The people that walked in darkness
have seen a great light;
on the inhabitants of a country
in shadow dark of death
light has blazed forth' (Is 9:1).

5 Prayer

As we progress in *Prepare the Way* we need to be familiar with two aspects of prayer, namely, praying with prose and Scripture, and faith-sharing. Whatever is said about praying with prose or Scripture in the context of *Light out of Darkness*, I understand as relevant for prayer at all times.

Using a prose passage in prayer

In Part Two of *Prepare the Way*, pp. 124–126, I show how we go about using a prose passage on a specific theme which I have written, for example, 'I speak to God.' The *remote preparation* which has been mentioned before, such as looking forward to prayer, slowing down, focusing on God is relevant here. *Immediate preparation* includes knowing the subject matter which one intends to pray, the time, place, posture, etc. which seem appropriate. (See pages 39, 40).

In any prayer time where due preparation is made, and the desire of the one praying is a genuine seeking of God, one may expect to be moved in some measure by the Spirit. These movements, as already indicated, will be centred around *insights* which one receives, arising usually out of the material one is praying.

An 'insight' is only the starting point. It remains barren until one reflects on its meaning for one's life. The *feelings* play a role at this time, alerting one to one's response, be it of attraction to the insight given, or a resistance to it. Even then, there is a further step in this sequence of fruitful awareness of the initial 'insight'. It deals with a *decision* that has to be made. Since the Holy Spirit has moved in prayer to alert one to a way of looking at something, it means that one's present attitude is either being confirmed or challenged. One is either being called to decide to remain faithful to a course of action or to change an attitude or approach.

Reflection is vital, if prayer is to deepen. Unless one is a reflective person in ordinary daily life, it is unlikely that one will be very reflective in prayer. Closely associated with reflection is *awareness*. Again, one will find it difficult to be aware of the 'interior' experience unless one is accustomed to being aware of what is happening all around one in life.

Until one becomes more mature in prayer, it helps to have the kind of discipline that is stressed here. In *Prepare the Way*, questions are suggested after the prayer on the prose passage, so as to stimulate awareness and reflection. The best questions are those that one instinctively asks oneself which, under the guidance of the Spirit, arise out of one's interest in the subject.

Praying Scripture

In *Light out of Darkness* the Scriptures are always proposed as a follow-up on the prose passage which deals with the same theme. Both should deal with similar themes. It helps to have pondered the material in the prose, to have applied it to oneself and to have come to certain decisions. Praying a passage from Scripture on the same theme makes for much greater depth. The way has been prepared through reflection on the prose passage, so that the soil has become more receptive to hearing God's own word. I am always reminded, at this time in the programme, of the words of

Isaiah: '. . . my thoughts are not your thoughts, my ways not your ways – it is Yahweh who speaks' (55:8).

I feel that the reflection on the prose has revealed to the one who prays some measure at least of how thoughts and ways can deviate from God's thoughts. At least a seed has been sown; awareness has been sharpened, decisions taken.

Consequently, in praying the word of God in Scripture, there is more hope that, as Isaiah says of Yahweh, 'the word that goes from my mouth does not return to me empty, without carrying out my will and succeeding in what it was sent to do' (Is 55:11).

Praying Scripture, like praying prose, means reading slowly and reflectively, pausing as soon as something strikes one. It helps to think about the thought that spoke to one's mind and let it move one to the heart, to the feelings. Inviting the Holy Spirit to help one see the relevance of the thought to one's life and one's seeking of God in all things, is wisdom.

It is indeed wisdom to aim at depth in one or two lines of Scripture, rather than covering a lot of material superficially. Eventually, one gathers one's own scriptural gems. The oftener one prays these, the richer the insights become. It is like a person who yields up deep secrets after some time to the trusted friend who has treated reverently treasures that are prized.

Whether one is reading a spiritual book or praying with Scripture, the results will be all the greater the more one reflects, becomes aware, and applies insights to one's own life. It is such a loss if the Spirit of God keeps alerting us to potential growth points in our life, and we miss recognising His action!

Faith-sharing

This prayer experience has become popular in the last two decades. There was a time when people were advised not to talk about their interior life, except to a spiritual director! The thinking behind this exhortation seemed to be that one might become proud, or at least less humble, if one talked about these matters to others 'supposedly' less blessed.

In fact, the advice was based on sound principles, strange though that may now seem to us, who have gained so much from the practice of faith-sharing. It was, I think, an effort to safeguard people from the inexperienced and the unwise.

Consequently, in *Light out of Darkness*, no comment on the faith-sharing of another person is allowed. The leader acknowledges the sharing of a member by a simple 'thank you'. Only when a trained spiritual director leads a group are comments from such a leader encouraged, so as to enrich the participants. Faith-sharing is not the same as sharing about our faith. The latter deals with the content of what we are taught and believe as the doctrine of the Church.

Faith-sharing on the other hand is sharing with another, or others, the fruit of my particular discernment with regard to God moving me, speaking to me, in my prayer and my life. This discernment, as I have said before, needs to be confirmed. If the listener(s) has been genuinely touched, challenged, convicted or inspired, this is indeed confirmation for the one who is sharing. Nor is it necessary for the listener to express that in words to the speaker. The Spirit reveals His presence in myriad ways. It is relatively easy to distinguish the genuine from the false in faith-sharing. If one is sharing an experience of consolation, where God seems to be close and comforting, then humility, honesty and simplicity will mark the speaker and be obvious to the listener. Moreover, the real confirmation comes from the quality of *life-experience* which results from or is accompanied by this consoling experience. The neighbour will benefit from God's presence in consolation.

The charlatan is easily exposed. When faith-sharing is shallow or lacking in truth or depth, one usually finds that *prayer* has been neglected. Nor has there been any service towards the neighbour, at the personal expense of the one who is now sharing.

The faith-sharing which seems to touch people most deeply is when someone, as he listens to the Spirit, discovers his own frailties. Others could have told him, for example, about his arrogance, or his tendency to control people. They could have told someone else about her jealousy, or envy, or anger. But it is only when we discover for ourselves, through the goodness of God, that we have been blind or deaf or dumb, that we seem to be able to claim it and do something about it. When a person is led by God to say in truth, 'I did not see my behaviour like that until now. I did not know I was so very blind. Thanks be to God for His goodness. Now, I am beginning to see,' all rejoice. Honest, sincere faith-sharing like that speaks directly to the heart of the listeners.

There is, however, no discussion at all about the content of a person's faith-sharing, as you will see later. When someone is sharing a faith-experience, a listener may say eventually: 'Your sharing helped me enormously. It was only when I heard you speak that I understood what was going on in myself.' But there should be no comment about the content.

Faith-sharing can be very simple or very deep. That does not matter. What is important is that it is real, that it is genuine; that I share with others not only the movement in prayer, but especially how that affected my life, because I clearly had seen the need to change.

A few simple examples of faith-sharing may help: A lady had been praying and reflecting on her attitudes and relationships with others. The following was her honest and practical faith-sharing:

I've come to know myself better, to recognise my fears and my inhibitions. My mother was domineering. But I must take my own responsibility for the situation that I allowed to develop. I'm discovering a new freedom within myself now. That is important for me after all these years. I cannot thank God enough. I am slowly learning to trust Him more and more. My daily prayer has helped me come to this. Reflection on it helped me see. Sharing with a friend has brought me new strength and courage. Thanks be to God.

A man who was shy and kept a safe distance from others discovered this truth about himself through *Light out of Darkness*. He longed to be set free. He listened to the faith-sharing of others and ventured to open up a little in his turn. The warm, accepting attitude of a group made him feel more and more comfortable. It did not pose a threat to him. Gradually, the presence and support of the Holy Spirit in his prayer and then in his life did for him at deeper level what human beings had begun. It was a joyful experience when he was able to share this experience with others. Eventually he became a group leader.

Common sense

In faith-sharing, we must recognise that God has given us a precious gift which is our common sense! What we share must be the truth, but common sense may dictate that we do not share everything. We have responsibilities to other people as well! We discern what it is right for us to share. That means that we discern what is my true experience; what will best glorify God and witness to His action in my life, and yet observe the rights of other people in my life. Here are some guidelines that help us in discerning our faith-sharing:

- What helped me discover my blindness, or deafness, or central weakness, etc?
- What revealed to me my self-centredness?
- What helped me be more honest about myself?

- What focused me more on God, on my neighbour and less on myself?
- What helped me be more real, more aware of others, more in touch with reality?

Confidentiality

The importance of confidentiality in a group situation can never be over-emphasised. In faith-sharing people make themselves vulnerable by trusting the group. A breach of confidentiality could seriously damage a person. It would also damage the growth of the group. Experience teaches that people value having a 'safe place', namely a group of like-minded people, where they can feel confident about sharing their search for God and sharing also some of their pain and their darkness. Confidentiality, therefore, means *noblesse oblige*.

No discussion

In a group, or even when an individual shares with a friend, experience has taught us not to encourage discussion about the content of the faith-sharing. A person is sharing what he has discerned as the word and action of God in his prayer and in his life. It would be foolhardy for any other person to venture into that sacred ground. 'Thank you' is sufficient. The most that is acceptable is the comment above, namely, 'Your sharing helped me. It was only then I understood what was happening to me.' That is a general comment which refers to yourself, what is happening to you. It does not include a comment on the content of another's faith-sharing. If a trained spiritual director is leading a group, that is a different matter. The director may then discern what else is appropriate to be said.

Faith-sharing is richer when done in a group because one learns from the sharing of others. Outside the formal group situation, friends who are open and honest with one another can also derive much fruit from faith-sharing. Faith-sharing is so important that it can even be fruitful if individuals share by telephone, when a meeting with friends would be difficult.

The essential thing is to prayerfully pause and discern those changes in our behaviour which are necessary, to reflect on the whole process and draw the main threads together. This drawing together is in itself another form of discernment. One cannot give a blow-by-blow description of each day in each week! The essential point is to identify what God has really taught me in this experience. That is the fruit that is worth sharing.

**Your word is a lamp to my feet,
a light on my path'** (Ps 119:105)

6 Freedom – fruit of repentance

In *Prepare the Way* we need to plumb the depths of our sinfulness, particularly of our sinful attitudes. We need to come to a deeper awareness of these attitudes. By claiming them humbly before Christ we can be brought by His healing love from darkness into the radiance of His light and love. This is freedom.

Repentance of sin brings one to a new reality in life. In Luke we read: 'For this reason I tell you that her sins, her many sins, must have been forgiven her, or she would not have shown such great love. It is the man who is forgiven little who shows little love' (7:47).

Our awareness of what constitutes sin – mainly a rejection of God's love and saving presence in all the gifts and giftedness of life – can become dim indeed. This is a result of blind, ingrained sinfulness. Sinfulness is so much wider and often so much more insidious than sin. Sinfulness is the poisonous root, the deceptive, contaminating attitude which can make a potentially good act evil. Sinfulness can render acts less good than they might have been, thus insidiously introducing a 'neither hot nor cold approach', which is so condemned by the Lord. The attraction, or invitation, to plumb the depths of our sinfulness is really a gift from the Lord. He alone acts and achieves, but we like to see ourselves as the achievers. I can only open my being to receive insight, wisdom and growth. I cannot press buttons, do the right things to get moving, or take charge of the process, though I may well be tempted in my darkness to try to do so! Plumbing the depths is truly a letting go process, a letting God use His power and His wisdom, while I keep my place and trust in faith and hope and love. A delicate awareness begins to grow. By faith I perceive that the Lord is near, is holding and cherishing me, and in His infinite awareness of the truth of my being is calling me into a deeper knowledge of this darkness, so that He can bring me to new life. Light out of darkness. And this is freedom.

Thoughts such as these, I remember, moved me with a longing on one occasion to come closer to God; at the same time I had an awareness that to do so I needed to know my real self better. I knew that it meant going deeper than where I was. God was calling me, I felt sure of that, and I felt that He wanted to teach me many things. I had a sense that this teaching was closely related to getting to know better the *real* me. I was strengthened by a sense of God's closeness, which took me a little by surprise.

On a summer day in August I was walking down O'Connell Street in Dublin which was crowded with tourists. I felt called to do an experiment on myself. I didn't know how it would begin or end! I had very little to guide me, but there was a sense of excitement, a sense of urgency within me. I felt held in the protection of God. It seemed to me that the key to entering deeper into my being would be *through my feelings*. I may say that this experience and experiment happened a good number of years ago, long before we became so knowledgeable and sophisticated about feelings as related to spirituality! I had just completed two and a half years in America and my horizons had greatly widened. This new breadth owed something to the various disciplines

I had enjoyed but still more, I think, to the experience of new places and new ways, the combination of support and friendliness which did not obliterate the teaching value of deep loneliness. All had combined to draw me to an experiment which would, I hope, lead me into great depths of my being, through my feelings. I got quite a surprise.

I stepped out briskly. I was passing Clery's department store when a woman with a child in a pram seemed to shoot across my path. Normally in such circumstances, I would have muttered impatiently to myself something like 'botheration'. Indeed I was just on the verge of saying that, when I stopped suddenly. I remembered the experiment I was intent on doing. This must be the beginning! I was hoping to come to know my real self through my feelings. I hoped that through this, I would somehow come to know Christ better, too. An unusual sense of expectancy held me. My heart was strangely alight. I have never forgotten that feeling, despite the discoveries I made!

I began questioning myself. It became a kind of unusual dialogue between my inner reality which was a challenging voice and my exterior me, which was the defendant. I will call the inner, deeper me, the Voice; the external defendant is Me.

VOICE: How are you feeling now about that incident with the woman and the child?

ME: She nearly tripped me!

VOICE: I didn't see that. But how are you feeling about it now?

ME: I'm annoyed.

VOICE: What exactly has annoyed you?

ME: She could have looked where she was going. (*I began to feel a little ashamed at this stage, but not yet ready to admit that.*)

VOICE: She was burdened with a child in a pram in a crowded thoroughfare. You are carrying only a handbag! Are you in earnest about this experiment? If so cut out the excuses, see what is really going on and learn.

ME: (I have no more words!)

I felt that I was on the brink of some discovery that was important to me. My excitement was growing and with it a sense of comfort and presence. I felt it was so good to be alive. I felt ready to discover even unpleasant things about myself. I sensed vaguely that in this way, I would also come to know the real God better.

I crossed the street, walking on air. Yet I was reflecting deeply. The outcome of what is here a very abridged version of the reality took me completely by surprise. I had attributed rights to myself to which I had no claim, rights to an untramelled passage through a crowded area! I was unwilling to grant those same rights to a mother with a child in a pram.

I kept asking myself awkward questions to lead me deeper into the truth. I discovered that the roots of such an unwarranted attitude lay in arrogance and pride. I should have been shattered, but that did not come until later. My spiritual director advised me to spend as much time as it took to reflect on the whole experience. It took me three days. I wrote it out in detail as a reflective meditation.

I discovered that through this Socratic method of question and answer, I was led to truth. I was also led into a deeper place in my being. The result of it all was a new and almost heady experience of freedom. Combined with this a joy kept bubbling up from deep within. I truly felt like an explorer on discovering a new land. Out of childhood sprang the memory of Cortez,* when he gazed, dumbfounded, at the vast expanse of the Pacific, stretched before him for the first time. The mystery and wonder of his discovery of that vast ocean imprinted itself on my being as a child. The impact of it recurs, whenever the 'infinite' touches my life in an unexpected way.

The fruit of that experiment on O'Connell Street has never left me. In fact, it has deepened. Reflection on the 'new awareness' deepened the actual experience. I was taught by the Spirit the need to recognise the truth of my discovery. Without recognition, I could not claim the truth. This is an

* 'On First Looking in Chapman's Homer' by John Keats.

important distinction, between recognition and claiming. It is only when I claim something as true, as part of the real me, that I am able to proceed to do something about it.

Feelings help me to understand where I am in a situation. These feelings need to be sorted out or discerned as to their direction, in helping me reach God and His truth. All of this is a form of growth into freedom. It is a gift of God. It was important for me to continue reflecting on freedom. What did it mean? What did it feel like?

I discovered that for me freedom happens when I am moved by God out of a certain darkness. It may be the darkness of being unaware, insensitive, the darkness perhaps of my refusing to look at what is really going on, the darkness therefore of being out of touch with reality.

Freedom therefore for me is associated with the rejection of darkness in some form. The desire to move is at least a beginning. Freedom is not something that I do, that I earn. It is not done by me. It is rather a movement of the Spirit within me, alerting me to new life which is opening up – though I may be unaware of that, at the time.

It is the Spirit awakening a desire in me; a desire for deeper things, a desire to be somehow more free, yet more surrendered to what is greater than me.

I am not in control. I cannot be. The initial action, the beginning of a new movement, a new journey can only come from the Spirit.

I am unaware of where the journey will lead. I am, however, in touch with movements within; with a sense of newness; of new life. To let that go would be a deep bereavement, a kind of abortion. Freedom presages a new depth of living as a Christian. It seems to take many forms, depending on God's call and on my response.

For me, freedom in this particular case resulted in no longer fearing to discover my darker self; no longer being caught by negatives or fear of failure. I had learnt a definite lesson: light always comes out of darkness when it is surrendered to God.

I began to understand better St Paul's statement, which had always appealed to me: 'So I shall be very happy to make my weaknesses my special boast so that the power of Christ may stay over me' (2 Cor 12:9).

Christ's strength is infinite. It behoves us to keep discovering our weaknesses. There is a long journey ahead!

Though the light has come into the world, people have shown they prefer darkness to the light because their deeds were evil (Jn 3:19).

Part Two: Prepare the Way –
Walking with Christ

Introduction

Leaders of groups need to understand the foregoing sections relative to the function of *Prepare the Way*. This function is to recognise and claim the reality of personal and corporate sin and the need for repentance. *Prepare the Way* leads from darkness to light and to *Building the Temple*.

Structure
Whether you are following this as an *individual* or as a *group member*, a structure helps. The following very simple structure is used from now until the end of the programme, as a way of bringing together prayer and life – one of the aims of this book.

The beginning
Hand over the whole prayer period to the Holy Spirit. Become still. *Glory be to the Father*: Say it slowly and reverently including others who may need prayers.

Faith-sharing
Individuals may share with God their awareness of how He has moved them in prayer and called them to practise the

insight He gave them in their daily living. *Group members* share with the group, as directed by their leader.

Prose passage on the specific theme of the chapter
Let the 'movements' speak to you – as already explained on page 23.
Talk to God about anything that strikes you.
If it helps, make a note of the thought that most moves you.

Questions to help you deepen your awareness and your reflection
Stay with any question that reveals you more truly to yourself.
If you feel resistance, pray all the more for light and strength.

Scripture passages on the same theme
Do the same as with the prose passage above.
Use the same questions if they help.
Follow the guidance of the Spirit.
Before finishing the prayer on Scripture, take time to draw together the main thread of what moved you.
Pray to discern the most important truth that you learnt.

Prepare for your next faith-sharing
Follow the guidelines given in the section on faith-sharing (page 107). Out of the section just now completed, what was the most important growth point for you? What was your experience, as you practised that in your daily life circumstances? That is the content of your faith-sharing which happens when you begin the next section.

The end: Glory be . . .
Finish by including in this final prayer the wounded and broken in the world. Rest reverently for a little while at the conclusion of the prayer.

Nightly reflection
It is understood from now to the end of *Prepare the Way* that the nightly reflection forms an integral part of daily prayer and living.

As we move on to the next step in *Light out of Darkness*, here is a summary, in table form, of the themes of the next eight sections of *Prepare the Way*, along with a list of the corresponding human qualities that help us to develop. Recall that *Light out of Darkness* is a human-spiritual growth process: development of the person is through the integration and inter-penetration of the human and the spiritual.

Section	Human Dimension	Spiritual Dimension
1	Awareness, desire, feeling	My relationship with God
2	Words, actions, attitudes	I speak to God
3	Events, movements, fears, hopes	God speaks to me
4	Positive and negative attitudes	My prayer
5	Goodness innate in me	God's goodness revealed in me
6	My human struggle	God's tenderness in my struggle
7	My neighbour	God's love for my neighbour. My love?
8	Trust	My trustworthiness

1 My relationship with God

Beginning
Let us hand over this coming prayer time to God. Be still, thanking Him for being with us. As we say the *Glory be*

. . ., let us remember those for whom we want to pray, people who may not have this opportunity that we have.

Glory be to the Father . . .

Faith-sharing

You completed *First Steps*, and as an individual, or as a group member, you may like to talk to God about what was most important for you out of *First Steps*. What did you learn? How did it affect your life? Were you more open to other people as a result of having done *First Steps*? Did you tell others about your experience with it? In short, have you witnessed to others about what God has done in you, for you and through you? Get in touch with God and thank Him for being with you, as you recall the time since *First Steps*. Share (as an individual with God or as a group member with the group).

Prose passage on the specific theme: Relationship with God

When you pray, to whom do you actually pray? That may seem a foolish question, but it isn't. We need to sharpen our awareness about many things, if we want to grow as Christians. Some pray to the Father, or the Son, or the Holy Spirit. Others may pray to the Blessed Trinity, or to God.

What is *real* for you? Take your time with this important question. For many people this became a new starting point in their lives. They discovered that they hadn't given much thought at all to this question. What about you? It matters to God that you are interested. God is interested! It is God who attracted you to pray to one Person rather than another. It is God who moves us at certain times to make a change. Have you thought of that? Is it important to you now? It means that there is a special relationship between you and God. It matters to Him! He is interested in everything that concerns us, but He will not intrude. He waits until you invite Him into your life, perhaps not formally, but always He reads the depths of hearts!

How often do you pause to say a 'thank you' to God,

or how seldom? Our good manners are sometimes lacking where gratitude to God is concerned. Yet we are very alert about what concerns ourselves, that appreciation is duly expressed! Relationships grow when we truly appreciate and value another and when we learn to express that. We all need affirmation! In this matter of developing relationship with God, *desires* are important.

Did you know that it is the Spirit of God Himself who 'desires' good desires into us? And we thought we were doing it! But we need to become more aware of our desires, so that we can thank God for them. We will talk a lot about awareness in these programmes and you will be amazed to discover, I think, how unaware you have been up to this time.

For example, you seem to desire to know God more intimately or why are you reading this book? You seem to desire to grow as a fully developed human-spiritual person. Pause to become aware that you and God share the same desire for you! At this stage, you may be tempted to say: 'This is all too much for me. I could never live up to this relationship with God.'

You are becoming aware now of anxieties and fears! That awareness is good. You are growing already! But about fears, for the moment hand them over to God. He will take care of them until I say more later about fears. God knows about your 'fear' before you become aware of it. He never leaves you. He is always with you, as He promised.

By admitting to fears, to lack of awareness, or to anything else you have discovered, you have become more real. God loves us to be real people, who are in touch with reality.

Questions to help you deepen your awareness and reflection

What has struck you in this prose passage?

How are you feeling about it? Surprised? Anxious? Happy? Excited? or what?

Do you desire to deepen your relationship with God?

Do you realise that deepening human relationships helps to deepen our relationship with God? More about that later.

Have any special questions occurred to you? Stay with them for a while, especially when you have more time.

Before moving on to praying Scripture, *pause*.

Out of all the *awareness* and *reflection*, what has struck you most? What has been the most important thought or awareness for you? Bring that to God. Talk to Him and listen to Him. This prepares you to listen more keenly when you pray God's word to you in Scripture, as you are about to do now.

Scripture

So far some thoughts have struck you. You have been attracted by them, or maybe you were a bit stunned or frightened. Whatever you felt, you can always talk to God about it.

Read now some of the passages from Scripture. Think about them. Reflect on them. What do they say to you about relationship with God? about the relationship of prayer? about desires? You do not need to pray through all the passages, unless they speak to you and are helpful.

The following passages are examples of scriptures you can reflect on which deal with relationship and the desire for relationship with God:

Jesus said: 'Follow Me and I will make you into fishers of people' (Mk 1:18).

Jesus said: 'If anyone wants to be a follower of mine, let him renounce himself and take up his cross every day and follow Me' (Lk 9:23).

'When you seek me you shall find me, when you seek me with all your heart; I will let you find me' (Jer 29:13–14).

'I tell you therefore: everything you ask and pray for, believe that you have it already, and it will be yours' (Mk 11:24).

Each day, pray some of this material. It is better to go slowly, to reflect, and to pause to talk to God about it all.

Become *aware* of your feelings, and your responses. It may help you to re-read the initial sections on *Awareness, Listening, Feelings, Discerning*. Be sure to decide *how* you are going to let the prayer-insights you receive affect your daily living. It may help to write down the particular thought or insight that struck you most. How can you 'flesh that out' today?

Preparation for your next faith-sharing
Before you start Section Two, become aware of what your faith-sharing on the material now in hand is going to be. How did it focus you on God? What action did that lead you to? Bring this faith-sharing, as an *individual* to God, or as a member to the *group*.

The end: Glory be . . .
Say this slowly, reverently, as already suggested. Include all those who have nobody to pray for them. *Glory be to the Father* . . .

Nightly reflection
Follow the directions you were given in First Steps. The Nightly Reflection is an integral part of *daily prayer and living*.

2 I speak to God

To individual readers: Before ending each section, individuals are advised to spend time drawing together what you learnt from the section. Discern what is the most important point in that for your growth. What helped you most to grow, to be less concerned about self, more centred on God and on your neighbour? The answer to these questions will help you in your faith-sharing. Talk to God about it. If it helps you, write out the points that struck you most.

To group members: Each week, when you meet as a group, you always do your faith-sharing on the prayer-life experience of the preceding week. This is now taken as understood, both by individuals and groups, to the end of the book. In case of doubt, check out this page again. Also read *Faith-Sharing* on pages 107–111.

Beginning
Welcome to you again! Let us begin as usual by handing over to God this precious time, to praise and glorify Him and ask His blessing. Become still. Together we say the *Glory be to the Father* . . . asking God's blessing on us and on our families and friends.

Faith-sharing
Recall what you were guided to discern as your experience of God moving in your prayer and life. You did that before you finished the last section. Please share now, as the Spirit moves you. Individuals may like to write their faith-sharing as a 'letter' to God. Group members listen to each other. If you are in a group, the leader then thanks you all for your faith-sharing.

Prose passage on the theme: I speak to God
There are many ways in which we can speak to God. Perhaps you are unaware of the variety of ways. Human beings speak to one another through words, actions, and attitudes. So we do with God! Human beings, as well as God, hear 'speech' in what has no words, for example, in the way we listen or don't, whether we are reflective, or feeling people, whether we discern God's presence or not. All is speech. God hears that kind of speech, too!

It is worth noting at this point that in whatever way we human beings relate to one another, we do the same with God. We have only one body, one heart, one set of senses. We tend to use them in the same way, whether we are relating with one another or with God. If, for example, we do not 'listen' to our neighbour, we will not listen to

God. Our lack of 'trust' in our neighbour will reflect itself in lack of trust in God! We are the *same* person, whether we are relating to people or to God. We cannot separate the human and the spiritual. The more we become aware of the inter-relatedness of the human and the spiritual, the more **real** we become.

Today, however, we choose three ways of speaking to God: through *words, actions* and *attitudes*.

Words

In the last section, on relationships, you used *words* to express to yourself what was happening within you. They were probably spoken in the silence of your heart. Those particular words were probably not intended by you for God's ears, yet of course He heard them all. Everything about you is important to Him. Always be *real*, because God likes that.

You also used words to speak directly to God. This is what we call 'formal prayer'. There is a place for both. The words about God are a preparation for the direct talking to Him, or listening to Him, or just being with Him, which is what we usually call prayer.

Actions

Have you ever been aware that words and actions don't always seem to be in tune? For example, a parent may say to a child: 'Be a person whose word is your bond.' Then for the flimsiest of reasons, a promise to the young person is broken. Confusion and distrust can grow between them as a result. Unfortunately this distrust can spread to others, and even to God! Are our words and actions always in harmony?

Attitudes

I cannot sufficiently stress the importance of attitudes. They are a deep inner reality from which actions spring. Our attitudes are often hidden, even from ourselves. Yet God, who reads the heart, is never deceived!

Look again at the example given above about the breaking of a promise to another. The actual 'breaking' was an action.

But that action of breaking comes from deep within us, from an *attitude*. It could come from inner selfishness, from a self-centred attitude that puts self first on all occasions; perhaps from pride, from deep anger. That attitude needs to be recognised for what it truly is, then claimed before God, and changed as a matter of personal responsibility.

It is possible however, that at times, the same action, 'breaking a promise', may spring from a good attitude – something like loyalty to a client which has to take precedence in certain circumstances. In such a case, while observing confidentiality and prudence, the young person is owed a reasonable explanation. Consequently, no damage results. God is a good 'listener'. He hears 'situations' correctly and will always help us to help others.

Questions to deepen your awareness and reflection on above passage

What thought(s) moved you, awakened your awareness? Reflect on that and see what implications that may have for your approach to life or to others?

Did anything surprise you? Pause with anything that holds you. Hand it over to the Holy Spirit, and ask Him to help you come to a deeper truth.

Are you clearer about your own reality with regard to the harmony or disharmony between your words, actions and attitudes?

What will you do today, and every day, to change what needs changing?

Scripture on the same theme

A passage from St Luke speaks of the relationship between good and rotten trees and good and bad fruit respectively. It is the same with attitudes, actions and words. All affect relationships. Good attitudes will bear the good fruit of words and actions. Bad attitudes poison actions or words.

There is no sound tree that produces rotten fruit, nor again a rotten tree that produces sound fruit. For every tree can be told by its own fruit: people do not pick figs from thorns,

nor gather grapes from brambles. A good man draws what
is good from the store of goodness in his heart; a bad man
draws what is bad from the store of badness. For a man's
words flow out of what fills his heart (Lk 6:43–5).

Psalm 40 speaks of relationship with God, especially from
the point of view of trust. Trust is essential to building good
relationships with God and with one another.

> I waited and waited for Yahweh,
> now at last he has stooped to me
> and heard my cry for help.
>
> He has pulled me out of the horrible pit,
> out of the slough of the marsh,
> has settled my feet on a rock
> and steadied my steps.
>
> He has put a new song in my mouth,
> a song of praise to our God;
> dread will seize many at the sight,
> and they will put their trust in Yahweh.
>
> Happy the man who puts
> his trust in Yahweh,
> and does not side with rebels
> who stray after false gods.
>
> How many wonders you have done for us,
> Yahweh, my God!
> How many plans you have made for us;
> You have no equal!
> I want to proclaim them, again and again,
> but they are more than I can count.
>
> You, who wanted no sacrifice or oblation,
> opened my ear,
> you asked no holocaust or sacrifice for sin;
> then I said, 'Here I am! I am coming!'

In the scroll of the book am I not commanded
to obey your will?
My God, I have always loved your Law
from the depths of my being.

To me, poor wretch,
come quickly, Lord! (Ps 40:1–8,17)

Get in touch with the feelings that you experience as you
pray this Psalm.

Become still; listen to God. Re-read, if necessary the
section on 'Praying with Prose and Scripture', page 104–5.
Recall that it is better to do a little Scripture well than to
cover too much ground in a shallow way. Aim at depth
rather than a shallow spread. At the end, use the above
questions again, or others that occur to you.

Preparation for your next faith-sharing

Before starting the next section, prepare at an appropriate
time for your faith-sharing. Discern what most helped you
grow when you prayed this chapter. How did it affect
your living?

The end: Glory be . . .

We finish with the *Glory be to the Father* . . . Bring into your
prayer the wider world. In this way you share with them what
you have received here of God's goodness. Rest for a while
in God's presence.

Nightly reflection

This follows its usual course.

3 God speaks to me

Beginning

Welcome again. Let us be *still*. Draw into our prayer our
families and friends. Now let us say slowly and reverently:
Glory be to the Father . . .

Faith-sharing
Recall what you were guided to discern as your experience of God moving in your prayer and life. You did that before you finished the last section. Now share, as the Spirit moves you. At the end of each sharing, the leader says, 'Thank you'.

Prose passage on the new theme: God speaks to me
God speaks, but not as we speak to one another. God speaks clearly, if we have ears to hear! The problem is rarely with the way God speaks but with our unwillingness to listen. We can become so 'hard of hearing'. I wonder what is our underlying attitude here! Why are we 'hard of hearing'?

I have chosen Psalm 40 again, but using it as the basis for the prose passage.

It is a powerful Psalm in itself. It is also illustrative of the *dialogue* that continually goes on between God and me, if I become attuned. It shows, too, various ways in which God speaks.

Identify with the psalmist, so that as I comment, you feel as if you alone are being addressed. Pay attention, therefore, to words or phrases in the Psalm that move you, whether this attracts you or arouses resistance. Note these, and perhaps later, return to them. God has spoken to you through them.

In Psalm 40, an event threatened the psalmist – *you*, as identified with the psalmist! You became afraid. That event was God speaking to you through your fears, and you dialogued with God both by your patient waiting and your crying out to Him in trust. God then acted, by bringing you to a safe place and making you secure. God's speech of 'caring' moved you so deeply that you responded in a song of praise. We see how the relationship changed through mutual 'speech', from a fear-filled cry to a trust-filled song of praise.

Between you and God, there has been speech in word, action and attitude! Because of that, the focus moved from you and your plight to a desire for the well-being of others.

You hope now that others will place their trust likewise in God.

Trust has entered in between you and God, and so He can now show you your past *idols*, the false gods from which He saved you. Discovering false idols is not a pleasant experience, but it is a step to new growth for you. God spoke 'truth' to you! You recognised your weakness, you desired healing and that took place. Note that God's speech is very effective!

You proclaim joyfully, 'You have no equal', and in true humility, you assign God His rightful place. There is no one like Him. Your idols are dethroned!

God continues to speak to you through favours and graces. You value highly 'having ears that hear', because your self-love no longer blocks your hearing. The dialogue continues: 'Here I am, Lord.' Here is the generous response of your commitment to His voice, His speech. 'Come quickly, Lord.'

Summary of prose passage
Psalm 40 therefore reveals how God speaks to us in various ways – through danger, confrontation, action, grace, call to follow and obey, in recognising frailties, facing the truth, trusting the Saviour, accepting God's help and co-operating with Him.

Let us thank God for the gift of speech and hearing!

Questions to help you deepen your awareness and reflection on above
What new form of speech from God did you discover in Psalm 40? What demands does it make on you, on your attitudes, on your responses?

Were you aware before this of your dialoguing with God? Will you continue?

Do you instinctively turn to God when danger threatens you?

Have you discovered your false idols? All have some!

Is your response 'Here I am, Lord' or are your ears – and heart – still blocked?

Scripture on the same theme

Psalm 40 again. Spend more time on it and continue to learn from it. Use the same questions as above or have you questions of your own? How did you apply the prayer-insights to your daily living? With what results?

1 Samuel 3:1–21. God calls Samuel. Reflect prayerfully on God's speech with Samuel.

Preparation for your next faith-sharing

Before starting the next section, prepare at an appropriate time for your faith-sharing. Discern what most helped you grow in this last section. How did it affect your living?

The end: Glory be . . .

As we end with this prayer, gather up in it the broken people in this world who don't know how to listen to God perhaps, but who need your prayer. Rest in God for a little after the prayer. *Glory be to the Father . . .*

Nightly reflection.

As usual.

4 My prayer

Beginning

Welcome again. Become still. Let us praise God and be ready to listen to His Spirit. As we say the *Glory be* . . . let us remember those for whom we have promised to pray.

Faith-sharing

Recall what you were guided to discern as your experience of God moving in your prayer and life. You did that before you finished the last section. Now share, in any order, as the Spirit moves you. Thank you for sharing.

Prose passage on the theme: Prayer: positive and negative attitudes

In this book, quite a lot has been written on prayer. If it helps you, read the three sections on prayer in this book (see pp. 34–43, 104–111 and 170–177).

You recall what was said about being clear about the *time, place*, and *material* for prayer. It helps greatly, if we gradually let go of our activity, as our prayer-time approaches.

Look forward to your time with God. Become more *aware* of the great honour to be able to spend time with God.

Today, I want to speak about the *attitudes* that help us in prayer.

Humility is so necessary. Christ emptied himself for me; do I really want to come before Him now filled with myself and my own importance! Beg for humility and to understand the truth of my relationship with God. He is all . . . I am nothing without Him.

Gratitude is an attitude that befits my coming before God in prayer. He holds me in being, He protects me, He speaks to me, He loves me. Do I *really* tell God that I appreciate it all and am grateful? Is there no danger at all that I grumble, for example, at the kind of prayer I had this morning? Do I not act at times as if God were at fault, that I deserve to be consoled and made to feel I was progressing? When prayer is dry or difficult, do I complain, or do I show both *gratitude* and *humility*, by staying with Him even five minutes longer? God was speaking to me through the 'event' of dry prayer. But I didn't even listen! God reads our hearts, and in wisdom, gives me always what is best for me.

A misleading attitude in prayer is when I think that I should be achieving something! God is the one who achieves in me and through me. I am an unprofitable servant, totally dependent on God for all. Pride is at the root of a lot of my wrong attitudes. I even tend to lay false expectations on God, as if He were demanding high achievement from me! I am deceiving only myself. God is never deceived.

A further danger awaits me in prayer, if I am not careful. Because, in pride, I want to feel that I am 'getting' somewhere, I get frantic and anxious, when 'nothing' seems to be happening. I forget to listen to what God is really saying through my actual prayer, be it filled with distractions, dryness or whatever. Instead, I may almost force myself to think 'good thoughts', 'nice-sounding thoughts'! I can count up 'insights' forgetting that insights are only barren thoughts, until the Spirit of God transforms them – using my co-operation – into a change of heart! It is always God who achieves. By His power I hear, I receive, and glorify Him. Amen.

Questions to help you deepen your awareness and your reflection

Be concrete about what you have learned in this section.
What attitudes helped you?
What were unhelpful attitudes?
Where were you placing yourself before God?
What did you learn?
What decisions have you made to change your approach?

Scripture passages on the same theme: Psalm 104; The prodigal son

Psalm 104. From your reflection on the positive and negative attitudes in prayer, you probably realise that you need to spend time reflecting on who God really is. You need to meet the Almighty God of the universe! Psalm 104 will be a great help.

While praying this Psalm, delight in being able to sing the praises of your God who loves you, sinner though you are!

Bless Yahweh, my soul.
Yahweh my god, how great you are! . . .
You made the moon to tell the seasons,
the sun knows when to set:
you bring darkness on, night falls,
all the forest animals come out:
savage lions roaring for their prey,

claiming their food from God.
The sun rises, they retire,
going back to lie down in their lairs,
and man goes out to work,
and to labour until dusk.
Yahweh, what variety you have created,
arranging everything so wisely
Earth is completely full of things you have made . . .
All creatures depend on you
to feed them throughout the year;
you provide the food they eat,
with generous hand you satisfy their hunger.
You turn your face away, they suffer,
you stop their breath, they die
and revert to dust.
You give breath, fresh life begins,
you keep renewing the world.
Glory for ever to Yahweh!
May Yahweh find joy in what he creates . . .

I mean to sing to Yahweh all my life,
I mean to play for my God as long as I live.
May these reflections of mine give him pleasure,
as much as Yahweh gives me!
May sinners vanish from the earth
and the wicked exist no more!

(Ps 104:1, 19–24, 27–31, 33–5)

The words of this Psalm establish an attitude of gratitude and
worship to Almighty God. We are weak but God is mighty.
Yet we need to grow in our understanding of God's attitude
to us. One of the best ways of doing this is to pray through the
story of the Prodigal Son (Lk 15:11–32). These two passages
present us with Almighty God and the compassionate God
of love.

Preparation for your next faith-sharing
Before starting the next section, prepare at an appropriate
time for your faith-sharing. Discern what most helped you

grow in this last section. How did it affect your living? As I said before, if you are an individual reader and if you found any difficulty at all in sharing vocally your faith-sharing with God, why not try 'writing' it to Him. This could be a weekly *letter to God*. The advantages are that at a later date you can re-read the various 'movements of the Spirit' which you experienced. You could do a 'quiet day' on these gifts from God and be able to go deeper into the experience, when you have more time for reflection. Try it. Then choose whichever way suits you best.

The end: Glory be . . .
Now, let us gratefully think of how good God has been to us and how much he has taught us even in this section. Let us pray for all who need our prayers. Rest a little while in God. *Glory be to the Father* . . .

Nightly reflection
As usual.

5 God's goodness revealed in me

Beginning
Welcome! Now become still. Take ten minutes if possible, so as to let go the hassle of the day. When your body is quiet and your mind and heart are stilled, you are more free to 'wait' for the coming of the Spirit. *Glory be to the Father* . . .

Faith-sharing
Recall what you were guided to discern as your experience of God moving in your prayer and life. You did that before you finished the last section. Now share, in any order, as the Spirit moves you. Thank you.

Prose passage on the new theme: God's goodness revealed in me

The mark of our true greatness and of our potential is that we are made in the image and likeness of God. God created human beings as the peak of His creation. He made us 'little less than a god' (Ps 8:5; Gn 1:26,28; Ws 2:23). Our innate goodness, therefore, is the result of all this goodness of God.

God is the potter who moulded us (cf Jer 18:1–12). We wish to praise, glorify and thank the potter, who is God, the Creator. We can appreciate more the gift of humanity in itself, when we recognise that the Son of God, Jesus Christ, took on the same humanity as we have – sin alone excepted.

It is essential that we learn to esteem highly the richness, the dignity, the potential of being a 'human being', if we are to grasp in any measure the way God loved us when He created us. Unless we believe in the goodness of our 'visible' humanity, how can we believe in the 'invisible', namely that we are children of God and co-heirs with Christ!

A real block to our appreciating and valuing highly our gift of humanity is our poor self-image. Some are very aware of this poor self-image. Others tend to deny – at times somewhat strongly – that they experience this phenomenon at all. I wonder how such people account for their over-aggression, over-weening need to exercise control over others, an exaggerated need to please, to be successful, to be the life and soul of the party, to name but a few manifestations of a possible poor self-image.

To grow out of a poor self-image, we need to grow out of a subtle form of 'pride'. Pride focuses us on ourselves – in numerous inscrutable ways – one of which is this 'poor, deprived me' attitude. We need to grow out of our blindness, which can be wilful. We are really often saying to God: 'You did a poor job in creating me. I am worthy of a lot more!'

To all of us, God has given the 'one thing necessary' for salvation. That is the potential to love. People who love God and love their neighbour in word and action and attitude, are well on the way to the freedom which ousts the poor self-image. It is true that some people are more nervous than others, more highly tuned. That is not the same as a poor self-image, which craves attention. People who are more highly tuned than others are usually willing to accept help from others and to admit who they really are. Then they grow in trust.

Our hope and our confidence are not in ourselves who are sinners, but in Christ who is our Saviour. It is true that in ourselves, apart from God, we are nothing. But it is also true that in Him and with Him, all things are possible. Let us put our energy into living in Him and with Him. This is how we discover the wonder of our being and how His goodness becomes revealed in us.

Let us grasp two points: we are talking about God's goodness, not about our goodness. His goodness is that He created us in His image, which can never be destroyed. He also created us in His likeness, which unfortunately is damaged but can be restored. That depends on our human-spiritual growth in Christ, which is what *Light out of Darkness* is all about.

The second point is that God loved us when He created us and found the work of His hands 'very good'. God's love is unchanging. He continues to love us as He continues to re-create us. This re-creation happens when we genuinely co-operate with His love and try to use all His gifts to the best of our ability. Above all, we must remember to act *with* God, never apart from Him, trying to do it alone.

Questions to help you deepen your awareness and reflection

What have you learnt about how you see God and how you see yourself?

Have you a poor self-image? What have you learnt here about this kind of image? How can you do something positive about it?

Do you see how cultivating a poor self-image keeps you centre-stage in getting attention?

Have you grasped that serving and loving others in words, thoughts, actions and attitudes, help quickly to eradicate

unwanted weeds from our being? Put others centre-stage
and serve them! Do you think that doing this would truly
reveal God's goodness in you?

Scripture passages on the same theme
'God created man in the image of himself . . . male and
female he created them' (Gn 1:27).
'God saw all that he had made, and indeed it was very good'
(Gn 1:31).
'Ah, what is man that you should spare a thought for him,
The son of man that you should care for him?' (Ps 8:4).

> 'Yet you have made him little less than a god,
> You have crowned him with glory and splendour,
> Made him lord over the work of your hands,
> Set all things under his feet' (Ps 8:5,6).

Read Psalm 139, pondering especially, God's love, the
wonder of our being, and the constant presence of God
in our lives.
  Other possible texts: Is 43:1–3; Jer 1:5; Dt 32:6,7.
  Use the questions above, or your own.

Preparation for your next faith-sharing
Before starting the next section, prepare at an appropriate
time for your faith-sharing. Discern what most helped you
grow in this last section. How did it affect your living?

The end: Glory be . . .
Bring the whole world into your praise, glory and thanksgiving to God, as you say *Glory be to the Father* . . .

Nightly reflection
As usual.

6 God's tenderness in my struggle

Beginning
Welcome! Let us become still, in body, mind and heart. This is how we prepare for the coming of the Spirit upon us. *Glory be to the Father . . .*

Faith-sharing
Recall what you were guided to discern as your experience of God moving in your prayer and life. You did that before you finished the last section. Now share, as the Spirit moves you. Thank you for sharing.

Prose passage on the new theme: God's tenderness in my struggle
In the last section, we became more aware of God's goodness revealed in us. At the same time, we recognised that sin and sinfulness damage our likeness to God. We want to get to grips with that sinfulness, so that God can gradually restore us to His likeness. We must face this question of our sin honestly. St Paul helps us greatly in this. He says to us: 'I cannot understand my own behaviour. I fail to carry out the things I want to do, and I find myself doing the very things I hate' (Rm 7:15).

This encourages us who are truly sinners. We must approach this matter, however, with hope and sincerity. St Paul says that our hope is in God. He adds: 'and this hope is not deceptive, because the love of God has been poured into our hearts by the Holy Spirit which has been given for us. We were still helpless when at his appointed moment Christ died for sinful men . . . what proves that God loves us is that Christ died for us while we were still sinners. Having died to make us righteous, *is it likely that he would not fail to save us from God's anger?* . . . we are filled with joyful trust in God, through our Lord Jesus Christ, through whom we have already gained our reconciliation (Rm 5:5–11, italics the author's).

We need to be faithful in our prayer and living, at all times. We need to know the areas of our sinfulness and take appropriate action, but with our hearts and hope focused on God, not on ourselves.

The following prose passage, 'Love me as you are', is adapted from an anonymous French writer. He knows that we all seek the mercy and forgiveness of God and that, though we are sinners, we need to be loved and cherished. Let us love and cherish our neighbour as well! Listen to what he says:

I know your misery, the inner struggle of your heart. I also know the weaknesses of your heart. I am aware of your cowardice, your sins and your falls. I still tell you 'Love me as you are'. If you wait to be an angel before you give me your love, you will never love me. Even if you often fall again into sins you are ashamed of, even if you are poor in the practice of virtue, I do not allow you not to love me. Love me as you are! Yes, give me your heart at all times and in whatever dispositions you may be, in fervour or in dryness, faithful or unfaithful, love me as you are.

I want the love of your poor heart. If you want to be perfect before giving me your heart, you will never love me. What can prevent me from turning every grain of sand into a shining radiant archangel of great nobility? Don't you believe that I could bring into being thousands of saints, more perfect and loving than those I have created? Am I not the Almighty God? But if I choose to be loved, here and now, by your limited heart in preference to more perfect love . . . will you refuse . . . can you refuse . . . ?

Allow me to love you, my dear child. I long to win your heart. Oh, yes, I do want to mould you to better things, but in the meantime I love you as you are. I only wish you could do the same! I desire the very kind of love you can give me; the love that comes up from the bottom of your misery, because I truly love you in your very weakness, I treasure the love of the poor, the love of the weak that cries without sound: 'Lord, I love you.' It is this cry that comes from the bottom of your heart, that matters to me, because this is real.

I don't need your achievements, your gifts, your virtues. I have not laid down high goals for you. I created you for the purpose of loving, of loving me, and not that you become puffed-up and self-centred. When you are centred on loving me as you are, then you free me to do great things for you. In this present moment, therefore, in these circumstances, just love me! Then I will achieve in you more than you could ever have dreamed.

Today I, the Lord of Lords, stand at the door of your heart as a beggar. I knock and I wait. Do hurry to open, my heart is eager. Do not make your misery an excuse. Your misery is my excuse for loving you more! Yes, you are poor and weak, even more than you know. But I know it, and I love you all the more with tender compassion. Believe me, trust me, love me. This is all I ask. I will do the rest.

I want you to think of me during the day as often as you can. I want you to think of me as a friend, as one on whom you can rely, who will never let you down. Will you do that for me as a way to love me as your are? I want you to act out of love, no matter how small it may seem to you. When you act out of love, you are loving me as you are. Do you know that? When doubts or suffering come your way, remember me and call on me. I will be with you and will give you strength. Above all, when temptation comes your way, then cry out, cry out with trust and determination. I am with you, and I will answer. Then we are both loving one another as we are.

Questions to help you deepen your awareness and reflection

Reflect. Take time. What have you discovered about the darker side of your being? Do you keep your eyes on the

Saviour? Do you above all beg Him for help and do you
listen to Him? What do you need to do to let God and your
neighbour 'increase' while you 'decrease'? Be very honest
and humble. Make necessary decisions.

Scripture on the theme

Use the texts from Paul: Rm 7:15; 5:5–11; use especially
Psalm 51, all of it if possible, but especially these lines:

> Have mercy on me, O God, in your goodness
> in your great tenderness wipe away my faults;
> wash me clean of my guilt,
> purify me from my sin.
>
> Instil some joy and gladness into me,
> let the bones you have crushed rejoice again.
> Hide your face from my sins,
> wipe out all my guilt.
>
> God, create a clean heart in me,
> put into me a new and constant spirit,
> do not banish me from your presence,
> do not deprive me of your Holy Spirit.
>
> Be my saviour again, renew my joy,
> keep my spirit steady and willing;
> and I shall teach transgressors the way to you,
> and to you the sinners will return.
>
> My sacrifice is this broken spirit,
> you will not scorn this crushed and broken heart.

Try to give some extra time to this section. Read and pray
Psalms 6, 32, 38, 102, 143, some time in the future. These
Psalms help us get in touch with our feelings of love and
remorse. When you reflect on these Psalms, beg God to

give you the grace of a change of heart, which is what we call conversion of heart.

Preparation for your next faith-sharing
Before starting the next section, prepare at an appropriate time for your faith-sharing. Discern what most helped you grow in this last section. How did it affect your living?

The end: Glory be . . .
Now we end this section, bringing into our praise and glory to God all those who have nobody to pray for them, who need our prayers or who have asked us to pray for them. *Glory be to the Father* . . .

Nightly reflection
As usual.

7 God's love for my neighbour

Beginning
Welcome. Become still and at peace waiting and preparing for the coming of the Spirit upon us. We now say: *Glory be to the Father* . . .

Faith-sharing
Recall what you were guided to discern as your experience of God moving in your prayer and life. You did that before you finished the last section. Now share in any order, as the Spirit moves you. Thank you.

Prose passage on the new theme: God's love of my neighbour
We are gradually beginning to see how important are our words and thoughts, our actions and our attitudes. They can build up our neighbour or they can intimidate, or 'tear down' our neighbour's efforts to grow into Christ! This is serious

for all of us. The question of our neighbour and who he or she is in the eyes of Christ, is brought home to us clearly and unequivocally in the story of St Paul's experience on the road to Damascus.

Jesus knew well the integrity of the man Saul, and He longed to mould him to a deeper vision. Saul was persecuting 'his neighbour', so it was through teaching on the same theme, 'the neighbour', that Paul eventually saw the light and was converted. So it often is with us in our encounters with 'neighbours' whom we do not like. When we begin to see the neighbour 'with the heart of compassion' rather than with antagonism, we too experience true conversion.

St Paul was led to a very deep experience of how Jesus Christ saw the 'neighbour'. On that Damascus road, Saul heard a 'voice'. 'Saul, Saul, why are you persecuting me?' Saul, soon to become Paul, answered, 'Who are you, Lord?' 'I am Jesus, and you are persecuting me,' was the response.

Could Jesus have declared to Paul and to us more clearly how He sees the neighbour! Is it not what He said in His preaching before that: 'In so far as you did this to one of the least of these brothers of mine, you did it to me' (Mt 25:40). My neighbour, therefore, is the one whom Jesus loves, whose troubles, burdens, sorrows, fears, He takes as His own; the one whose burden of sin He has taken upon Himself to pay with His life-blood. The tender heart of Jesus – tender not only towards me but likewise towards every neighbour of mine – experiences the least slight, as also the greatest injury, as done to Himself.

Where do I stand in all this? Have I a hard or unloving heart for anyone? If so, then Jesus experiences me as having that heart towards Him! Has my behaviour to my neighbour been a joy or a heartbreak to Christ? Do I really listen to my neighbour, to what she is saying, to what her silent communication tells me if I but listen?

Has anyone ever expressed a heart-cry to me like the following one here? If so, then I need to repent if I refused to hear. Why? That is an answer that you alone can give and to Jesus!

(Adapted from an anonymous writer)
Please hear what I'm not saying.
Don't be fooled by me, by the face I wear,
for I wear a mask, a thousand masks
and none of them are me.
Pretending is an art that's second nature with me,
For God's sake don't be fooled.

I create a mask to hide behind
to shield me from the glance that knows.
But such a glance is my salvation,
but only if it's followed by *love and acceptance*,
the only thing that liberates me from me,
that assures me I am worth something.
But I'm afraid to tell you this,
afraid you'll laugh, will see I'm nothing
and reject me.

Please listen and hear what I'd like to be able to say,
what for survival I need to say.

Questions to help you deepen your awareness and reflection

What must change within you in regard to your neighbour? What decisions have you to make with regard to behaviour?

Would you have recognised Jesus on Calvary? Do you recognise Him in the man at the door who comes in rags and tatters?

Was it 'believers' or another 'criminal' who recognised Jesus on Calvary?

What did Christ say to Thomas: 'You believe because you can see me. Happy are those who have not seen and yet believe' (Jn 20:29).

Am I aware now of the great measure of unbelief that there is in my 'belief'?

Sum up for yourself all that this prayer on the neighbour

says to you. Are you ready to take it seriously and to discern what the 'voice' is saying to you, today?

Scripture passages on the same theme
Acts 9:1–19 (the story of Paul on the road to Damascus).
Luke 10:29–37 (the story of the Good Samaritan).

Ask yourself, with whom to you identify in these stories, with the persecuting Saul or the repentant Paul; with the merciful Samaritan, with those who didn't want to get involved, or with the one left half dead on the road?
Matthew 22:37–40 and Matthew 5:43–8 will repay prayer and reflection.

Preparation for your next faith-sharing
Before starting the next section, prepare at an appropriate time for your faith-sharing. Discern what most helped you grow in this last section. How did it affect your living?

The end: Glory be . . .
As we end this section, include in our praise and thanksgiving all whom you feel called to remember before God. *Glory be to the Father* . . .

Nightly reflection
As usual.

8 My trustworthiness

Beginning
Welcome. Be still. Wait on the Lord in peace. *Glory be to the Father* . . .

Faith-sharing
Recall what you were guided to discern as your experience of God moving in your prayer and life. You did that before

you finished the last section. Now share, in any order, as the Spirit moves you. Thank you.

Prose passage on the new theme:
My trustworthiness

Trust is a necessary basis for genuine communication. There can be no building a real relationship with God or with others, without trust. If I don't trust myself, I will not trust my neighbour. If I don't trust other people, I will find it very difficult to trust God.

Trust in another person means that I accept that other, as I hope to be accepted. When I trust another I can risk being my true self, without wearing a mask. When I learn to trust myself, I can open my door wide and say to others: 'Come in.' When I trust in God, I trust myself and my neighbour more deeply. Trust helps me believe the near-incredible: God loves me, is constantly labouring for and with me, moulding my image to be like himself! When I trust God like that, He is free to use me as His instrument, to further His plans for me, for my neighbour, and for all His people.

Trusting God and trusting other people makes me more trustworthy. That means that I know God's rightful place, and I know my own. God is all, and I am nothing without Him! I delight to give God what is truly His, namely, all, and to receive everything from the hands of God, without whom I am destitute in a true sense. Being trustworthy means that I also recognise my neighbour's claims on me and try to respond to them. The Good Samaritan was a trustworthy person. To be trustworthy means that God can trust himself to me, and – what is so important to God – He can trust my neighbour to me. Saul, as Paul, became trustworthy.

Trust, therefore, is important. If I desire it greatly, and if I pray for it and am willing to accept the consequences of growing in trust, then I will receive this gift.

Questions to help you deepen your awareness and reflection

Is your basic tendency to trust or to distrust?

Can you trace that tendency back to childhood? If your

tendency is to 'trust', then give praise, glory and thanks to Almighty God. If, on the other hand, you discover that you basically tend to 'distrust', you need to have a healing for those childhood experiences. Pray for that to God, who hears your need.

You may, however, discover that you tend to distrust another without any real cause. You could have let 'distrust' become a bad habit. Here, too, listen to your deepest core. Attitudes of jealousy, ambition, fear, pride, natural dislike can be the root causes here. You need to attack the root first.

I can 'project' distrust on to another, because I am not able to carry the burden of it myself. Is any of this true for you?

Ask God to take away the heart of stone, or of distrust that may be in you and to replace it with a heart of flesh, of 'trust'.

We can only achieve 'trust' by risking trust! Try it.

Scripture passages on the same theme
2 Samuel:22, 2–4, 19–20, 29–30, 36, 47:

> Yahweh is my rock, and my bastion,
> my deliverer is my God.
> I take refuge in him, my rock,
> my shield, my horn of salvation,
> my stronghold and my refuge.
> From violence you rescue me.
> He is to be praised; on Yahweh I call
> and am saved from my enemies.
> They assailed me on my day of disaster,
> but Yahweh was my support;
> he freed me; set me at large,
> he rescued me, since he loves me . . .
> Yahweh, you yourself are my lamp,
> my God lights up my darkness;
> with you I storm the barbican,
> with my God I leap the rampart . . .
> You give me your saving shield

and your armour covers me over.
Wide room you have made for my steps under me;
my feet have never faltered.
Life to Yahweh! Blessed be my rock!
Exalted be the God of my salvation.

Psalm 56: 3, 4, 9, 11–13:

Raise me up when I am most afraid,
I put my trust in you;
in God whose word I praise,
in God I put my trust, fearing nothing.
What can man do to me?

This I know: that God is on my side . . .
in God I put my trust fearing nothing;
what can man do to me?
I must fulfil the vows I made you, God;
I shall pay you my thank offerings,
for you have rescued me from Death
to walk in the presence of God
in the light of the living.

Psalm 52:8.

I, for my part, like an olive tree
growing in the house of God,
put my trust in God's love
for ever and ever.

Preparation for your next faith-sharing
Before starting the next section, prepare at an appropriate
time for your faith-sharing. Discern what most helped you
grow in this last section. How did it affect your living?

The end: Glory be . . .
Now we end this section, include in our praise and thanks-
giving all whom you feel called to remember before God.
Glory be to the Father . . .

Nightly reflection
Re-cap
Before the end of this section, spend a lot of time on what you have learnt from the beginning of the programme. Perhaps you kept a journal of your faith-sharing? You could profitably spend a few hours, or a quiet day, reflecting, praising the Lord, giving thanks.

You need to ensure that you have a strong foundation before beginning with the next programme, *Building the Temple*.

You would be greatly helped at this time – when you have finished *Prepare the Way* – if you re-read slowly and reflectively the sections that introduce *Prepare the Way*.

STAGE THREE

BUILDING THE TEMPLE

Part One: Building the Temple – Discovering New Growth in Christ

Introduction

We have faithfully dealt with the basics of *First Steps*. In *Prepare the Way* we have looked at the reality of darkness in many of our relationships. We have recognised the obstacles that needed to be removed. Thus we prepared for the coming of Christ with new life.

In Stage Three, *Building the Temple*, we experience the dynamic of the Spirit leading us more deeply into new life, new growth, new experience of life in Christ. Relationships were the heart of *Prepare the Way*, so here, the concept of gift is the heart of *Building the Temple*. Growth comes now not so much from brokenness to wholeness but rather from a greater sensitivity to the brokenness of the body of Christ which we all are.

Incarnational reality is the centre of all this giftedness. It is by dwelling in the temple within us guided by the Holy Spirit, that we become deeply bonded with our brothers and sisters, co-members. These two gifts, the Spirit acting within us, and our bondedness in the body of Christ, draw us to living out the Pauline experience of 'I live now not with my own life but with the life of Christ who lives in me' (Gal 2:20). Fullness of life in Christ is achieved in us through the Spirit when Christ becomes the source and the

153

sustainer of every thought and action. This is never fully achieved in this life, but we have travelled a long road from the day we began taking our First Steps.

For the third time we take up again the common themes of light and darkness, the sower, prayer and freedom. In this third stage we come to a new depth of experience.

Light and Darkness

The more deeply we live in Christ, the more we can expect to experience *spiritual warfare*. The chapter on spiritual warfare is of great importance. The battle is engaged, now more than ever, and the victory in Christ is ensured to those who turn to Him. But it is incumbent on us to be familiar with the tactics of the enemy and to know how to protect ourselves against his deceits.

The Sower

The parable offers us consolation which invigorates us.

Prayer

It is fitting that prayer moves into deeper relationship with Christ, into the area of preparing for contemplation. Oneness with Christ is growing. The struggle is lessening, though one is always on the alert, but it is fitting that prayer too should become more quiet, resting in our Lord and God.

Freedom

As always, a new measure of freedom is the signal that darkness has been more truly conquered and Christ's victory is being celebrated. *Interior transformation* is taking place. We have reached a goal for the present. For the moment, we can rest in Christ.

Part Two, as always, uses the material presented in Part One and each person is able to move at his or her own pace to assimilate and to absorb what is pertinent to life.

1 Incarnational reality today

Incarnational reality today brings together all that I have been trying to say about who we are in our human-spiritual reality.

We are the temple, the home in which the Holy Spirit lives every moment of our lives. We are His body, the body of Christ. When, individually and corporately, we try to apply the fruits of redemption to our situation, we become the glory of the Lord.

This glory is incarnation realised in us in every moment of each day, through the experience of the birth and the life of Christ within us.

It is incarnation realised through the power of the Spirit active in each member of His body.

It is incarnation happening *now* in hearts that desire close union with Jesus Christ.

It is incarnation made possible through a process of self-emptying so that we become like Christ who 'was emptied'.

It is uniting our sufferings with the sufferings of Christ.

It is dying to self so as to live in and with Christ.

It is sharing in the death of Christ by our sufferings for the sake of the body.

St Paul says: 'It makes me happy to suffer for you, as I am suffering now, and in my own body to do what I can to make up all that has still to be undergone by Christ for the sake of His body, the Church' (Col 1:14). Here Paul explains how our suffering can become an incarnational experience when it is accepted for the sake of Christ's body, the Church. To the Corinthians, Paul says: 'Always wherever we may be, we carry with us in our body the death of Jesus, so that the life of Jesus, too, may always be seen in our body. Indeed, while we are still alive, we are consigned to our death every day, for the sake of Jesus, so that in our mortal flesh the life of Jesus, too, may be openly shown (2 Cor 4:10–11).

To separate death from resurrection in Christ's paschal mystery is not possible, neither is it possible to separate our 'dying' from our 'rising' experience of incarnation today. St Paul says: 'I have been crucified with Christ and I live now not with my own life but with the life of Christ who lives in me' (Ga 2:20).

This is a clear statement, not only of Paul's personal experience but a statement for all who would follow Christ closely. Purification precedes new life. Christ's words take on a richer meaning in the light of incarnation today. He said: 'If anyone wants to be a follower of mine, let him renounce himself and take up his cross every day and follow me. For anyone who wants to save his life will lose it; but anyone who loses his life for my sake, that man will save it' (Lk 9:23,24). When we surrender our lives to the guidance of the Holy Spirit, we save it. What we 'gain' is what Paul describes as his living 'now not with my own life, but with the life of Christ who lives in me' (Ga 2:20).

The magnitude of what is offered in exchange for our own life can overwhelm us. Christ emptied himself the moment He became a human being. For love like His, that was not enough. He died and rose again so as to save us. He did not leave us alone. He left us His living presence in the Eucharist. He left us His Spirit. What more can even He do? He keeps emptying Himself to live, act, dwell in the vessels of clay that we are, so that we can live by the power of the treasure within. To the Corinthians, Paul said: 'It is the same God that said, "Let there be light shining out of darkness", who has shone in our minds to radiate the light of the knowledge of God's glory, the glory on the face of Christ. We are only the earthenware jars that hold this treasure, to make it clear that such an overwhelming power comes from God and not from us' (2 Cor 4:6,7).

Through the gracious generosity of Christ, we are empowered, by His Spirit, to live with the very life of Christ within us. As I have said, the very magnitude of that gift can not only overwhelm us, but even intimidate us. The reality is almost too much. No matter where we are, how we are, Christ is there with us, in us, together with us. When we are sunk in a pit, we do not have to reach up to Christ, we do not have to shout aloud to catch His attention, His strength is supporting us before we even recognise it. This is the union of love, and God is love. We, in our darkness, tend to modify the immensity of the gift, even while we genuinely desire Him. We strive to 'remember' to call upon the help of Christ when our need is great. At our best, we try to stay with Christ while yet solving our own problems! At other times, usually when life is flowing more smoothly, we try to recall the importance of 'the present moment'. By this we mean that 'Now is the favourable time; this is the day of salvation' (2 Cor 6:1), as Paul tells us when he reminded the Corinthians of the words of Isaiah: 'Thus says Yahweh: At the favourable time I will answer you, on the day of salvation I will help you' (Is 49:8).

To live in the present moment is wisdom indeed, especially if, in that moment, we not only meet Christ but let Him live in us. If we find ourselves betrayed, rejected, wounded, deserted, maligned, Christ is there in that experience with us. Our pain is Christ's pain and His pain, by a most gracious gift, becomes ours.

An experience a few days ago taught me this in a way that I will always remember. An ecumenical group of us spent a weekend praying, praising and glorifying God by sharing and by assessing many activities. There was much joy but also much pain. On the Sunday, all attended the Catholic and the Anglican liturgies, communicating according to the rite of our own particular church. In the past, this separation has always been a painful experience for me. But I do believe that the suffering involved will eventually bring healing and union.

The experience of this particular Sunday was for me momentous. As the paten was passed round the circle, the familiar pain at our separation hit me. When the chalice reached me, I was unprepared for an onslaught of such pain as I had never previously experienced. It left me gasping. I felt devastated. It all happened probably in a second, but for me, time stood still. The blood ceased to be just blood. The pain ceased to be *my* pain. Christ became *invisibly* present in His pain, His tears, His brokenness. It was almost unbearable. When the celebration was over and the celebrant held me, I was able to sob, as I do not remembering doing since I was a child. Only then, when we two were of one mind and one heart in Christ, did the pain, Christ's in me, begin to ease. Later I discovered that a man directly across the room from me had had a very similar experience. He too believed that he was sharing in the pain and the tears of Christ, because of our separation. Our prayers, our praising denoted 'one mind, one heart', yet the body of Christ was torn apart.

In my anguish I turned to Christ the Way, the Truth and the Life (Jn 14:6). He reminded me that He is still praying for us: 'I pray not only for these but for those also who through their words will believe in me. May they all be one. Father, may they be one in us, as you are in me and I am in you, so that the world may believe it was you who sent me' (Jn 17:20–2).

Our 'oneness' therefore must eventually be realised, since Jesus Himself continually prays for its accomplishment. He is the Way. What is the truth that sets us free? Jesus says: 'I am not asking you to remove them from the world, but to protect them from the evil one . . . consecrate them in the truth; your word is truth' (Jn 17:15). The advocate, whom the Father will send to be with us for ever is 'that spirit of truth whom the world can never receive since it neither sees nor knows him' (Jn 14:17) . . . 'when the spirit of truth comes he will lead you to the complete truth' (Jn 16:13).

Jesus, not only the Way and the Truth, but also the Life, has fulfilled His promise not to leave us orphans. He remains with us in the power of the Spirit who lives within us. The Spirit of Jesus ensures the possibility of this fullness of life for us. 'I tell you most solemnly, whoever believes in me will perform the same works as I do myself, he will perform even *greater works*' (Jn 14:12 italics the author's).

What are these 'greater works'?

They are that Jesus Christ, no longer incarnate in human flesh – as once through the overshadowing of Mary by the

Holy Spirit – is now in a different way, through the power of the same Holy Spirit, living within each of us. Jesus says: 'if anyone loves me he will keep my word, and my Father will love him, and we shall come to him and make our home with him' (Jn 14:23).

St Paul confirms in Galatians 2:20 that this in fact is his own personal experience: 'I have been crucified with Christ, and I live now not with my own life but with the life of Christ who lives in me.'

This is the reality of incarnation today. Through the Spirit of truth it is possible for us to know the way that is Jesus, to know the truth and to enjoy the fullness of life which has been promised to us.

What are the implications of incarnational reality?

The prime implication of incarnational reality is that the same Jesus, who redeemed us while living on earth as a human being, is now, as the risen Lord, empowering us to apply the merits of redemption subjectively to ourselves. All this is accomplished in the power of the Spirit of Jesus who lives within us. It implies that in all things we try to put on the mind and the heart of Christ. Jesus Christ incarnate was an emptied human being. His way was to learn, from personal experience, to reflect and gradually to grow, through that personal experience in everyday life. In all the events of His personal experience, Jesus was led by the Spirit.

We too, therefore, must be emptied, so that we too can be filled with the light and guidance of the Spirit of Christ. We too, as we have already seen, have our personal everyday experience. We too have the guidance of the Holy Spirit. We too must follow Christ's way of reflecting on our experience, learn from it, listen to its teaching, discern the meaning of our feelings and hand over every moment to the Holy Spirit. Of ourselves we are nothing and have nothing. Like St Paul, we too will frequently 'be crucified with Christ' through carrying the daily cross, whatever form that may take. But in Christ, we have all. 'There is only Christ: he is everything and he is in everything' (Col 3:11).

How is this reality of incarnation to be accomplished?

Essentially the reality of the incarnation is the work of the Holy Spirit from beginning to end. Our best response to the action of the Spirit is to hand over each event and each experience to the power and guidance of the Spirit. This requires a continuous self-emptying. It means keeping the focus of our whole being on Christ. Our aim is to live as Christ lived, namely under the guidance of the Spirit. Therefore in each present moment, we try to discern the movements within us and follow the Spirit confidently.

We do not foolishly ask ourselves: 'What would Christ have done in this situation?' This is something we cannot possibly know. It is wiser to live in the 'present situation', where Christ Himself is alive and active in the Spirit. In the present situation we can listen to His Spirit, become aware of all the factors relevant to the situation, and discern to the best of our ability what He wants of us. We are always aware that our discernment is limited and temporary. Limited, because as fallen human beings, we can misinterpret or be misled by our ego; temporary, because emerging new factors always necessitate a new discernment process.

In my experience, the programme set out in *Light out of Darkness* is one practical way to try to make incarnational living a reality today. There are others. This is the one I can vouch for, as a way to help people to grow in Christ, through reflection on experience and through the leading of the Holy Spirit. This is one way to keep our focus on Christ. This requires not only that one follows sincerely, in the best possible way, the programmes laid down here, but that one continues to live them. This means that each one discerns how best to apply the experience of *Light out of Darkness* to discerning her own way of life as applicable to her individual circumstances. The principles will always be the same. Only the details of circumstances differ.

Let us listen to St Paul, who values the place of faith in his following of Christ: 'The life I now live in this body I live in faith: faith in the Son of God who loved me and who sacrificed himself for my sake' (Ga 2:21). In short –

each moment in my day can be a moment where the risen Christ, alive in me through His Spirit, can take over my thoughts, my words, my actions, my attitudes, my hopes, my desires – if I wish to invite Him to do so. By handing over to God all that I am and have, by receiving back the gift of myself, I receive a gift that is continuously cleansed, purified, and renewed in the abundance of life which was promised. When this happens, as I have seen it happen in *Light out of Darkness*, the invisible becomes visible, and the visible transformed leads into the invisible. Then the gift of contemplative prayer is offered by God.

When prayer-insights, given by the Spirit, lead a person to the action, the attitude in daily living, which best 'enfleshes' the prayer insight, the Spirit is at work, weaving a thread of gold between Spirit and spirit. When such a person prays, the quality of prayer gradually changes. It becomes a form of contemplative prayer, a resting in God, praising, glorifying, thanking, surrendering. Prayer becomes a wordless, image-less, *being with* God, in deep humility. It is always in God's time, in His choice of circumstances, always in love, as His Spirit reads the readiness of the waiting heart.

When in our frail mortality we experience great pressures and weariness, with unavoidable demands being made upon us, we become vulnerable. Old habits and attitudes strive to assert their former power. Our response to what is happening counts! The response of the 'surrendered' being, the response that speaks 'freedom', the response that is aware of our frailty. This awareness, however, is filled with grateful humility that 'surprise visits of frailty' are not more frequent! Why should one be 'surprised' by visits of frailty, since such a person is realistically rooted in the truth of his or her 'unworthiness'? The fact and the truth are clear! There is no need to protest overmuch. It is better to recognise, claim and surrender!

This gift from the Spirit of the living Christ, who is incarnate today in a redeemed and loved sinner, clarifies I think, the meaning of *incarnational reality*.

St Ignatius Loyola puts it succinctly and powerfully: 'Take, Lord, and receive all my liberty, my memory, my intellect and all my will – all that I have and possess. You gave it to me: to You, Lord, I return it! All is Yours, dispose of it according to Your will. Give me Your love and grace, for this is enough for me' (*The Spiritual Exercises* No 234).

We can join with the Franciscans in praying:

> Inwardly cleansed
> interiorly enlightened
> and inflamed by the fire of the Holy Spirit
> may we be able to follow
> in the footprints of your beloved Son
> our Lord Jesus Christ (St Francis of Assisi).

All that came to be had life in him
and that life was the light of men,
a light that shines in the dark,
a light that darkness could not overpower (Jn 1:4,5).

2 The concept of gift – the heart of spiritual growth

A foundation for *Building the Temple* was laid in *Prepare the Way*. To ensure that the foundation was strong and solid, we engaged in excavations. This involved looking at the darker side of ourselves, especially in the area of *relationships*. Because we discovered how tender God can be in our struggles, we faced our frailties and darkness more courageously. This ensured a good measure of freedom, which is the fruit of growth.

We are the temple that is now being built. The temple in question therefore is not a place but a person, the person that I am in the heart of God. The reality of *the concept of gift* is the pivot of this building programme of the human-spiritual me. St James says: 'It is all that is good, everything that is perfect, which is given from above; it comes down from the Father of all light' (Jm 1:16–17).

That which Jesus said to the Samaritan woman about 'gift' could so easily be said to us: 'If you only knew what God is offering and who it is that is saying to you: Give me a drink, you would have been the one to ask, and he would have given you living water' (Jn 4:10).

We, in fact, are the people who, throughout *Light out of Darkness*, continuously keep asking Jesus for the gift of living water. Our need and our thirst keep growing. We become more keenly aware that 'unless the Lord build the house, its builders labour in vain' (Ps 127:1). We are also more aware, with awe, that we are co-workers with Christ. We are involved in building a temple of the Holy Spirit, of which we are the living stones.

The scriptural background to the building of this temple comes, aptly I think, from Nehemiah. After the exile, in about 444 BC, the Jews returned to Jerusalem. Despite the surrounding and mocking enemies, the temple and city walls were re-built. Their faith and indomitable spirit could not be gainsaid: 'The God of heaven will give us success. We, his servants, are going to build' (Ne 2:20). 'The walls were soon finished, since the people put their hearts into the work' (Ne 4:6).

In the face of ridicule and attack, Nehemiah's answer was always the same, *prayer and action*: 'Do not be afraid of them. Keep your minds on the Lord, who is great and to be feared, and fight for your kinsmen' (Ne 4:14). 'Then we called on our God and set a watch against them day and night to guard the city' (Ne 4:9–10). Ultimately, even the enemies were impressed by the effect of prayer, work and determination to trust God and fight. They acknowledged that '*this work had been accomplished by the power of our God*' (Ne 6:16 author's italics.)

'This work has been accomplished by the power of God' is a clarion call that must challenge and inspire every Christian. It is what we have hoped for and experienced in and through *Light out of Darkness*. Commitment is needed to follow this way, as it is demanding in time, energy, openness and trust.

Like the returned exiles, we too need *faith* in the power of God, *action* which results from discernment, and *fidelity* to the whole body of Christ. This is not a form of privatised religion. Our solidarity with all our brothers and sisters is a priority. Nehemiah's words can rouse us too: 'Do not be afraid . . . Keep your minds on the Lord who is great and to be feared. Fight for your kinsmen, your sons and daughters, your wives and your homes' (Ne 4:8). At all times, we too want to keep our focus on God, to be led by His Spirit for the sake of the body of Christ. This is the gift above all gifts that we beg Christ to give us, the gift of His Spirit.

**The night is over
and the real light is already shining** (1 Jn 2:8)

3 Light and darkness – spiritual warfare

In the preparatory sections of *Prepare the Way*, I stressed personal and corporate sin, healing and reconciliation. To prepare for *Building the Temple*, I emphasise incarnational reality, namely the fulfilment of being indwelt by the Spirit of the Risen Christ. This is the gift of gifts which we know in our heads but do not always allow to change our lives. When this truth informs our spirituality and we try to live it, we may expect disturbances from the enemy. How else is he to be conquered by the Spirit of Christ within us? He will not give up his toehold grip without a struggle!

There is a strong tendency today to speak, to act, to behave as if Satan were non-existent, almost a figment of our imagination. Through Scripture, therefore, let us get the picture clear about the adversary, the devil, who 'is prowling round like a roaring lion, looking for someone to eat. Stand up to him, strong in faith and in the knowledge that [people] all over the world are suffering the same things' (1 Pet 5:9–10).

St Paul heard Jesus say to him: 'I shall deliver you from the people and from the pagans, to whom I am sending you to open their eyes, so that they may turn from darkness to light, from the dominion of Satan to God, and receive, through faith in me, forgiveness of their sins and a share in the inheritance of the sanctified' (Acts 26:17,18).

St Paul reminds the Ephesians that they are not struggling against human enemies but 'against the Sovereignties and the Powers who originate the darkness in this world, the spiritual army of evil in the heavens'. He exhorts them to rely on God's armour so that they will be able to resist and hold their ground. 'So stand your ground', he says, 'with truth buckled around your waist and integrity for a breastplate, wearing for shoes on your feet the eagerness to spread the gospel of peace and always carrying the shield of faith so that you can use it to put out the burning arrows of the evil one. And then you must accept salvation from God to be your helmet and receive the word of God from the Spirit to use as a sword. Pray all the time, asking for what you need, praying in the Spirit on every possible occasion' (Ep 6:12–18).

Paul spoke strongly to the Corinthians. He tells them that there must be no weakening on their part. There must be no watering down the word of God. They must speak the truth openly, so that it may reach the unbelievers 'whose minds the god of this world has blinded', says Paul, 'to stop them seeing the light shed by the Good News of the glory of Christ who is the image of God' (2 Cor 4:2–5).

I wonder what St Paul would say to our generation! What do we say to ourselves in view of what Jesus has said: 'He who is not with me is against me' (Mt 12:30). The conflict between light and darkness fills the Bible. We must take a stand. 'Choose today whom you wish to serve' (Jos 24:15). 'I have set before you life and death . . . Choose life, then, so that you and your descendants may live' (Dt 30:19). But we remain neither hot nor cold. 'I wish you were one or the other, but since you are neither, but only lukewarm, I will spit you out of my mouth' (Rev 3:15–17).

We are seemingly not ready even to stand in the gap for the sake of the Lord: 'I have been looking for someone among them to build a wall and man the breach in front of me, to defend the country and prevent me from destroying it; but *I have not found anyone*' (Ez 22:30, italics the author's). No wonder Elijah went before the people on Mount Carmel and said: 'how long will you waver between two opinions? If the Lord is God, follow him; but if Baal is God, follow him' (1 Ki 18–21 NIV). Why the fear and hesitation where withstanding Satan is concerned? Has not Christ said: 'In the world you will have trouble. But be brave: *I have conquered the world*' (Jn 16:33 italics the author's). Did Jesus not personally confront Satan in the desert and score a victory over him? 'Then the devil left him, and angels appeared and looked after him' (Mt 4:11). Has the faith throughout the centuries not been proclaimed in: 'So let us thank God for giving us the victory through our Lord Jesus Christ' (1 Cor 15:57).

St Ignatius of Loyola guides us well on how to deport ourselves with regard to Satan. We see this in the discernment of spirits in the *Spiritual Exercises* (Nos 313–36). In brief, he advises us to stand up to the enemy, be firm, relying on God, and the enemy will flee (325); on the other hand, if we are afraid and lose heart, then 'there is no beast so wild on the face of the earth as the enemy of human nature . . . ' (325). Again this 'father of lies', this 'deceiver' tries to draw us further into his grasp, by urging us to keep silent about our fears, our temptations (326). The solution is, of course, to bring such into the open to a trustworthy, capable person, if a spiritual guide is not available.

Another ploy of this wily enemy is to attack us at weak points in our defence. Where he finds us 'weakest and most in need for our eternal salvation, there he attacks us and aims at taking us'. Another point of attack can be 'the weakness of complacent strength which is pride' (327).

Satan will not try to disturb anyone who is on the downward

slippery slope. He is more interested in those who are trying to lead a good life. Christians must expect to be the subject of attack if they are doing the work of the Lord. One has to be on one's guard against this 'angel of light', as St Paul called him when he was speaking to the Corinthians (2 Cor 11:14). As an angel of light, he is truly a deceiver (332). He enters, for example into a good thought which we have, or a holy desire. Then he moves us from the 'good thought' to 'complacent thoughts' about our spiritual progress, or something similar. Soon that original 'good' thought is contaminated and we are caught in pride or selfishness or spiritual greed.

I have mentioned only a few of the helps given us in the *Spiritual Exercises*. These are pertinent to our recognising and discerning the presence of the enemy, who never ceases to try to win from Christ those who are seeking Him in earnest. We must never fear, however, as St Ignatius warns us in No 325. Besides, Jesus Christ tells us: 'Be brave, I have conquered the world' (Jn 16:33). Jesus prayed to His Father for all of us: 'I am not asking you to remove them from the world, but to protect them from the evil one' (Jn 17:15).

Finally the writer to the Hebrews assures us 'God himself has said: *I will not fail you or desert you*, and so we can say with confidence: *With the Lord to help me, I fear nothing: what can man do to me?*' (Heb 13:6).

In a *Light out of Darkness* retreat, I find that the enemy often tries to disturb and upset those who are seeking God with all their heart. That is a good sign. I would worry if there were no such movement! The remedy is, of course, what Paul told the Ephesians, as already cited: 'Pray all the time, asking for what you need, praying in the Spirit on every possible occasion (Ep 6:18). There are certain points where the enemy hopes to weaken defences, cause anxiety, and lessen trust. And always it is the same story: *the power of the group, of the body of Christ filled with the Spirit, wins through*. The victory is Christ's and the group itself experiences joy and renewed strength, often without knowing why it is so.

Sometimes a group member may be slow in deciding for Christ, may give a toehold of entrance to the enemy, thus holding back the saving action of Christ. It is then that the team leading the retreat redoubles its prayer and sacrifice. Ultimately victory is certain. 'Since God is for us, who can be against us?' Then we can hear and rejoice with the words of Isaiah:

> Arise, shine out, for your light has come,
> The glory of Yahweh is rising on you,
> though night still covers the earth
> and darkness the peoples.
> Above you Yahweh now rises
> and above you his glory appears . . .
> and you shall know that I, Yahweh, am your saviour,
> that your redeemer is the Mighty One of Jacob
> (Is 60:1–3,16).

The issue could not be clearer.

Now a sentence is being passed on this world; now the prince of this world is to be overthrown (Jn 12:31).

4 The Sower – Mark 4:20

'And there are those who have received the seed in rich soil: they hear the word and accept it and yield a harvest, thirty and sixty and a hundredfold.'

One of the truths that we gradually learn from the parables of Jesus, is that we usually have a stake in every part of a parable. For example, in the 'Prodigal Son' we may, in the beginning, identify with one or other brother, depending on who we ourselves are. Wisdom eventually reveals to us that we can, in some respects, abuse the goodness of those who love us, like the prodigal, but can be redeemed by acknowledging our mistake, and coming home. Still later, perhaps, we see that the lack of love on the part of the elder son, and his hard, self-righteous approach to life, are faults that at first perhaps were hidden from us. We 'saw' with the eyes of the world, with the accepted canons of what the world considers is good behaviour. We can learn from both brothers, because we can err like both.

So, in this parable of the sower, there is much to be learned. We can all, at different stages of life and at different times in the same stage, welcome God's word with joy at first, and then lose it. We can withstand a difficulty, even suffer a little persecution perhaps and remain faithful, at first. Then, one day, we may choose the easier way, we may opt for 'riches'. Then we have to be careful and repent!

We may even in due time, reap a good harvest, not only thirty and sixty but a hundredfold. But on our own, we can never make it. We must never make that mistake! Only when we are empty and dependent on Christ and on the power of His Spirit, can we rise when we are weak; only when we continue to choose Christ above every other delight, can we be blessed by a rich harvest and new growth. At all times, we must remember that we are 'unprofitable servants'. Of ourselves we are nothing. We need to rest in trust and in surrender in the hand of our Father, who is God.

When we know our true place and continue to give Almighty God His place of sovereignty in our lives, then with quiet confidence we can say with the psalmist: 'In peace I lie down, and fall asleep at once, since you alone, Yahweh, make me rest secure' (Ps 4:8).

Yahweh will be your everlasting light (Is 60:20).

5 Prayer – contemplative moments

Fidelity to prayer, as described in the preceding sections on prayer, results in growth in the following of Christ. This fidelity prepares one for a more intimate relationship with God. In prayer, this will probably be a form of *contemplative prayer*; in living, this will probably take the form of *incarnational living* throughout each moment of the day and night.

The particular form of contemplative prayer will be God's special gift to each person. I concern myself only with preparing ourselves, in whatever way we feel attracted, to being more open to receive from the Lord His gift of prayer for us today.

I give therefore some ways in which to become still, passively alert to His presence or to His absence. I give some ways which help us focus on God in this present moment, ways, also, which help to hold us in His presence, aware of Him, in the midst of busy-ness and preoccupation with human affairs.

Some of you will be familiar with these; others may be coming to this awareness for the first time. I think that we all need, at times, to become steeped again in simple methods such as those proposed. We may discover that our own new depths release new life even from the familiar; or we may discover that we are more in need than we thought of a simplicity which opens us to God!

Be still (Ps 46:10)
Sooner or later, I think that we all get caught by rushing into the actual 'prayer' without proper preparation. The contamination of the over-busy world is still with us! We need to rid ourselves of this, before we can 'be with God' in such a way that we truly listen, hear and surrender.

I assume that you have taken care of the 'remote preparation' and the 'immediate preparation', as described on
pages 39 and 40. We are preparing here for deeper prayer,
therefore a more sensitive approach of love.

Rooted in Christ
Our body can often be the cause of our restlessness. This
simple exercise not only calms the body but focuses the mind
and the heart.

Remove your shoes if that helps you. Plant your feet
'firmly' on the ground, moving them until you feel that
you are one with the ground, wherein you also find the
ground of your being.

Relax your body: Shake your head, wriggle your shoulders,
let your hands hang loosely. Take special care of your head!
Some tend to jut out the chin. Avoid that. Others may lower
the chin too close to the breast. The correct position is when
the top of your head seems to be parallel to the floor.

Your shoulders: as with the head, avoid having the
shoulders slumping forward. Avoid also shoving them back
so much that you appear to be in a strained position. Look
straight ahead at a fixed object, or close your eyes, if you
prefer. Once you have got the correct position, it happens
almost automatically after that.

If you come to prayer reasonably well prepared, this will
take only a few moments. If, however, you are distracted,
it is worth while to remain rooted in Christ like this for as
long as it takes. In fact, this exercise of being rooted in Christ
may even move into a contemplative 'being with Christ'.

This approach can be used throughout the day as well, to
keep you in the presence of Christ. You are sitting in your
office, or the train, or your car. You are gardening or ironing,
playing golf, or having a drink at home or in the bar!

Prayer should be woven into the rhythm of our lives. We
are able to pray at any time by becoming aware, by silently
saying to ourselves, 'I am rooted in Christ, all is well.'
Nobody will notice, or be aware. But you can be 'aware'
of them and cover them with the peace of Christ.

If you want to deepen this simple experience for yourself,

you can at a convenient time reflect prayerfully on the scriptural background. In Colossians 2:7, we read: 'You must be rooted in Christ and built on him and held firm by the faith you have been taught, and full of thanksgiving.' In Ephesians 3:16–20, we have a passage that speaks not only of the way to prepare for prayer by being planted in Christ, but a scriptural background to *incarnational living* each day: 'Out of his infinite glory, may he give you the power through his Spirit for your hidden self to grow strong, so that Christ may live in your hearts through faith, and then, planted in love and built on love, you will with all the saints have strength to grasp the breadth and the length, and height and the depth; until, knowing the love of Christ, which is beyond all knowledge, you are filled with the utter fullness of God. Glory be to him whose power, working in us, can do infinitely more than we can ask or imagine.'

Other ways to bring us to stillness are, *breathing*; becoming *aware* of what distracts us – like sounds, and then letting them go; or handing over our *senses* one by one to the Holy Spirit; asking him to cleanse them of all that is not of God or helpful at this moment, surrendering them to be emptied of self and refilled with God's Spirit.

We have spoken before of *breathing* and of *awareness, listening, getting in touch with feelings*; these can also be used in this way of coming to stillness in preparation for prayer.

Freely choose to hand that listening, awareness, or feeling over to God. Surrender whatever is not helpful in it. Ask God to cleanse it of anything that is not of Him. Open to receive instead the power of the Spirit filling you, especially filling your interior listening, interior senses, so as to be drawn into God.

It is worth while to spend time in these simple exercises. Your actual prayer will deepen, but, in addition, your stillness throughout the day will develop. This helps incarnational living, or as I also call it, 'contemplative living'.

A variation on handing your being over to the Holy Spirit is to enter into an experience in the following way:

Breathe deeply, focusing on your breathing.

Become aware of your mind, the thoughts that are filling it, in this moment.

Deepen your awareness of that one main thought.

Choose to let it go into God's care. Rest, focused on God, gratefully . . .

Move past your thoughts, move deeper into your being. Become aware of your feelings, now.

Hand the dominant feeling over to God. Rest in Him . . . letting go even more . . .

Move past your feelings, deeper into your desires and hopes . . . Centre on your deepest desire for God. Deepen that desire by resting in it . . . Choose now to let it go, even that deep desire for God, let it go to Him and choose to rest in God Himself instead . . .

Move deeper still into your being, led by the Spirit who desires all that is good within you. Let the Spirit draw you deeper still into your being, where you now have *nothing of your own*. You have let go even good desires for God. You are in the deepest place, where you have nothing, no one but God! You are in His presence where you long to surrender to this great love, to God who is love. Rest there in surrender until the Spirit who holds and protects you, draws you back again to familiar surroundings.

Slowly, gently, let go where you were. Be present to God's call to come to prayer, now.

When you have prepared for prayer like this, you can safely leave the actual prayer to the Holy Spirit who is guiding you.

Minute oasis

I call a minute oasis those momentary withdrawals from the noise or distraction of the world, whereby we are renewed and recharged with the energy and love of God. Some of those ways of coming to stillness can also become a minute oasis, as I already mentioned.

The purpose of these 'minute oases' is to remain aware of God even when we are busily working. We must, of course, give our whole attention to whatever work is entrusted to us. But does 'withdrawing' have to detract from the work? Look at your own experience of human loving! Provided that a wise balance is observed, is the work of a balanced and committed young man or woman endangered by a momentary warm remembrance of the loved one? Does not the work actually improve because of the awareness that one loves and is loved? So it is with us and God, who is love.

Let us now look at some instances of a minute oasis.

Become keenly aware of this present moment.

Marvel at it. Learn from it. One moment at a time. God, Almighty God, is present in that moment, present for me, in my life!

Pause; be present to Him; listen to Him; or just *be* . . . alive . . . with the Creator!

Let me offer a brief scriptural background to that important 'present moment': St Paul says: 'We beg you once again not to neglect the grace of God that you have received. For he says: *At the favourable time, I have listened to you; on the day of salvation I came to your help*. Well, now is the favourable time; this is the day of salvation' (2 Cor 6:1–2).

We are well advised therefore to live in the present moment, learning from the past but letting it go; not moving into the future which is not yet. God is in each present moment. We need to be there in His presence.

We need reminders of God's presence in the 'now', as we can become too engrossed in other things. A few examples may stimulate you to find your own oasis, whatever suits you and your circumstances.

A very busy priest was concerned about this problem. As he walked down the stairs, reflecting on the necessity of being aware of God in the present moment he felt the wood of the staircase under his hand. Something stirred within him. As he finally grasped the newel post, he knew he had found a treasure: 'Every time that I touch wood,' he said, 'it will become for me a reminder of God – a minute oasis.' This momentary withdrawal into the reality of God's presence at this moment enriched his daily living.

I heard of a business tycoon, who was a good Christian.

Whenever his secretary let him know that there was a business call for him, he used to say: 'One moment please.' Then he pulled out the shallow drawer in his desk in which only one item lay: a prayer-card with the holy name 'Jesus' on it. The man used to place his hand on the card, say quietly in his heart, 'All for you, Jesus', and take the phone call.

I recalled this story when I became a headmistress. The phone was my enemy! So I decided to 'use it for God'. When the phone rang, I used to say to myself before answering, 'It is Your voice I want to be, and Your voice I want to hear.' This was a great help on numerous occasions, especially when some calls were a test of patience and understanding.

I was deeply touched on one occasion when I was sharing with members of a Mothers' Union. I told them the above story. Later, a dear lady whispered to me: 'Let me tell you what I do. Every time I pour out tea, I pour the first few drops in honour of the Father, then for the Son and finally for the Holy Spirit.' The mischievous light in her eye alerted me, not only to her humour – which blends so well with God's ways – but that something good was coming. 'And let me tell you,' she added, 'it improves the tea as well!'

Anthony de Mello SJ on a teaching video, confirmed for me something which I had already found worked well. This was: '*Do only one thing at a time*.' I used to pride myself on doing at least three things at the same time. On reflection, I soon discovered that this was disrespectful to people and prevented my giving my full attention to whatever was in hand.

Later I discovered that it was necessary not only to do one thing only, but necessary to give one's whole self to that thing, at that time. This became clear, when I recognised that God was the one for whom I was working and He was present in that moment. His presence drew one's whole attention.

You will probably discover other helpful ways of meeting God in the present moment. Let me say a few words now on contemplative eating.

Try it! Really taste potatoes, or carrots, or meat, or . . . or . . . Savour them in themselves. Each is unique. Even as a reality of our human existence, food deserves this kind of attention.

Add to that, awareness of the many hands, the many people who have given a little of their lives, even a few moments, to nourish us. Consider the love of God present, throughout all the time, from the seed in the ground or whatever until we have it now here before us. This is a mystery, an experience that has life in it for each of us!

Then there is contemplative drinking – I had in mind, coffee, tea, milk, water! But there is no reason at all to confine it to those drinks. Christ enjoyed wine! Be led by the Spirit and discover for yourself new ways of meeting, of being with, and of being united with your God.

Sleeping

My own experience has taught me how God continues to labour for us even while we sleep. How often when I have entrusted a problem, a burden or a worry to the Holy Spirit before going to sleep, I awaken with a more positive attitude to it. Of course, the whole of my being, body, mind and spirit, has contributed to this release from tension, but God is in it all. When we sleep in the recognition of His continuing presence with us in our unconsciousness, we open ourselves to His continuing healing and blessing.

I find it helpful to prepare for sleep by doing the *Awareness Prayer* well (see pp. 189, 190). Reading Romans 8:26–7 prayerfully and reflecting on it at some time is also very worthwhile: 'The Spirit too comes to help us in our weakness. For when we cannot choose words in order to pray properly, the Spirit himself expresses our plea in a way that could never be put into words, and God who knows everything in our hearts knows perfectly well what he means, and that the pleas of the saints expressed by the Spirit are according to the mind of God.'

It is an enrichment for me at any rate, if I hand over my sleep to the Holy Spirit, asking that every move of my limbs, every beat of my heart, every breath be transformed by the Spirit into praise, glory and worship of Almighty God. Listen to Scripture:

'Now I can lie down and go to sleep
and then awake, for Yahweh has hold of me' (Ps 3:5).

And again in Psalm 4:8.

'In peace I lie down, and fall asleep at once,
since you alone, Yahweh, make me rest secure'.

Or in Proverbs 3:24.

'When you sit down, you will not be afraid,
When you lie down, sweet will be your sleep.'

On awakening
The result of this trust in God's Holy Spirit is:

'Let us wake in the morning filled with your love
and sing and be happy all our days' (Ps 90:14).

or:

'For me the reward of virtuc is to see your face,
and, on waking, to gaze my fill on your likeness'
(Ps 17:15).

A more prosaic way of starting a new day is simply to say:
'Thank you God for another lovely day, in which to love
You and be loved by You!'
If we begin each day in some such way, if throughout
the day we keep using reminders, 'hallowed moments of
withdrawal', if finally we entrust even our sleep to the
Holy Spirit, then, without doubt, we will be taught how
to pray!

**May Yahweh let his face shine on you and be gracious
to you.
May Yahweh uncover his face to you and bring you peace**
(Nb 6:25,26).

6 Freedom – interior transformation

We have seen in previous sections on freedom that this grace marks a liberation from the bondage of darkness, a rejection of sin. Every step of our struggle, when it is sincere and our focus is truly on the power of God, is graced by a new measure of freedom. We have also seen that freedom is 'given' us by God. It is not a medal we earn for good conduct.

Freedom is an interior experience. It is not tangible. At times it is not even *felt*! Yet when we are free, when we experience freedom, we know it, because our outlook is different. Difficult undertakings are still difficult, but interiorly we have changed. We are not alone. We are working from a different power base, one that doesn't tie us up, but untangles us.

What is different about the freedom we enjoy, when prayer and living are a walking with God through every experience, in the power of the Spirit? Does it mean that one is already transformed? Definitely not! Does it mean that old tapes won't play, that old frailties are now dead and buried, never to rise again? Certainly not! Think that way and there is a very rude awakening in store.

Yet there is a difference, and it seems to be this. The person or persons that we were, still live. Nobody changes that much. Therefore one may have to struggle until one dies with the 'sting of the flesh', as Paul did. But the *inner reality* is different. Before, one strove to be better with quite a mix of motivation. The person who is more free has a different *vision*. That word seems to strike the right note, the right tone. What does it mean?

It means that for the free person, 'striving', for example, could have a touch of violence in it. The free person sees the goal as different, and the striving towards one's own

perfection no longer causes the spiritual adrenaline to rise.
That has become a bit irrelevant. What then? When the goal
posts move, an entirely new game is in play. Not only is there
a new vision, but the old rules aren't a guide any more. In
fact what are the rules? How does one move so as not to put
a foot wrong in this new pitch? The simple answer, I think,
is: one doesn't! The old constraints no longer help. When one
becomes a new person – and that is the meaning of freedom,
of this new inner reality – one begins to savour the newness.
It's another case of new wine and old wine-skins. They just
can't fit together again. It is, in fact, the savouring of the
newness, pondering its deep, hidden meaning through the
only guide who can ensure the continuity of this life-giving
freedom, that the next step becomes clear. In a very real
sense, one becomes a child, but not childish. Only a child
can dare to risk; a childish, unfree person needs a clearly
charted course, today, tomorrow and every tomorrow. To
the free person, this is prison.

Apart from Jesus, the best model for true freedom that
I know is His mother, Mary. Did anyone else face such an
uncharted journey through life? Responsible for her child,
for her Son, she could only ponder. All the rules had been
broken and thrown away. The rabbis and high priests were
no longer the clear voice of God. Their hopes were broken,
shattered, unreal, unfree. They could not offer freedom from
old wine that had soured with jealousy, self interest, injustice
and violence.

Nothing was certain any more in human terms, neither
the behaviour of a good son, nor a mother's ability to
understand her child. Mary could only ponder the one
certain reality in her life. Yahweh, her God, would not
desert her. She had to ponder. She had to be free to fall
in with His plans, whatever, wherever, however. Mary did
this. Leaving Nazareth for Bethlehem, then for Egypt, then
back to Nazareth, she learned the 'way' – not the rules – by
reflection in hindsight. The baptism in the Jordan, the pilgrim
preacher and miracle worker, the rough followers, the attacks
even from within her kindred, had no precedent. Mary was
a free woman! She let go and learnt the hard way.

Calvary found her in a new place, another vineyard to become fruitful with her Son's blood. Mary was free, undramatic even, in her grief. No tearing of veils, no struggling to die with her Son. Mary was free. She stood at His cross and watched Him die.

At His brief word on that hill, she left her home – the home laden with memories – for that of another. Life was not for living in the past. Life was to be lived to abundance, even of pain, in the present. Mary learnt what it was to be free, by living each moment as it presented itself, with her gaze on Yahweh, her spirit in the care of God's Spirit and her heart with her Son.

Let us continue to keep our focus on God so that we too be taught and set free:

> Lord God Almighty, to You be
> praise, glory and thanks without ceasing
> for the wonder of Your mysterious ways.
> In Your great mercy, O Lord, grant to us,
>   Your children
> humility, the grace of surrender and the wonder of
>   love. Amen.

See to it then that the light inside you is not darkness. If, therefore, your whole body is filled with light, and no trace of darkness, it will be light entirely, as when the lamp shines on you with its rays (Lk 11:35,36).

7 Shalom

This is an excerpt from 'A Shalom Prayer' by Dennis Wrigley – a prayer for peace with God.*

I come as myself.
Just as I am.
This moment.
My feelings, my fears
My joys, my sadnesses.
You see me as I really am
You know me
Through and through
You see all
All that I am
Or ever have been.

As I kneel before You
I give You my heart and all my emotions
All my deepest feelings that lie
Hidden within me.
I give You my stillness
But I also give You the turbulence, the cross
    currents of my life,
My feelings of failure and rejection.

I give You every relationship
Every situation in my life
All my reactions
All my outbursts of joy and of anger,
All my moments of elation and despair.

Lord I give You my intellect,
I lay before You all my frail thoughts and ideas,
I give You all my searching and striving,
My grasping after truth.

I give You all my ignorance and confusion,
I give You all my questions and doubts,
I acknowledge You to be truth,
Truth in its entirety,
Total truth in all its purity.
The Truth which can set me free, in my body,
    my mind and my spirit.

Free from all the bondage,
Free from all the lies and deceit of the world,
Free from my own selfishness and pride and greed.
Break the chains which hold me back, Lord,
Fling open the door of my prison,
That I may pass from the darkness of this world –
     my world
And walk out into the bright light of Your presence.
Father, may I now feel the radiance of Your love upon
     my life,
May I feel the warmth of Your fatherly love upon me,
     your child.
Trusting, depending, loving
Help me to know what joy my response brings to You.
Give me the grace in my weakness to cry 'Abba', Father.
Help me to know that beneath me are Your everlasting
arms
     bearing me up.

* This prayer is used widely in personal and corporate healing and can
be obtained in its full form from The Maranatha Community, Westway,
Western Road, Flixton, Manchester M31 3LE.

I am the light of the world;
anyone who follows me will not be walking in the dark;
he will have the light of life (Jn 8:12).

Part Two: Building the Temple – Building with the Spirit

Introduction

This next part of the programme aims at *a development of depth, a deeper spirituality*. This is necessary, if *Light out of Darkness* is to become one way of experiencing incarnational reality in our lives today. 'I live now not with my own life but with the life of Christ who lives in me' (Ga 2:20). The 'temple' that is being built is the human-spiritual person that I am. The 'builder' is the Holy Spirit of God – who makes His home within us. We are the co-workers, the body of Christ, using every means given to us in this great work of faith, hope and love. All is done to the praise and glory of almighty God, creator, redeemer and sanctifier.

There are ten sections in this second part of *Building the Temple*. In the first four, the aim is to deepen our awareness of God, our neighbour and ourselves, from the angle of following Christ more realistically. To indicate a change in depth, the 'Nightly reflection' exercise changes its name to the *Awareness prayer*. Fidelity to this prayer, making it an essential part of our individual way of life to the end of our days, is a guarantee of growth.

In section five, we come to a watershed. Here we deal with the concept of 'gift'. This is a vital point in the whole programme. There is time to draw breath, time to recognise that the proper use of God's gifts ensures salvation, personal and corporate, whereas the abuse of gift opens the door to perdition.

It is right and fitting that the theme of the following section is the theme of 'freedom'. From there to the end of Part Two, nothing can stop the flow of the dynamic. It is truly an experience of *God-with-us*.

The structure of *Building the Temple* closely resembles that of *Prepare the Way*. It provides, however, for greater depth experience. Here it is in summary:

The beginning

Hand over the whole experience to the Spirit. Become still. Relax body, mind and heart to prepare for the coming of the Holy Spirit. Welcome! Let us glorify the Lord together, as we say: *Glory be to the Father* . . .

Feelings: the 'Now' experience

To take account of our 'human' self, we get in touch with our *feelings*. We express that awareness, in one word, with the group (or, for individuals, with God). For example, 'elated', 'weary', 'anxious', 'hopeful', 'disturbed', 'peaceful'.

The purpose of recognising and claiming how we are feeling now is to stress the importance of the *present moment*: we find God present in each moment. It emphasises also the value of being in touch with our feelings. The Holy Spirit alerts us to the importance of our feelings in the gift of *discernment*. To share negative feelings is a first step to doing something about them so that they become positive. Such a sharing is not faith-sharing however. It is simply sharing how we are feeling. All this is followed by a short prayer.

Faith-sharing

The faith-sharing experience will hopefully be gaining in depth for people as we move now into this more positive approach to God. Darkness is always there, but the light of Christ is also shining more strongly.

Pause for a few moments before starting the faith-sharing. This is to give time to recall again the insights each received, and how these were enfleshed in daily living.

Thank you for that faith-sharing which witnessed to God's generosity in your prayer and living. Through honest faith-sharing, you build up your fellow Christians, who are 'living stones' in the temple of God.

The theme

Each section looks at two dimensions of its theme: the human and the spiritual. These two dimensions form the prayer content for the next week. Pray the material. Reflect on it. Apply it to yourself. Discern what decision(s) you have to make to ensure that the prayer-insights are translated into daily action. Use the prose passage and scripture for prayer in which you will get your insights relative to your own life. At night, pray the *Awareness prayer*, which reveals how faithfully you have integrated your insights into your daily living.

Prayer, living, sacrifice for the coming week

The themes outlined in each section form the basis of prayer, living and sacrifice for the coming week.

Prayer: The prose passage, scripture, or poem are tabulated. Use the table for easy access at prayer time during the next week.

Living: At this point in the prayer experience we also issue ourselves a clear reminder, through questions, of the necessity to flesh out in *living* what each insight demands.

Sacrifice: Linked to this is our reflection on the *sacrifice* that is appropriate to the insight we have been given. This is a different approach to the normal understanding of sacrifice. It has not got a negative meaning, such as 'doing without something'. Its purpose is to obtain the necessary psychic or spiritual energy to translate each insight into daily action. For example: if the insight is to have greater concern for a neighbour who is difficult, then one looks first to one's own frailties! If I find the neighbour's company tedious, then, in faith, I visit or communicate with my neighbour. This is at my own cost! If I recognise, however, that my neighbour is a nervous person and I am a threat to her, then I look to my own obligation first to develop gentleness and humility. The sacrifice chosen must be appropriate to the insight given and to the action that is desired. It is at my expense, not costing my neighbour more!

Preparation for faith-sharing

This is done at the end of each section. What do I discern as God's special teaching to me in the last section? What am I learning about myself from prayer? What am I learning from my efforts to enflesh the insight in action? Am I in earnest about the approach to sacrifice?

The end: Glory be . . .

Finish as always, gathering into prayer the marginalised, or needy. Rest as long as possible, within the temple of one's being where the Spirit lives. Say the *Glory be* . . .

This table presents the ten themes of the next section of the programme, showing how each spiritual dimension has a corresponding human dimension or gift:

Section	Human Dimension	Spiritual Dimension
1.	Communication in prayer and life	Relationship with God and others
2.	Gifts: breathing, breath of God, persons	Deepening Relationships
3.	Awareness	How God sees me
4.	Deepening awareness through memory	How I see God
5.	The concept of gift	Temple of the Holy Spirit
6.	Finding God through my	The gift of freedom

senses

7.	Forgiving, being forgiven	God's forgiveness
8.	Desire for God	Conversion of heart
9.	Trust and commitment	Following Christ
10.	Faith, surrender, peace	Surrender – Mary as model

1 Relationship with God and others

Beginning
We hand over this prayer-life experience to the Holy Spirit. Relax and be still. Prepare for the coming of the Spirit.

Welcome! Let us glorify the Lord, and include families, friends and needy people, as we say together: *Glory be to the Father* . . . (A moment's pause.)

The 'Now' experience
Getting in touch with how you are feeling, in this present moment, helps your human growth. If you are in a group, sharing that builds relationship. If the feeling is negative, claiming it is the first step in making it more positive. This is not faith-sharing. Give one word that describes your present feeling like: weary, excited, happy, upset, anxious, hopeful.

Prayer

You keep him in perfect trust
whose mind is stayed on you
because he trusts in you.
Trust in the Lord forever,
for the Lord is an everlasting rock
(Is 26:3–4, RSV adapted).

Faith-sharing

You have experienced *First Steps* and *Prepare the Way* and you may wish to witness to the things God has done for you through each programme. In addition, you may wish to share something about the effect of *Light out of Darkness* on your prayer and life from the time you began *First Steps* until this present moment.

When you are ready, please begin your faith-sharing.

If you are in a group, the leader says 'Thank you' to each person. When all are finished, the leader says something like: 'Let us pause for a moment before God, to thank Him. Let us be with the group before Him, asking God to continue blessing each person.'

The theme for Section 1: Relationship with God and others

This has two dimensions, *the human and the spiritual*. The *human* deals with the question of *gifts* and *fears*. The *spiritual* deals with trust and confidence in God, and the important *awareness* prayer.

Gifts

In communicating with God and with each other, we use several gifts: listening, sharing, speaking, thinking, reflecting, feeling, being generous and courageous, taking action despite fear, building relationships with God and with each other. All gifts come from God, and we are free to use them or reject them. We use the same gifts in our ordinary daily living as in prayer! It helps to be aware of that. By communicating with others, we build a relationship with them and get to know and love them; by communicating with God, we do the same thing, but we call the communication with God, prayer. There is meant to be a close connection between prayer and our daily living, especially in the way we relate to our neighbour. Prayer is *real* when, as a result of our prayer, our way of living becomes more Christian, that is, using all that we are, human and spiritual, with gratitude, and by recognising that all is a gift from God. Prayer deepens when we discover that God is as much at home in our life as in our prayer! Prayer and life are not separate entities but a whole; it is a gradual learning with its normal ups and downs.

Fears

As ordinary human beings, we are often more aware of our fears than we are of trust, or of the gifts that God has given us.

It is a good thing to look fear in the face, to name it, to claim it, and resolutely to take personal responsibility for lessening its grip. This happens when we share our fear with others. You may discover that others too have fears; perhaps they share your fears! At any rate, sharing with others tends to break the stranglehold of fear. The enemy likes to keep us enslaved by our fears. Keeping silent about them does not help us to become liberated from them.

Be honest and courageous. Trust in the group; trust in God; and above all trust in yourself, because you are the temple of the Holy Spirit. One way to build up that temple is to face and to name your fears *because you trust in God*.

Reflect and apply to your daily life.

Scripture

A passage from Deuteronomy is the material for the *spiritual dimension*. You are accustomed now to being aware of 'movements' within you, alerting you to God's call. Do this in every piece of Scripture. First, become still. Listen with all of your being, mind, heart and will.

'Do not take fright, do not be afraid . . . Yahweh your God goes in front of you and will be fighting on your side as you saw him fight for you in Egypt. In the wilderness, too, you saw him: how Yahweh carried you, as a man carries his child, all along the road you travelled on the way to this place' (Dt 1:29–31). *Reflect and apply to your daily life.*

Awareness prayer

We mentioned before that the *Nightly reflection*, which you practised from *First Steps* on, is deepening. Therefore the name has changed to *Awareness prayer* to indicate the deepening process. The value and importance of this prayer cannot be over-stressed. Fidelity to it is a guarantee of continued human and spiritual growth. Keep begging for the grace of light to illumine your darkness. It is said usually at the end of each day.

The *Awareness prayer* is an intimate prayer of love, gratitude and sorrow. Be still. Rest in His love. Wait until His Spirit moves you to the next step. You are not alone! Look back on your day. God never left you all the time. Always He held you in awareness and in love. During the day as you prayed and tried to live as befits a Christian, He never forgot! Did you?

Recall the times when you were graced with awareness of His presence. Look at what He achieved in and through you when you were thus rooted in Him.

Pause. Give thanks to Him, in your own words. Sometimes you may want to use the words of Judith, 'Lord, you are great, you are glorious. Wonderfully strong, unconquerable.' (Judith 16:16).

Go through your day, slowly, gratefully. Hand yourself over to Him, continuously. Praise and glorify Him.

Recall the movements of the Spirit within your being as you prayed. Recall the many insights He gave you, the courage and fidelity to enflesh them in your daily behaviour. Thank Him.

Recall how He helped you during the day to live in the spirit of prayer, to be recollected, to enjoy contemplative silence, to enjoy a 'minute oasis', when you withdrew and rested in Him. Thank Him, praise Him.

But now, recall how despite His help and closeness, you allowed some measure of darkness to enter into your being. You were unaware of Him, who holds you always before His loving eyes. When you became angry, put another down, spoke sharply, neglected your duty, you had forgotten Him. Ask yourself why this happened. That is a very important question for you. The root of your darkness lies hidden in the answer. Was it laziness, sloth, pride, anger, jealousy – why? Beg God to help you become *aware*. He reads the heart. He is aware of your sincerity or your half-heartedness. He needs your sincerity and integrity. Ask yourself, what is the root cause of your neglect of God? What was so engrossing that it came before your commitment to Him? Answer that, and you will know your real priorities. You will know then what you must do, so as to be faithful and aware of God in your life. Tell Him of your sorrow. Humbly beg for light to see and to understand.

What positive sacrifice can you make to ensure that you become aware of God in your life?

Praise Him, thank Him, intercede for others as you pray for yourself. End the *Awareness prayer* at night with whatever suits you, the 'Our Father' perhaps.

Reflect and apply to your daily life.

Prayer, living, sacrifice for the coming week

This is the programme of prayer for the coming week. It is also a reminder of how prayer affects living. Sacrifice strengthens the morale to let prayer change our behaviour in the ordinary, little things of daily life.

Prayer: In the coming week, talk to God about your gifts. Thank Him. You may discover that you did not recognise some things as gifts at all! Perhaps you could have used these gifts better and been more aware of God's presence in them, while you were using them. For example, you are now more *aware*, or more *discerning*. God is present in these gifts. Become aware of that presence. Praise Him and thank Him. Use the *Awareness prayer* to develop a great sensitivity to God, present in every aspect of your life. Keep asking humbly for the gift of light for yourself and others to illumine your darkness. *Pause, reflect, worship*. Then move on to *Scripture*. Isaiah 26:3–4 is the short prayer at the beginning. Then reflect on Dt 1:29–31. A special passage to encourage you throughout the week comes from Jer 29:13–14.

'When you seek me with all your heart, I will let you find me.'

Living: What 'insights' in prayer did you get? What deci-
              sions have you made to let those insights affect
              your behaviour? Check out in your *Awareness
              prayer* how faithful you have been and what
              changes are happening in your life.

Sacrifice: Re-read the section on 'sacrifice' on page 185
              until you fully understand it. By a proper choice
              of sacrifice, you gain psychic and spiritual energy,
              to help you pray well and live better.

Preparation for faith-sharing for your next meeting

This is done by you at the end of each section, when you
will have *prayed, lived* and *made sacrifice* as laid out above.
Discern what God is teaching you; what you are learning
about yourself in prayer; about relationships with others in
living; and about genuine love of God through sacrifice.

The end: Glory be . . .

Finish as always, gathering into prayer the marginalised, or
needy. Rest as long as possible within the temple of one's
being where the Spirit lives.

2 Deepening relationships

Beginning

We hand over this prayer-life experience to the Holy Spirit.
Relax and be still. Prepare for the coming of the Spirit.

Welcome! Let us glorify the Lord, and include families,
friends, and needy people, as we say: *Glory be to the
Father* . . . (A moment's pause.)

The 'Now' experience

Getting in touch with how your are feeling, in this present
moment, helps your human growth. Sharing it builds relationship in the group. If the feeling is negative, claiming it
is the first step in making it more positive.

This is *not* faith-sharing. Give one word that describes your present feeling, like: weary, excited, happy, upset, anxious, hopeful.

Prayer
Psalm 139:13–14 will help us discover more clearly who we are as the work of God's hands:

> It was you who created my inmost self,
> and put me together in my mother's womb;
> for all these mysteries I thank you:
> for the wonder of myself, for the wonder of
> your works.

Faith-sharing
You prepared your faith-sharing, when you finished the last section, Relationship with God and others.

Pause again now. Recall your experience of insights, of living those out in daily life and how sacrifice helped you.

When you are ready, begin your faith-sharing. If you are in a group, everyone listens respectfully to the one who is sharing.

Thank you for sharing.

The theme for Section 2: Deepening relationships
This theme has two dimensions, the *human* and the *spiritual*. The *human* deals with breathing as a natural, relaxing exercise; the *spiritual* deals with breathing as a prayerful communication using a meditation by George B. Nintemann, OP.

Breathing as a relaxing experience: the human dimension
Become aware of your breathing, but do not change its quality. Without this ordinary gift, you would die; it is so vital. Unobtrusively, it works for you all the time, even when you are quite unaware of it. Become aware of the gift now, accept it gratefully, and let it relax you. Draw in life-giving air, refreshing you as it flows through you; as you breathe out, let all your anxieties, weariness, problems flow away

with it. Relax, let go, let peace fill you! Thank God for this gift. *Reflect and apply to your daily living*.

Breathing as a prayerful communication: the spiritual dimension

God's spirit is the breath of God renewing the face of the earth; without this gift, we would die spiritually. Like our natural breath, God's breath, His Spirit, works for us even when we remain unaware of Him. Become aware of God's spirit all around us, and open to receive Him as you breathe. Unite yourself with the Spirit, filling the depths of your being as you breathe; let it heal you wherever you need healing; if you have injured anyone, send forth the Spirit of God to renew that person by your breathing peace upon him; breathe in God's gift of the Spirit, and breathe out that same gift on a weary, troubled world; become thus a channel of peace, of life, of love, through which God reaches His world. You will find this spiritual dimension of breathing life-giving, in your home, in the office, on the street; it restores your own peace of heart, and it can restore all things in Christ, if you open to receive His Spirit.

The following piece by George B. Nintemann, OP, 'Persons are gift', replaces Scripture in this section.

Persons are *gift* . . .
at least Jesus thought so: 'Father, I want those you have
given me to be where I am.'

Persons are gifts which the Father sends me wrapped.
Some are wrapped very beautifully;
They are very attractive when I first see them.
Some come in ordinary wrapping paper.
Others have been mishandled in the mail.
Once in a while there is a 'Special Delivery',
Some persons are gifts which are loosely wrapped;
Others very tightly.
But the wrapping is not the gift.
It is so easy to make this mistake.

Sometimes the gift is very easy to open,
Sometimes I need others to help.
Is it because they are afraid?
Does it hurt?

Maybe they have been opened up before and thrown
away.
Could it be that the gift is not for me?

I am a person,
therefore I am a gift, too.
A gift to myself, first of all,
the Father gave myself to me.
Have I ever really looked inside the wrappings?
Afraid to?
Perhaps I have never accepted the gift that I am . . .
Could it be that there is more inside the wrappings
than I think there is?
Maybe I've never seen the wonderful gift that I am.
Could the Father's gifts be anything but beautiful?
I love the gifts which those who love me give me;
Why not this gift from the Father?   ˙

And I am a gift to other persons.
Am I willing to be given by the Father to others?
A person for others?
Do others have to be content with the wrappings . . .
never permitted to enjoy the gift?

Every meeting of persons is an exchange of gifts.
But a gift without a giver is not a gift;
it is a thing, devoid of relationship to a giver or givee,
Friendship is a relationship between persons
who see themselves as they truly are:
gifts of the Father to each other, for others . . .
brothers, sisters.

A friend is a gift not just to me

but to others through me.
When I keep my friend and possess him, I destroy his
  'giftedness'.
If I save his life for me, I lose it;
If I lose it for others, I save it.

Persons are gifts, received and given, like the Son.
Friendship is the response of person-gifts to the Father-
  giver.
Friendship is Eucharist.

Reflect and apply to your daily life.

Prayer, living, sacrifice for the coming week

Prayer: Pray Psalm 139. Use breathing as a prayer experi-
             ence. Meditate on the piece, *'Persons are gift'*.
             Awareness prayer: Through it, develop a great
             sensitivity to God, present in every aspect of your
             life. Keep asking humbly for the gift of light for
             yourself and others to illumine your darkness.

Living: How can I relate to difficult people, and experi-
             ence them as 'gift'? Perhaps I need a more mature
             concept of gift – as related to my salvation? A gift
             can be helpful and useful without being pleasant!
             Whoever, or whatever helps me to a better
             understanding of myself, so that I recognise my
             need of God, is a gift! How does this concept
             affect me?

Sacrifice: Self-discipline is necessary if I am to mature as
             a fully human and spiritual person. Recall the
             positive attitude to sacrifice which we spoke about
             earlier.

Preparation for faith-sharing for your next meeting

This is done by you at the end of each section, when
you will have *prayed, lived* and *made sacrifice* as laid out

above. Discern what God is teaching you; what you are learning about yourself in prayer; about relationships with others in living; and about genuine love of God through sacrifice.

The end: Glory be . . .
Finish as always, gathering into prayer the marginalised, or needy. Rest as long as possible within the temple of one's being where the Spirit lives.

3 How God sees me

Beginning
We hand over this prayer-life experience to the Holy Spirit. Relax and be still. Prepare for the coming of the Spirit.

Welcome! Let us glorify the Lord, and include families, friends, and needy people, as we say: *Glory be to the Father* . . . (A moment's pause.)

The 'Now' experience
Getting in touch with how you are feeling, in this present moment, helps your human growth. Sharing it builds relationship in the group. If the feeling is negative, claiming it is the first step in making it more positive.

This is *not* faith-sharing. Give one word that describes your present feeling, like: weary, excited, happy, upset, anxious, hopeful.

Prayer
Pause a moment to become more aware of God, as we prepare to listen to His words of love for us: 'But now, thus says Yahweh, who created you, Jacob, who formed you, Israel: Do not be afraid, for I have redeemed you; I have called you by your name, you are mine. Should you pass through the sea, I will be with you; . . . for I

am Yahweh, your God . . . you are precious in my eyes
. . . and I love you' (Is 43:1–4).

Faith-sharing

You prepared your faith-sharing, when you finished the last
section 'Deepening relationships'.

Pause again now. Recall your experience of insights, of
living those out in daily life and how sacrifice helped you.

When you are ready, begin your faith-sharing. If you are
in a group, everyone listens respectfully to the one who is
sharing.

The theme for Section 3: How God sees me

This has two dimensions, the *human* and the *spiritual*.
The human deals with the gift of awareness; the spiritual
deals with how God sees me, using several passages from
Scripture.

Awareness: the human dimension

Through this valuable gift, I begin to know the 'real' me a
little better. I come to value and appreciate the potential of
my human gifts and also to know my frailty and my need
of my Saviour. I begin to see myself as God sees me, the
one whom He created, the 'work of His hands'. I see that
I am blessed with an abundance of gifts which He gave
me in love, so as to grow into His true likeness. This is
when I become 'real', relating to the 'real' God in a true
relationship, which is prayer. Too often, however, because
of anxiety or insecurity, this 'real' me hides away, together
with my problems.

Frequently the way we cope with problems is denial –
in the psychological sense – trying to pretend the problem
doesn't exist, that by ignoring it, all will be well and it will
disappear. It won't. We must face it, claim it, and decide to do
something about it. We discovered that our fears diminished
when we shared them with the group. We discovered that
we had a lot in common. If we want to grow into fully alive
human beings, then let us face whatever is causing us undue
concern or anxiety. Become *aware* of it. Have a good look

at it, and share just as much as you want to with the group. Listen to Christ, as He says to you now: 'Come to me, all you who labour and are overburdened, and I will give you rest' (Mt 11:28).

Reflect. Apply to your daily living.

How God sees me: The spiritual dimension

Once again in Scripture, God will tell us how deeply He loves us. His love is everlasting for each of us, His very own. Let us become aware of His message of love. 'Do not let your hearts be troubled. Trust in God still, and trust in me . . . I am going now to prepare a place for you . . . I shall return to take you with me; so that where I am you may be too' (Jn 14:1–3). And again: 'Do not be afraid, for I have redeemed you; I have called you by your name, you are mine. Should you pass through the sea, I will be with you, or through rivers, they will not swallow you up. For I am Yahweh, your God, the Holy One of Isracl, your saviour . . . you are precious in my eyes . . . and I love you . . . Do not be afraid, for I am with you' (Is 43:1–4).

Reflect and apply to your daily life

Prayer, living, sacrifice for the coming week

Prayer: Bring the new awareness of yourself to prayer. Talk confidently to God about your discoveries. It is the 'real' you that He seeks, to help you grow into His likeness.

    Awareness prayer: Through it, develop a great sensitivity to God, present in every aspect of your life. Keep begging for the grace of light to illumine your darkness.

    Scripture: Jn 14:1–3; 13:34; 14:18–23; 15:15; Is 43:1–4.

Living: Are you *aware* that God loves you, as you are? How is that reality affecting your life? Are you trying to love other people more? What other insights did you get? How do you plan on integrating them with life?

Sacrifice: It is your turn to sacrifice yourself now for Him

who 'emptied Himself' for you. He opened wide
His arms and died for you. What can *you* do that
you may live for Him? Action for the kingdom
flows from a deep inner life. The sacrifice must
be at your own expense, so as to help others.

Preparation for faith-sharing for your next meeting

This is done by you at the end of each section, when
you will have *prayed, lived* and *made sacrifice* as laid out
above. Discern what God is teaching you; what you are
learning about yourself in prayer; about relationships with
others in living; and about genuine love of God through
sacrifice.

The end: Glory be . . .

Finish as always, gathering into prayer the marginalised, or
needy. Rest as long as possible within the temple of one's
being where the Spirit lives.

4 How I see God

Beginning

We hand over this prayer-life experience to the Holy Spirit.
Relax and be still. Prepare for the coming of the Spirit.

Welcome! Let us glorify the Lord, and include families,
friends, and needy people, as we say: *Glory be to the
Father* . . . (A moment's pause.)

The 'Now' experience

Getting in touch with how you are feeling, in this present
moment, helps your human growth. Sharing it builds relationship in the group. If the feeling is negative, claiming it
is the first step in making it more positive.

This is *not* faith-sharing. Give one word that describes your present feelings like: weary, excited, happy, upset, anxious, hopeful.

Prayer
Substitute your own name for Israel, son, in this prayer:

> When Israel was a child I loved him,
> and I called my son out of Egypt . . .
> I myself taught Ephraim to walk,
> I took them in my arms . . .
> I led them with reins of kindness,
> with leading strings of love.
> I was like someone who lifts an infant close against
>   his cheek;
> stooping down to him I gave him his food
>
> (Ho 11:1,3,4).

Faith-sharing
You prepared your faith-sharing, when you finished the last section 'How God sees me'.

Pause again now. Recall your experience of insights, of living those out in daily life and how sacrifice helped you. When you are ready, and in any order, begin your faith-sharing. If you are in a group, everyone listens respectfully to the one who is sharing.

The theme for Section 4: How I see God
This has two dimensions, the human and the spiritual. The human deals with awareness deepened through memory; the spiritual deals with scripture on how I see God.

Awareness deepened through memory: the human dimension
Recall someone who had too strong an influence on your life, someone whom you experienced as unloving, not fully supporting you. At that time, what image would best describe how you experienced that person – tyrant, judge, lion, enemy, taskmaster? With insight, or with the wisdom of years you would probably now modify that earlier image. With greater maturity, you are free enough now to change

or modify your earlier experience. Let us see, therefore, if the same can happen with regard to God – if, for you, there is necessity to change an unfortunate earlier image.

Recall your earlier impressions of God and your image of Him then. Be very *real* about this. Does your behaviour testify to a loving God? Or does your behaviour, despite perhaps all the correct words, testify to a tyrant God, a God that has to be appeased, a God that watches to catch you out? What is the God like that you believe in? What kind of a God do you want to believe in? What kind of a God does the above passage from Hosea present to you?

Reflect. Apply to your daily living.

Scripture: the spiritual dimension

The spiritual draws on the Hosea passage on God quoted above, as well as Matthew 11:25–7 and Psalm 145. Is this the way that I see God? Deepen your awareness of the longing you experience to know this God, who cares for and loves you. Recall how much God longs for you. What 'movements' do you experience as you read Hosea? Stay with those movements and beg God to increase your love for Him.

At that time Jesus exclaimed, 'I bless you, Father, Lord of Heaven and of earth, for hiding these things from the learned and the clever and revealing them to mere children. Yes, Father, for that is what it pleased you to do. Everything has been entrusted to me by my Father; and no one knows the Son except the Father, just as no one knows the Father except the Son and those to whom the Son chooses to reveal him' (Mt 11:25–7).

Reflect and apply to your daily life.

Prayer, living, sacrifice for the coming week

Prayer: Talk to God about the discoveries you have made with regard to images of people and of God. Desire to relate to the 'real' God and not to a caricature of Him.

Awareness prayer: Through it, develop a great sensitivity to God, present in every aspect of your life. Keep begging for the grace of light to illumine your darkness.

Scripture: Hosea 11:1–5; Mt 11:25–7; Psalm 145.

Living: Let the *awareness prayer* change the way you live. Are you becoming more aware? Is the deeper awareness affecting the way you live and relate to other people?

Sacrifice: Make it real. It needs to be constant rather than great. Be discerning in your choice; a sacrifice is something that helps you change your behaviour.

Preparation for faith-sharing for your next meeting

This is done by you at the end of each section, when you will have prayed, lived and made sacrifice as laid out above. Discern what God is teaching you; what you are learning about yourself in prayer; about relationships with others in living; and about genuine love of God through sacrifice.

The end: Glory be . . .

Finish as always, gathering into prayer the marginalised, or needy. Rest as long as possible within the temple of one's being where the Spirit lives.

5 Temple of the Holy Spirit

Beginning

We hand over this prayer-life experience to the Holy Spirit. Relax and be still. Prepare for the coming of the Spirit.

Welcome! Let us glorify the Lord, and include families, friends, and needy people, as we say: *Glory be to the Father* . . . (A moment's pause.)

The 'Now' experience
Getting in touch with how you are feeling, in this present moment, helps your human growth. Sharing it builds relationship in the group. If the feeling is negative, claiming it is the first step in making it more positive.

This is *not* faith-sharing. Give one word that describes your present feeling, like: weary, excited, happy, upset, anxious, hopeful.

Prayer
Christ has waited a long time for us to express our thanks for His generosity. As we hear His voice speaking to us in Revelation, let us open wide our hearts:

Look, I am standing at the door, knocking.
If one of you hears me calling and opens the door,
I will come in to share his meal, side by side with
him . . . If anyone has ears to hear,
let him listen to what the Spirit is saying (Rev 3:20–2).

Faith-sharing
You prepared your faith-sharing, when you finished the last section, 'How I see God.' *Pause again now*. Recall your experience of insights, of living those out in daily life and how sacrifice helped you.

When you are ready, begin your faith-sharing. Everyone listens respectfully to the one who is sharing.

The theme for Section 5: Temple of the Holy Spirit
This has two dimensions, the *human* and the *spiritual*. The human deals with the concept of gift, the spiritual deals with Nehemiah and the re-building of the temple of Jerusalem.

The concept of gift: the human dimension
This section is a watershed. It gives us time to draw breath and to draw strands together. It is crucial for the whole

programme. From Section 5 to the end, the dynamic cannot easily be interrupted or stopped.

The *concept of gift* is at the heart of the Christian mystery. All that we are and have is gift from God. His first gift to each of us is His eternal and everlasting love. From that flows the gift of creation, when He gave us the gift of life, the potential to grow as full human beings who are children of God. To this end, He gave us the gift of all animate and inanimate creation, especially people, with whom we can grow and praise God. God gave us Himself as loving creator, saviour and sanctifier, whom we worship through the proper use of His gifts. In constantly drawing human beings to Himself through adoration and love, He continues to create us in His own image and likeness.

Misappropriation, or abuse of gift, lies at the heart of the mystery of sin. Sin is the rejection of God's love present in each gift. Misappropriation of gift is when we refuse to acknowledge that everything we are and have comes from God. This is to abuse gift by denying the giver. We have nothing of ourselves. When we accept this truth, then we want to worship God and surrender to Him; when we claim gifts as our own, we hope to be independent and great in our own esteem! This idolatry of 'self' is sin. A simple way to recall the truth of gift is as follows: 'All that I am and have is God's gift of love to me; God Himself is present in each gift of love; He gifts me so as to save me and give me abundance of life which I can share with others.'

In the coming week, spend time discovering gifts that you did not recognise before – yourself, others, events, things. A gift need not be a pleasant experience! If it's a life-giving experience, putting reality clearly before you, it is a precious gift, however challenging and unpalatable. Whatever frees you to acknowledge your proper place before God is a gift. St Paul expresses it well: 'I shall be very happy to make my weaknesses my special boast so that the power of Christ may stay over me . . . For it is when I am weak that I am strong' (2 Cor 12:9–10).

Reflect. Apply to your daily living.

Scripture

We move to Scripture to get the background for the structure of *Building the Temple*. The Scripture passage is from Nehemiah. After the exile, the Jews returned to Jerusalem about 444 BC. The Temple was rebuilt first. Then the walls were strengthened to protect the city. The people had 'a will to work', but they had to face the ridicule and attacks of their enemies. Nehemiah's answer was always the same, *prayer* plus *action*: 'We prayed and set a guard', or 'Remember the Lord and fight'. Soon the walls were built and the city protected, and even the enemies acknowledged God's hand in it.

In *Building the Temple*, we too rely on God and action: we *pray*, and we *live* according to the grace of our prayer; we strengthen our hands by *sacrifice*, and we gladly acknowledge that the hand of God is achieving great things in us. Thanks to God, the enemy within us is being gradually conquered, though we know we are frail and must 'stay awake and watch'. The 'Temple of the Spirit' is being built, but we are still earthbound and keenly aware that 'unless the Lord build the house, they labour in vain who build it'.

Adaptation from Nehemiah 2, 3 and 6:

'Come,' said the Jews, 'let us rebuild the walls of Jerusalem and suffer this indignity no longer. Let us start,' they exclaimed, 'let us build', and with willing hands they set about the good work. Enemies said, 'What are you doing?' but Nehemiah gave them this answer, 'The God of heaven will give us success. We, his servants are going to build.'

Enemies ridiculed the Jews and exclaimed: 'What are these pathetic Jews trying to do? Do they think they can put new life into these charred stones?' Another enemy said: 'Let them build; a jackal jumping on their walls will soon knock the stones down again.' Meanwhile the Jews were rebuilding the wall, which was soon finished, since the people put their hearts into their work. When the enemies heard that the gaps in the wall were being made good, they were furious and conspired to attack Jerusalem and upset the building plans. The Jews called on their God and set a watch, day and night, to guard the city. So they took up positions. Nehemiah had seen the fear of his people. He stood up and said, 'Do not be afraid of them. Keep your minds on the Lord who is great and to be feared.' The enemies withdrew when they heard that God had thwarted their plan, that the Jews were prepared and had gone back to work on the wall. Again the enemies tried to frighten them, thinking: 'Their hands will tire of the work, and it will never be finished.' But the Jews meanwhile were making their hands even stronger.

The walls were finally finished. When the enemies and all the surrounding nations had seen the walls, they were deeply impressed and acknowledged that this work had been accomplished by the power of God.

Reflect and apply to your daily life.

Prayer, living, sacrifice for the coming week

Prayer: *Discover* in prayer, gifts that hitherto you did not recognise or claim, including the less pleasant.

Pray on the content of this week's material.

Awareness prayer: Through it, develop a great sensitivity to God, present in every aspect of your life. Keep begging for the grace of light to illumine your darkness.

Scripture: Reflect on this adaptation of Nehemiah and its significance for your participation in *Building the Temple*, which you yourself are.

Living: Are you living in such a way that others are encouraged to build the temple of the Spirit with you? What more do you need to do? Why? What steps do you need to take to deepen your awareness of gift?

Sacrifice: Our hands, too, like the hands of the Jews of old, need to be strengthened for the building programme through sacrifice that costs. Be discerning about this.

Preparation for faith-sharing for your next meeting

This is done by you at the end of each section, when you will have prayed, lived and made sacrifice as laid out above.

Discern what God is teaching you; what you are learning about yourself in prayer; about relationships with others in living; and about genuine love of God through sacrifice.

The end: Glory be . . .
Finish as always, gathering into prayer the marginalised, or needy. Rest as long as possible within the temple of one's being where the Spirit lives.

6 The gift of freedom

Beginning
We hand over this prayer-life experience to the Holy Spirit. Relax and be still. Prepare for the coming of the Spirit.

Welcome! Let us glorify the Lord, and include families, friends, and needy people, as we say: *Glory be to the Father* . . . (A moment's pause.)

The 'Now' experience
Getting in touch with how you are feeling, in this present moment, helps your human growth. Sharing it builds relationship in the group. If the feeling is negative, claiming it is the first step in making it more positive.

This is *not* faith-sharing. Give one word that describes your present feeling, like: weary, excited, happy, upset, anxious, hopeful.

Prayer
When Jesus opened the scroll in the synagogue of Nazareth, he read: 'He has sent me to bring the good news to the poor, to proclaim liberty to captives . . . to set the down-trodden free' (Lk 4:18). And in John we read: 'The truth will make you free . . . So if the Son makes you free, you will be free indeed' (Jn 8:32,36).

Faith-sharing
You prepared your faith-sharing, when you finished the last
section, 'Temple of the Holy Spirit'. *Pause again now.* Recall
your experience of insights, of living those out in daily life
and how sacrifice helped you. When you are ready, begin
your faith-sharing. If you are in a group, everyone listens
respectfully to the one who is sharing.

The theme for Section 6: The gift of freedom
This has two dimensions, the *human* and the *spiritual*. The
human deals with finding God through our senses; the
spiritual deals with freedom.

Finding God through our senses: the human dimension
We will now look at the gift of our five senses, which are
meant to be five avenues of freedom reaching to God. These
natural gifts can indeed be ways of seeking and finding God
in our daily living but, too often, our eyes, our ears, our
touch, our taste and our sense of smell lead us into areas
of our greatest unfreedom, into sinfulness.

Here I am using Scripture so as to learn more about this
wonderful human gift.

The following texts from Scripture reveal the mind and
the heart of God with regard to the use of our senses.
Isaiah says:

> The Lord Yahweh has given me
> a disciple's tongue.
> So that I may know how to reply to the wearied
> he provides me with speech.
> Each morning he wakes me to hear,
> to listen like a disciple.
> The Lord Yahweh has opened my ear (Is 50:4–5).

The Psalms are also expressive of the mind of God on
this point:

> Who else is God but Yahweh . . .
> who makes my feet like the hinds'
> and holds me from falling on the heights (Ps 18:31–3).

Hear my voice, raised in petition,
as I cry to you for help,
as I raise my hands, Yahweh,
toward your Holy of Holies (Ps 28:2).

Who has the right to climb the mountain of Yahweh,
who has the right to stand in his holy place?
He whose hands are clean, whose heart is pure . . .
(Ps 24:3–4).

This following quote from Revelation is rich in many aspects
of the senses, real and symbolical, as also on the union with
Jesus that can result from the proper use of the senses:

Look, I am standing at the door, knocking.
If one of you hears me calling and opens the door,
I will come in to share his meal,
side by side with him (Rev 3:20).

Finally, this Prayer of the Grail can be a constant reminder
of how to grow, by using the gift of the senses:

Lord Jesus,
I give you my hands to do your work.
I give you my feet to go your way.
I give you my eyes to see as you do.
I give you my tongue to speak your words.
I give you my mind that you may think in me.
I give you my spirit that you may pray in me.
Above all I give you my heart, that you may love in me
Your Father and all mankind.
I give you my whole self that you may grow in me,
so that it is you, Lord Jesus, who live and work and
pray in me. *Prayer of the Grail.*

Reflect. Apply to your daily living.

The spiritual dimension of freedom
Freedom is one of the most important gifts for us if we are
to grow on the human and spiritual level. By clinging to

anything, we are creating a lack of freedom – an unfreedom – in ourselves which limits us. For example, if I cling to the position that I have been unjustly treated, that the 'other' is in the wrong and has made me angry, then I soon become stuck and am no longer as free as I could be. Movement towards improved relations is impossible, unless I am free enough to allow the possibility of another point of view emerging. I can begin by taking some personal responsibility and stating the truth: 'I became angry'. With this slight shift of position, I have let a breath of freedom blow into my world, and I'm in a better position to discover more about my real self – which is always an experience of growth.

A true example of this is the following story. A mother got hurt at the changed behaviour of a dearly loved son, with whom she enjoyed a good relationship. She experienced a lack of freedom and each withdrew from the other. Prayer helped the mother to keep communication open, but she knew she needed help. As a result of getting help, she discovered that her hurt and anger were so deep that, unconsciously, she was building a wall between herself and her son. On reflection, she recognised that her son was confused by her behaviour and was picking up her repressed feelings. He felt powerless to reach her, and this infuriated and upset him. He vented his distress and anger in worse behaviour!

The vicious circle was broken by the mother, when she took personal responsibility for her own part in the problem. She could not deny that his behaviour was unacceptable, but she was freed to move and to take a more liberating approach. In freedom, she let go her hurt and self-righteous attitude and allowed her maternal feelings of love to predominate. Her son picked up her change of heart. He recognised that she loved him, but he instinctively knew that she was not condoning his behaviour. Later when they were able to talk together again, she shared with him her experience of freedom. He understood and began to respond in a more mature and loving way.

Turn now to the section on freedom on page 178–180. Re-read it and try to grasp its deep spiritual significance.

Reflect and apply to your daily life.

Prayer, living, sacrifice for the coming week

Prayer: Talk to God about the action you must take to
              ensure your growth into freedom. Where must
              you avoid clinging to anything?
              How can you best delight the Lord by enjoying
              the gift of your senses as He intends?
              Awareness prayer: Through it, develop a great
              sensitivity to God, present in every aspect of your
              life. Keep begging for the grace of light to illumine
              your darkness.
              Scripture: Pray Psalm 139 and discover 'the won-
              der of your being'. Lk 4:18; Jn 8:32,36; Is 50:4–5;
              Ps 18:31–3; Ps 24:3–4; Rev 3:20.
              Use the Prayer of the Grail.
Living: Are you using your senses with gratitude and
              appreciation? Are you growing in freedom? What
              more can you do?
Sacrifice: Where lack of freedom or excess threatens, use
              your senses with wisdom and restraint.

Preparation for faith-sharing for your next meeting

This is done by you at the end of each section, when you
will have prayed, lived and made sacrifice as laid out above.
Discern what God is teaching you; what you are learning
about yourself in prayer; about relationships with others in
living; and about genuine love of God through sacrifice.

The end: Glory be . . .

Finish as always, gathering into prayer the marginalised, or
needy. Rest as long as possible within the temple of one's
being where the Spirit lives.

7 God's forgiveness

Beginning
We hand over this prayer-life experience to the Holy Spirit.
Relax and be still. Prepare for the coming of the Spirit.

Welcome! Let us glorify the Lord, and include families,
friends, and needy people, as we say: *Glory be to the Father*
. . . (A moment's pause.)

The 'Now' experience
Getting in touch with how you are feeling, in this present
moment, helps your human growth. Sharing it builds relationship in the group. If the feeling is negative, claiming it
is the first step in making it more positive.

This is *not* faith-sharing. Give one word that describes your
present feeling, like: weary, excited, happy, upset, anxious,
hopeful.

Prayer

> Lord, I hold quietly in my mind before you
> those for whom I have a hard heart,
> whom I find it difficult to forgive.
> Lord, pardon all my sins and unfreedoms,
> fill me with your compassionate love.
> Give me a heart of flesh,
> the gift of your forgiving love,
> that I may truly forgive as I hope to be forgiven.
> Gather us all, wounding and wounded,
> within the healing of your mercy and love. Amen.

Faith-sharing

You prepared your faith-sharing, when you finished the last section 'The gift of freedom'. Pause again now. Recall your experience of insights, of living those out in daily life and how sacrifice helped you. When you are ready, begin your faith-sharing. If you are in a group, everyone listens respectfully to the one who is sharing.

The theme for Section 7: God's forgiveness

This has two dimensions, the *human* and the *spiritual*: the human deals with forgiving and being forgiven; the spiritual deals with the quality of God's forgiveness.

Forgiven and being forgiven: the human dimension

When you were a child, I'm sure you did something naughty, and dreaded being caught. Relive, now, that fear or anguish, but centre especially on the *dread of not being forgiven*. Any punishment is preferable. When, on occasion, forgiveness was withheld or even not fully given, recall what that did to you. How did your whole being, your body, your mind and your spirit react and recoil? Relive an experience of genuine forgiveness and contrast that with the experience of forgiveness being withheld.

Forgiving/not forgiving

We talked earlier about having a hard and unforgiving heart for someone. Relive the way that that destructive hardness seemed to permeate your being and freeze you into immobility at the sight of that person for whom you had a hard heart. Contrast with that the joy of the child that you were, when someone forgave you. Two images, the joy of forgiveness, the hardness of implacable unforgiveness. 'I do not know you,' says the Lord. 'Throw him out into the dark' (Mt 25:12,30).

Reflect. Apply to your daily living.

The quality of God's forgiveness: the spiritual dimension

There are times in our lives when only God Himself can 'melt us and mould us'. In listening to these Psalms, become aware, as you read, of the 'special' word addressed to you:

Lord God, you who are always merciful and
  tender-hearted,
slow to anger, always loving, always loyal,
turn to me and pity me (Ps 86:15–16).

From the depths I call to you, Yahweh,
Lord, listen to my cry for help!
Listen compassionately
to my pleading!
If you never overlooked our sins, Yahweh,
Lord, could anyone survive?
But you do forgive us:
and for that we revere you.
I wait for Yahweh, my soul waits for him,
I rely on his promise,
my soul relies on the Lord
more than a watchman on the coming of dawn
                                        (Ps 130:1–6).

Reflect and apply to your daily life.

Prayer, living, sacrifice for the coming week

Prayer: Reflect on the material of this meeting.
            Spend time on the feelings that arise in you, espe-
            cially on compassion and remorse. Pray especially
            the opening prayer: Lord I hold quietly in my mind
            before you . . .
            Beg for a 'heart of flesh' instead of a 'heart
            of stone'.
            Have you a hard, unforgiving heart for any
            person?
            Awareness prayer: Through it, develop a great
            sensitivity to God, present in every aspect of your
            life. Keep begging for the grace of light to illumine
            your darkness.
            Scripture: Mt 25:12,30; Ps 86:15; Ps 130; Ps 51.
            Pray the opening prayer and respond when you
            are moved.

Living: Do you need to beg for the compassionate heart
               of Jesus in your dealings with other people? Are
               you loving and forgiving? What is your actual
               experience when you are dealing with other
               people?
Sacrifice: Let your sacrifice equal the measure of your
               sorrow.

Preparation for faith-sharing for your next meeting

This is done by you at the end of each section, when you
will have prayed, lived and made sacrifice as laid out above.
Discern what God is teaching you; what you are learning
about yourself in prayer; about relationships with others in
living; and about genuine love of God through sacrifice.

The end: Glory be . . .

Finish as always, gathering into prayer the marginalised, or
needy. Rest as long as possible within the temple of one's
being where the Spirit lives.

8 Conversion of heart

Beginning

We hand over this prayer-life experience to the Holy Spirit.
Relax and be still. Prepare for the coming of the Spirit.

Welcome! Let us glorify the Lord, and include families,
friends, and needy people, as we say: *Glory be to the Father*
. . . (A moment's pause.)

The 'Now' experience

Getting in touch with how you are feeling, in this present
moment, helps your human growth. Sharing it builds relationship in the group. If the feeling is negative, claiming it

is the first step in making it more positive.

This is *not* faith-sharing. Give one word that describes your present feeling, like: weary, excited, happy, upset, anxious, hopeful.

Prayer

I am Yahweh, your God . . .
You know no God but me
there is no other saviour . . .
come back to Yahweh your God;
your iniquity was the cause of your downfall.
Provide yourself with words
and come back to Yahweh.
Say to him: 'Take all iniquity away
so that we may have happiness again
and offer you our words of praise . . . '

I will heal their disloyalty,
I will love them with all my heart,
for my anger has turned from them . . .
They will come back to live in my shade;
they will grow corn that flourishes,
they will cultivate vines . . .
I am like a cypress ever green,
all your fruitfulness comes from me
(Ho 13:4; 14:2–3,5; 14:8–9).

What is the *deepest desire* that awakens in you on hearing these words?

Faith-sharing

You prepared your faith-sharing, when you finished the last section 'God's forgiveness'. Pause again now. Recall your experience of insights, of living those out in daily life and how sacrifice helped you. When you are ready begin your faith-sharing. If you are in a group, everyone listens respectfully to the one who is sharing.

The theme for Section 8: Conversion of heart
This has two dimensions, the *human* and the *spiritual*: the human deals with the gift of desire; the spiritual with conversion of heart.

The gift of desire: the human dimension
To be able to desire is a gift that helps us transcend ourselves and our human limitations. It is very precious. It is, in fact, the very Spirit of God Himself who desires within us.

Recall again that 'deepest desire' that awakened in you as you listened to the opening prayer. That was God's Spirit speaking to you and drawing you beyond yourself to desire what He desires for you. Rest in that awareness again. Say to yourself, 'God's Spirit desired within me. I heard. I desired to respond. I want to be able to respond generously.'

Yet, we are frail sinners and can limit even God's desires for us, because, as we discovered in Section 6, He has given us the gift of freedom. Not only can we limit God's desire for us but we can go further and abuse the gifts He has given us and rebel against Him. Take, for example, the gift of other people. Christ says: 'Whatever you do to one of these, my least brethren, you do to me.' Does Christ feel loved or rejected by us in our dealings with other people? Abuse of gift means forgetting and rejecting God who loves and remembers us always.

> Does a woman forget her baby at the breast
> or fail to cherish the son of her womb?
> Yet even if these forget,
> I will never forget you (Is 49:15).

Beware of any limitations which you tend to place on your good desires, especially your desire for God. Such could be, for example, anxiety, fear, some measure of self-centredness, which puts self before God. Does your reflection show that you are truly seeking God 'with all your heart' and therefore 'will find him', as was promised in Jeremiah (29:14), or is self-interest a block to your finding Him? In other words, do you need conversion? Do you need to have your heart of stone replaced by a heart of flesh? Do you earnestly desire to put God first? If you want to change direction, to turn your life over to God, then, in your own words, say something like this: 'I recognise that I am truly a sinner and need my Saviour. I desire the gift of conversion, and I humbly beg for that grace in the loving and powerful name of Jesus.'

Reflect. Apply to your daily living.

Conversion of heart: the spiritual dimension.

Without great desire for a change of heart, to let go of a heart of stone, conversion will scarcely take place.

The story of St Paul's conversion is well known. As Saul, he was zealous in upholding the law and persecuting the followers of the new religion. As a person of integrity Saul was committed, according to his lights, to the destruction of what appeared to him to be evil. God read Saul's heart and saw there the desire to do what was 'good', so God's love and power achieved more in Saul than he himself 'could ask or imagine' (Ep 3:20). Blind to the limitations of the truth by which he was acting, he was mercifully blinded on the road to Damascus so that he might discover 'truth itself' and live. It was the beginning of the conversion story of Saul, who became Paul.

Conversion is usually a slow, continuous growth experience, never fully accomplished in us. It is the gradual dawning of a new light, a new truth. In the strength of that, we are moved forward to a new way of seeing, a new way of being. It is a gradual immersion in the light, which appears to us sometimes as darkness. The darkness is necessary for our cleansing and purification. Through the darkness transformed into light, we learn to leave what is of 'self' rather than of Christ. We begin to turn our lives towards Christ, who is the true Light of the world.

Conversion, at times, is like climbing a mountain for a beginner. The foothills appear quite steep and hard going. At the first plateau, there is a short respite, and then the

climb goes on and on. Gradually, the truth begins to dawn
that it is going to be a long, slow climb, and doubts begin to
surface. But somehow the climb continues. Eventually, the
climber ceases looking back at the foothills, ceases peering
upwards at the distant heights, and begins instead to trust the
guide. Then the experience becomes more real, and the climb
more enjoyable, because energy is going into the foothold of
the moment, an energy that seems to flow from the guide to
the climbers.

Out of his personal experience of the way of conversion,
Paul could thus write:

> Out of his infinite glory, may the Father give you the
> power through his Spirit for your hidden self to grow
> strong, so that Christ may live in your hearts through
> faith, and then, planted in love and built on love, you
> will with all the saints have strength to grasp the breadth
> and the length, the height and the depth; until, knowing
> the love of Christ, which is beyond all knowledge, you
> are filled with the utter fullness of God. Glory be to him
> whose power, working in us, can do infinitely more than
> we can ask or imagine; glory be to him from generation
> to generation in the Church and in Christ Jesus for ever
> and ever. Amen (Ep 3:16–21).

Reflect and apply to your daily life.

Prayer, living, sacrifice for the coming week

Prayer: Talk to God again about your reflections on the
material of this meeting. Reflect prayerfully on
desire and conversion, as it has been discussed.
Awareness prayer: Through it, develop a great
sensitivity to God, present in every aspect of your
life. Keep begging for the grace of light to illumine
your darkness.
Scripture: Ep 3:16–21; Is 49:15; Ho 13:41; 14:2–3,5;
14:8–9.

Living: Be very sensitive to His call to you to repent and be converted. 'Today, if you hear his voice, harden not your hearts.'

Are you becoming more concerned about other people, especially about people you do not like? Are you concerned about the poor and deprived?

Sacrifice: Be genuine in denying yourself, so that you may live. We have received so much while others have so little.

Preparation for faith-sharing for your next meeting

This is done by you at the end of each section, when you will have prayed, lived and made sacrifice as laid out above. Discern what God is teaching you; what you are learning about yourself in prayer; about relationships with others in living; and about genuine love of God through sacrifice.

The end: Glory be . . .

Finish as always, gathering into prayer the marginalised, or needy. Rest as long as possible within the temple of one's being where the Spirit lives.

9 Following Christ

Beginning

We hand over this prayer-life experience to the Holy Spirit. Relax and be still. Prepare for the coming of the Spirit.

Welcome! Let us glorify the Lord, and include families, friends, and needy people, as we say: *Glory be to the Father* . . . (A moment's pause.)

The 'Now' experience

Getting in touch with how you are feeling, in this present moment, helps your human growth. Sharing it builds relationship in the group. If the feeling is negative, claiming it is the first step in making it more positive.

This is *not* faith-sharing. Give one word that describes your present feeling, like: weary, excited, happy, upset, anxious, hopeful.

Prayer

> In God is my safety and glory,
> The rock of my strength.
> Take refuge in God all you people,
> Trust him at all times.
> Pour out your hearts before him
> For God is our refuge (Ps 62:5–8, adapted).

Faith-sharing

You prepared your faith-sharing, when you finished the last section, 'Conversion of Heart'. Pause again now. Recall your experience of insights, of living those out in daily life and how sacrifice helped you.

When you are ready begin your faith-sharing. If you are in a group, everyone listens respectfully to the one who is sharing.

The theme for Section 9: Following Christ

This has two dimensions, the *human* and the *spiritual*: the human deals with trust, commitment; the spiritual deals with commitment to Christ.

Trust, commitment: the human dimension

Trust is a very special gift to enable us to grow as human and spiritual persons. Growth, in fact, is impossible without some measure of mutual trust in our lives. Hence its great importance. We must take personal responsibility for building trust and letting it be built into our own lives and the lives of others.

Recall someone who is a trusted refuge and support in your life, someone who accepts you exactly as you are, warts and all. When you are so accepted, do you grow, or do you feel in any way diminished as a human being? Does your potential expand, or do you feel threatened? What happens to your confidence? Get in touch with your heart response, with your feelings, in regard to all this.

If you really desire to experience trust such as this, the answer is in your own hands. You must be open to receive this gift and to give it to others. It is a two-way stretch. Help others to grow by encouraging their strengths. Respect and accept the struggle of their frail humanity, as you hope to be accepted. Have a listening heart, so that others can unburden in trust to you. Be equally willing to accept all this service from others. Mindful of continuing conversion – which affects your human as well as your spiritual response – pinpoint attitudes and actions that must change for you in the area of trust, if you and others are to be able to grow.

Reflect. Apply to your daily living.

Commitment to Christ: the spiritual dimension

If we are to be converted and to turn our lives over to Christ, then we must desire this ardently. This again is a two-way stretch. We must receive everything from Christ, and we need to give Him the only thing He wants from us – our love, our heart. It is all, indeed, that we have to give, but it is the treasure which He desires. When we give Him our heart, we make ourselves vulnerable, because we are giving Him a blank cheque on our lives. This is not a state to be feared but to be greatly desired. God is love and acts always out of love in our best interests. When we love this way, then all God's people begin to be important to us, because they are important to Him, whom we love. Then He begins to teach us to give as freely as we have received.

Scripture helps us to understand these truths better:

You keep him in perfect peace whose mind is stayed on you because he trusts in you. Trust in the Lord forever for the Lord is an everlasting rock (Is 26:3–4, *adapted*).

> Give thanks to Yahweh, for he is good,
> his love is everlasting!
> I would rather take refuge in Yahweh
> than rely on men (Ps 118:1,8).

Jesus said to his disciples: 'It is not those who say to me "Lord, Lord", who will enter the kingdom of heaven, but the person who does the will of my Father in heaven . . . Therefore, everyone who listens to these words of mine and acts on them will be like a sensible man who built his house on rock. Rain came down, floods rose, gales blew and hurled themselves against that house, and it did not fall: it was founded on rock' (Mt 7:21,24–5).

Reflect and apply to your daily life.

Prayer, living, sacrifice for the coming week

Prayer:　Trust is both given and received. Reflect prayerfully on the material presented this week and see what it says about your commitment as a follower of Christ.

Scripture texts: Use the texts given or any others that help you in your commitment to Christ. Is 26:3–4; Ps 118:1,8; Mt 7:21,24–5.

Awareness prayer: Through it, develop a great sensitivity to God, present in every aspect of your life. Keep begging for the grace of light to illumine your darkness.

Living:　Has your trust grown since you began these programmes? What helped you most? Have you learnt to give thanks to God, spontaneously, for progress? That is the work of the Spirit within you.

Is your sense of personal responsibility growing? Do you see any difference, as a result, in your relationship with others?

What increases your confidence? What diminishes you? Do you treat others as you want to be treated?

Have you given more of your heart to Christ? Are you more *real* now than at the beginning of the programme?

Sacrifice: What is an obstacle to your growth in trust and commitment? What sacrifice can you make to gain the necessary psychic and spiritual energy?

Preparation for faith-sharing for your next meeting

This is done by you at the end of each section, when you will have *prayed, lived* and *made sacrifice* as laid out above. Discern what God is teaching you; what you are learning about yourself in prayer; about relationships with others in living; and about genuine love of God through sacrifice.

The end: Glory be . . .

Finish as always, gathering into prayer the marginalised, or needy. Rest as long as possible within the temple of one's being where the Spirit lives.

10 Surrender – Mary as model

Beginning

We hand over this prayer-life experience to the Holy Spirit. Relax and be still. Prepare for the coming of the Spirit.

Welcome! Let us glorify the Lord, and include families, friends, and needy people, as we say: *Glory be to the Father . . .*

The 'Now' experience

Getting in touch with how you are feeling, in this present

moment, helps your human growth. Sharing it builds relationship in the group. If the feeling is negative, claiming it is the first step in making it more positive.

This is *not* faith-sharing. Give one word that describes your present feeling, like: weary, excited, happy, upset, anxious, hopeful.

Prayer

Jesus, you taught us the way to surrender and to come to peace of heart. St Paul tells us (2 Cor 1:18) that with you, Jesus, it was always 'yes' to your Father. It was never 'no' but always 'yes' because you prayed long hours to know what he wanted. You trusted Him even when – as in the Garden of Gethsemane – your human nature did not want the pain of the Cross and all it meant. You kept on *praying* in trust, you *shared* your pain in trust, and finally you reached total *surrender*. You came to teach us that same way, and you give us the help of Mary, your Mother, who followed you most perfectly. Through the intercession of Mary, your Mother, and in the power of your holy name, Jesus, help us to deepen our faith, to come to true surrender and peace of heart. Amen.

Faith-sharing

You prepared your faith-sharing, when you finished the last section, 'Following Christ'. Pause again now. Recall your experience of insights, of living those out in daily life and how sacrifice helped you. When you are ready, begin your faith-sharing. If you are in a group, everyone listens respectfully to the one who is sharing.

The theme for Section 10: Surrender – Mary as model

This has two dimensions, the *human* and the *spiritual*: the human deals with surrender and peace; the spiritual deals with Mary as model.

Surrender and peace: the human dimension

A woman in labour is advised not to struggle against the pain of giving birth but to surrender to the pain, to enter into it, and the pain becomes less. Again, when our plans are upset, a lot of energy is wasted in negative outbursts of anger. Nothing constructive can be done until we stop threshing around blindly, accept the reality, and begin creatively and constructively to plan again. Recall an experience of pain or anger, when you went round in circles, confused and lashing out. Get in touch with how you felt, with the quality of your being, as you indulged your anger. Was the 'tone quality' a quiet peace, or was it noise, a deafening sound, full of commotion? Discover what spirits are moving within you.

Recall an experience when, eventually, you moved into positive behaviour. How did you feel when you 'let go' and moved to restored harmony within yourself or with another? Can you recall what helped you come to a better place? Throughout these programmes have you learned anything about yourself that can help you, in the future, to find a haven of peace in the midst of turmoil? Pause for a moment. Give thanks silently for any such gift which you have received.

Reflect. Apply to your daily living.

Mary as model: the spiritual dimension

We have heard the story of the Annunciation so often that, perhaps, we no longer hear it in our hearts. Let us take a few points from Luke 1:26–38 and try to listen with a discerning heart. Mary was a young Jewish girl of about sixteen years of age. The history of her people was well known to her, as were their expectations that a great and mighty saviour would liberate them from the hated yoke of the Romans. God asked this young, inexperienced girl to believe his word – so contradictory to all she had understood from parents, rabbis and tradition – a word that she did not even begin to understand. We tend to close our minds and hearts to the true greatness of Mary, to her trust, her courage, her surrender, and to find refuge from our blindness in a statement like: 'It was easy for her.' Let us see how easy it was.

According to the law, Mary would have been stoned to death if Joseph had revealed her condition. Mary knew this when she gave her consent, but she trusted God. She pondered, she prayed, she trusted, she shared her doubts and anxieties with Him, but she always surrendered, even without understanding. Let Scripture reveal to you a little of what Mary felt:

> 'Mary, do not be *afraid.*' Mary was *deeply disturbed* by the angel's words. 'You are to conceive and bear a son . . . he will be great and will be called Son of the Most High . . . ' to which Mary responded: '*How can this come about*, since I am a virgin?' 'The Holy Spirit will come upon you, and the power of the Most High will cover you with its shadow' (Lk 1:30–5, author's italics).

Recall how difficult *you* found it to believe, in these programmes, that God loves and desires you, that He calls you to do great things through His power, if only you allow Him freedom within you? Would *you* have believed the angel's message as coming from God? Would *you* have had the courage and trust to surrender as Mary did?

The truth is that we know that it is not sin that keeps us from God and from being able to do great things for him. It is our unwillingness to know and accept our frailty and to surrender our whole selves in trust to His almighty and healing power. We do not sufficiently believe in God's almighty power and infinite love, and so we do not trust enough. We must pray for the grace to trust in such a way that we can 'walk on water', totally surrendered as Mary was. Listen to the word of God, that moved over Mary's being and called forth that tremendous response, which changed our world:

> 'Know this too: your kinswoman Elizabeth has, in her old age, herself conceived a son, and she whom people called barren is now in her sixth month, *for nothing is impossible to God* (Lk 1:36–7).

To which Mary responded, holding nothing back:

'I am the handmaid of the Lord, let what you have said be done to me' (Lk 1:38).

We know that this was not the end for Mary, but only the beginning of a long road, that stopped on Calvary for a little and then continued, even to this day. As a pregnant mother, whose child is the Son of God, how did she respond, when all her plans were upset? Instead of frustrated anger, she pondered the mystery of God's ways in her life and moved to deeper trust, to co-operation and surrender. As she gave birth the hard way, having travelled far to unfamiliar surroundings, with no friends to greet her or to smooth the way, her heart, no doubt, still sang, 'My soul glorifies the Lord' (Lk 1:46–55). They were refugees, suffering especially because others – like the slain children of Bethlehem and their parents – suffered on their account. Like her Son, from whom she learned continuously, Mary said 'Yes' to the Father in the power of the Spirit.

We each approach Mary from a different position depending upon our church tradition and the particular stage we have reached in our spiritual journey. My own experience of Mary has always been a relationship of trust with a mother. Whenever things were flowing smoothly between her Son and me, she remained in the background. When, however, life got difficult for me, Mary, my mother, emerged from the shadows and was there.

As a young religious, in days when spiritual directors were not easily available, I used to talk everything over with Jesus. I was used to being heard and encouraged. I may have become complacent. One day, I felt I had been misunderstood by an authority figure and treated unjustly. I hurried off to Jesus, my confidant, to share my tale of woe. For the first time ever, I met with blank silence. I repeated my story, with a slightly tart, 'You weren't listening to me!' But the empty silence was deeper. By now, my hurt and anger with authority became transferred to Jesus. In addition I was frightened. If He failed me, where could I go? I stood up to leave the convent chapel, when my eye fell on His mother. I felt I needed a woman. 'Do you know what your Son has done to me, just when I need Him most?' I asked, and poured out my story and pain to her.

Then, in a gentle silence, I heard clearly within me: 'You can get bitter and you will wither, and everyone you touch will wither, and everything. Or, you can trust my Son, and you will grow, and everyone you touch will grow, and everything.' Eventually, I left the chapel, feeling that I was walking on air. As I ascended the stairs, I heard a voice say, 'Sister, you are smiling. How can you?' It was the authority figure! But my heart had changed radically. I said, 'I have learnt today from Mary, that Jesus is truly in heaven, and our hearts are His heaven upon earth.'

From Jesus I learnt later in prayer that darkness is the prelude to brighter light, when we trust in Him.

Reflect and apply to your daily life.

Prayer, living, sacrifice for the coming week

Prayer: Talk to God about 'surrender' as a rich human experience, built on knowledge, trust, courage and sharing. Listen to Him speaking through the gift of his presence in your life, through your Gospel story, your salvation history. Mary bore Emmanuel. You, too – in your life and your environment – are meant to be the 'Good News' of Christ with us today and within us through His Spirit. Is that the kind of witness you are prepared to give?

Awareness prayer: Through it, develop a great sensitivity to God, present in every aspect of your life. Keep begging for the grace of light to illumine your darkness.

In Scripture take any passage that helps you become like Mary. Begin with the Annunciation: Lk 1:26–38, 39–45, 46–55; 2:1–20, 22–38, 39–40, 51–2, 41–50.

Note that Mary, in response to all these mysteries, was actually afraid and amazed, and experienced difficulty and lack of understanding. In this, she is truly our Mother. Would that, in our response to the difficult problems of life, we proved ourselves to be her true child; at all times Mary 'ponders in her heart' and lets the Spirit of God live and act in her. We are the temple of the Holy Spirit who dwells within us in love, and who eagerly awaits our surrender. If we desire to surrender and are ready to take the consequences, this grace of surrender will be given to us.

Let us beg Mary to help us truly live the reality of incarnation today: 'I live now not I, but Christ lives in me.'

Living: Surrender in *little* things with fidelity and in God's time we will eventually surrender in *all* things by His power.

Sacrifice: Have I learned from my mother, who walked the way of the Cross, how I must take up my cross daily?

The end: Glory be . . .

Finish as always, gathering into prayer the marginalised, or needy. Rest as long as possible within the temple of one's being where the Spirit lives.

Epilogue

Jesus grew in wisdom, age and grace, a truly human-spiritual growth process. Thus He came to a full awareness of His identity as the Son of God.

In following a human-spiritual growth process in *Light out of Darkness*, we, too, come hopefully to a keener awareness of our true identity as beloved children of God.

Identity

Who am I?

This is the most basic question which a human being can ask. It is most necessary. I am a person. I am God's 'work of art, the work of His hands' (Fp 2:10).

Who am I in Christ?

I am the Temple of His Spirit. He dwells within me.
I am a member of His Body. Christ is the Head.
I live with the life of Christ, through His Spirit to the glory of the Father, though vessel of clay.

These three find expression in incarnational reality, as I journey in Christ from darkness to light, from disobedience to obedience, from frailty to strength, from fragility to wholeness.

Christ lives in each of us, to save, renew and reach His people, as Saviour and Healer.

Christ lives in us His Body, making our pains, our sorrow, His own.

Christ crucified allows His pain, His tears to become ours.

Joys, too, are a shared mutual experience.

With Christ we share, in some measure, humanity and divinity.

Christ, the Sinless One, had a body, a mind, a heart, a spirit – as we have.

Christ had senses, emotions, feelings, reflective and discerning powers – as we have.

Christ was led and guided by the Spirit – as we are.

Christ emptied, used fully His human and spiritual gifts to discern, through personal experience, His Identity.

Christ's identity, confirmed and accepted at the Jordan, led Him to mission and to death – out of love.

We, made in God's image, share Christ's divinity.

We, children of God, co-heirs of Christ, are continuously confirmed in our identity by Father, Son and Holy Spirit.

We, too, are led to mission by the Spirit – to spread the Gospel and live with the life of Christ.

We, too, are called to die daily to self – out of love; to die to self – as Jesus did, turning the other cheek, forgiving those who wound deeply, forgiving, loving, with the measure of Jesus being God's channel to heal the needy, being ourselves healed through this channelling, experiencing His Presence of love within us, doing infinitely more than we can ask or imagine.

Our response must echo that of Jesus, who said: 'What the Father has taught me is what I preach; He who sent me is with me, and He has not left me to myself, for I always do what pleases Him' (Jn 8:29). We are the disciples of Jesus, He is always with us. He lives within us. We live in His Spirit, who constantly guides and teaches us. How do you, how do I, wish to answer, so that we too may try to do always what pleases Him? Perhaps this prayer will help us articulate our response:

> Lord God
> Father, Son and Holy Spirit,
> Praise, glory and thanks to you
> For Your great mercy and love.
> Of myself, I gladly acknowledge I am nothing
> But with You all things are possible.
> Grant to me, Lord God Almighty,
> The heart of a child,
> Humility, surrender and love,
> The grace to say and to mean:
> 'Here I am, Lord,
> Do with me what You will.'
> Amen.

For further information concerning any aspect of this book, contact, with stamped, self-addressed envelope for reply:

Sr Kathleen O'Sullivan
St Louis Convent
Fordham Road
Newmarket
Suffolk
CB8 7AA

Appendix A – for group leaders

1 Benefits – human-spiritual growth

Individuals
In the various *Light out of Darkness* groups individuals are
helped to know and value themselves as human-spiritual
beings. They come to know the 'real' God and not the
caricature which many of them formerly knew. They are
exposed to His love which is greater than their transgressions.
As they come to know God's constancy and tenderness
they are better able to face both the reality of their own
unworthiness and the reality of their self-worth.

Groups
In groups these individuals are enabled to be freed from
confusion, poor teaching and a sense of isolation. When
they recognise that they are being helped by the honest
faith-sharing of others, they themselves take courage and
become more daring, more revealing.

Above all they discover that they are the 'Living Church',
that Christ is alive in them and is always with them. They
discover that they are not alone in their search for God.

Parishes
Light out of Darkness has been found to be especially
effective in a parish context, strengthening the faith of
individual men and women, who learnt to develop their

gifts and to become more widely involved in the life of the church and society.

Comments on human-spiritual growth from England and Ireland

A Methodist layman:
My own life has been transformed. It has been a great experience of renewal and growth. I have seen how others have been changed. Marriages have been healed. Gifts have been claimed by shy people and used powerfully in ministry.

An Anglican:
My faith has been enriched and my vision has been enlarged. This has affected my professional work. I listen more deeply and am no longer so selective in my listening. My vision sees each person as a messenger from Christ. I now receive from others as well as give to them.

A Roman Catholic:
My faith has sprung to life. Over the last five years my prayer life has changed. Prayer and living are more 'one' now. In each event I am learning to listen to the Spirit within me, guiding me. I discern what God is asking me to do, especially in regard to my neighbour, be that in my home, in the parish or at work. I find God in the little, daily events. Life has a new meaning. There is a savour to it.

2 Experiencing the programme *Light out of Darkness*

Individuals

Light out of Darkness can be an 'alone with God' experience in personal prayer, reflection and application to daily living.

The experience of *Light out of Darkness* can be deepened by sharing with a friend or in an informal group if so desired. After this, further growth can be encouraged by group activity.

Groups – Beginnings
Small groups can be introduced to *Light out of Darkness* by introductory talks, including excerpts from this book.

Alternatively a quiet day with prayer and reflection can be arranged and can include introductory excerpts from this book.

Groups on a parish or neighbourhood basis may be arranged with a trained leader (we have various teams for training leaders), perhaps having a series of weekly meetings with six weeks devoted to *First Steps*, eight weeks to *Prepare the Way* and ten weeks to *Building the Temple*.

3 Retreats – Development of human-spiritual growth

Light out of Darkness retreats are led by a trained leader, away from home in an atmosphere of contemplative silence. They involve three half-hour presentations of material daily with prayer and reflection on each presentation and faith-sharing on the prayer and reflection.

A variety of retreats is available:
- An eight-day retreat. (See p. 240: Leadership, paras two and three.)
- A six-day retreat covering all of *Light out of Darkness* with a healing ministry included.
- A series of three weekends covering respectively *First Steps*, *Prepare the Way*, *Building the Temple*.
- A two-day retreat covering excerpts only.
- A preached retreat. The duration of this retreat is by arrangement between organisers and leader, in which faith-sharing is optional, or not available at all. There are three presentations daily.

Participants:
- Most retreats are open to all Christians.
- On request or by arrangement, some retreats cater specifically for priests, ministers, religious.
- By arrangement some retreats cater for special groups like adult confirmation candidates, R.C.I.A. candidates, seminarians, deacons, or others.

4 Leadership

Light out of Darkness depends upon the training of good leaders to facilitate parish groups or to join teams leading retreats.

Priority should be given to the development of the personal spirituality of leaders. This is best done in the context of an eight-day retreat where six days are spent praying through *Light out of Darkness* in contemplative silence.

Two days training in a workshop follow, as an experience of contemplation in action. As a result lives are changed. Leaders recognise their own need to continue giving priority to their spiritual growth so that they can help groups in a more Christ-like way. The technique which they learn in the workshop gives them confidence. Leaders as well as groups need support. A team of two leaders provides the opportunity to pray together and have faith-sharing to assess their work and to prepare for the next meeting.

For potential leaders who cannot manage to get away from home for eight days, the three weekends are a possibility.

A special training weekend is offered to potential leaders who have done a six-day retreat, the series of three weekends, or have completed the six-months parish group experience.

Appendix B – for group leaders

1 Guidelines for Leaders

Personal spiritual growth is the priority for leaders. This involves:

(i) Commitment to daily prayer
(ii) Commitment to faith-sharing with a team partner
(iii) Fidelity to integrating prayer and life.

The temptation to substitute 'ministry' for personal prayer must be firmly resisted. A leader is on the dangerous 'slippery slope' once the team meeting or leading a group has become a substitute for personal daily prayer.

A team meeting

Leaders need a team partner. It ensures that they meet once a week for a team meeting, when they are leading a group. Groups always meet on the same day, at the same time, each week.

A team meeting for leaders is three-pronged:

(i) *Sharing how they are feeling.*
Faith-sharing for the leaders themselves is of prime importance. It ensures fidelity to daily prayer and to integration of prayer and life, and it prevents misunderstanding and builds up trust.

(ii) *Assessment of the last group meeting.*

– How did the leaders present the material? Was it obvious that they had reflected on it prayerfully and were familiar with it?

– Were the leaders there for the sake of the group rather than to satisfy themselves? Leaders need to keep their focus on Christ, and not on the impression which they themselves are making.

– Had the leaders good eye-contact with each member of the group? Are they aware that they may have a tendency to turn more often to one side of the group than to the other?

– Have the chairs been placed in a circle formation symbolic of the Trinity? Leaders sit side by side, but form part of the circle formation. Thus they are able to contact each person.

– Faith-sharing is a time when people are vulnerable. Are leaders aware of the need for great sensitivity to the group members at this time? When a member has shared, a leader says audibly: 'Thank you'. No discussion is permitted. Nor can the content of another's sharing be mentioned. Leaders have a responsibility to see that the space and privacy of each person is ensured.

– Have leaders alerted the members to the importance of observing confidentiality? Violation of confidentiality is a serious infringement.

– Does the group feel that they are in a 'safe' place and can be honest?

– Do members feel that they are accepted by each leader and valued for themselves?

– Does any member feel in any way pressurised to 'perform better'? This is not the same thing as taking responsibility to pull their weight.

– Were the 'ground rules' made clear to each member before commencing? Was it understood that certain 'ground rules', like confidentiality, are inviolable? Did members accept the commitment to daily prayer? to personal responsibility for punctuality? the attendance at the weekly meeting? to arriving ten minutes before a meeting actually started, so as to relax in body, mind and spirit, in preparation for the coming of the Spirit?

– Have you discussed whether or not to serve refreshments?

Chatter over coffee is not helpful to many who have experienced the Lord deeply. It is generally felt that people prefer to take home to their families or friends the peace and quiet which they experienced during the meeting.

– Are members clear about the meaning of faith-sharing? Do they know how to discern the content of their faith-sharing? Do they understand the need for honesty and openness? Do they understand the importance of listening to one another with respect and a non-judgemental attitude? Are group members familiar with the guidelines to fruitful faith-sharing? (pp. 109–110)

Each of the above points do not need attention at each meeting. If, however, leaders are anxious about commitment, or quality of faith-sharing, or any other point, it is valuable for leaders to check this list, and to pin-point any questionable area. In such a case, the actual meeting is not disturbed; leaders negotiate with the group for an extra ten minutes after the close of the meeting to give some teaching.

(iii)   *Preparation for the next group meeting*

Leaders decide first who will be leader 'one' and who leader 'two'. There is no kudos attached. It is purely a functional arrangement. In the following week leaders rotate with leader one becoming two, and vice versa!

Leader 'One' begins and takes	Leader 'Two' takes
Glory be	Faith-sharing
Prose passage	Questions to deepen
Scripture passages	awareness and reflection
	Preparation for next
Glory be	faith-sharing

The above holds for both *First Steps* and *Prepare the Way*.

In *Building the Temple*, leaders rotate as above; the structure differs slightly, however:

Leader 'One'	Leader 'Two'
Glory be	Faith-sharing

Human dimension	Spiritual dimension
Prayer, living, sacrifice	Preparation for next
Glory be	faith-sharing

Leaders need to ensure that there is first-rate communication between them especially with regard to clarifying the structure. In practice, this means that each leader, when completing the point for which he/she is responsible, mentions that the other leader will introduce the next point in the structure, naming it clearly.

Leaders avoid rush or undue haste. An atmosphere of unhurried calm promotes spiritual depth and listening to the Spirit.

Leaders try to help the group to be at ease with silence, whether during pauses, faith-sharing, or after the last Gloria. It is good for the group to remain quietly together in silence as the Spirit bonds them, the body of Christ, together.

In *Building the Temple* leaders need to remind the group frequently that each person is the temple of the Holy Spirit. The temple that is being built is that of each individual. At the end of the final 'Glory be' in each section, it is advisable to invite people to rest within themselves, where the Holy Spirit is waiting for them in His temple, which they are.

Parish work

Parish prayer-life groups have played a major role in using *Light out of Darkness* and in demonstrating its effectiveness in transforming lives. These are not prayer groups. The emphasis on prayer-life makes clear the central point of programmes, namely that prayer affects life.

Promotion

New leaders anxiously ask, how does one let parishioners know what they have to offer them. Many ways have been tried, but the most successful seems to be, by word of mouth. A notice in the parish bulletin to the effect that the 'undersigned' would like to share with those interested how *Light out of Darkness* has changed their outlook and affected their lives, has been successful. A date, time and venue are given. It is made clear that there are no strings attached. The speakers have something to offer. If anyone needs further information later, that will be forthcoming.

Such a group of leaders prepares a response sheet. There is a place for name, address, telephone number. It has three possible answers, one of which can be ticked at the appropriate place. (i) This is not for me; (ii) I am interested but need to know more; (iii) I am definitely interested.

Before the first meeting ends, the visitors are told of a second meeting (naming again venue, the time and date) for those who wish to come. This time, they will be told about the demands the programme makes, the ground rules, the commitment to daily prayer, beginning with a constant fifteen minutes for *First Steps*, which hopefully increases to thirty minutes before *Prepare the Way* begins.

The visitors will be invited to express their fears or doubts, or ask for any further information. They will be assured that they will get all possible help throughout the programmes.

2 Quiet days

Guidelines

The material and format of *Light out of Darkness* can be readily adapted to the running of quiet days. Attention to a few important principles will increase the likelihood of such a day being a rich and refreshing experience.

First and foremost, the organisers need to recognise the importance of prayerful preparation to ensure that the day is truly Spirit-led.

Practical points:

1. Find a suitable venue, in a peaceful setting. The ambience is very important, as is reasonable comfort, and the provision of enough rooms for everyone to have adequate space, toilet facilities and refreshments.

2. Know the audience you are aiming at – are they familiar with the concepts of *Light out of Darkness* or not?
3. Choose a theme and stick to it. Above all, do not try to include too much material. It is far better to have too little and leave people wanting more, than to include too much and have people going home with their heads in a whirl. That is not the function of a quiet day.
4. It is good to end the day with a simple act of worship.
5. Set out a programme, so that the participants have some idea what to expect. The start and finish times should be clearly stated to allow participants to plan baby-sitters or make other such arrangements. It is helpful if the Scripture and other material for use in the quiet time is listed, and any necessary handouts are copied in good time.
6. Make sure that adequate notice of the day is given. About six weeks seems right – long enough for most people's diaries not to be already booked up, and not so long that it is forgotten about.
7. Those who are leading the day should be freed from anxieties about the domestic arrangements by other helpers who look after these matters.
8. Everyone should wrap the whole day in prayer at all stages. Leaders should meet to pray about the material, to prepare practically, and to hold the participants, known and unknown in prayer during the lead-up to the day.

Programme for a quiet day using material from *First Steps* and *Building the Temple*

The theme develops the idea that we have an infinitely loving God, who is always ready to run out to meet us and lavish the best of everything upon us (like the prodigal's father) when we recognise our need of Him, and turn to Him. From this, we then move on to examining our own present position on life's human and spiritual journey, and finally in the third session, we look to Nehemiah for his example of prayer in action, which encapsulates the prayer-life interaction so central to *Light out of Darkness*.

10.00   Meet for coffee

10.30   Opening − 'God is in love with us' (based on *Prepare the Way*, Part Two, Section 5)

10.45   Prayer and music

11.00   Praying with Scripture
         − 'The Emmaus Road' (*First Steps*, Section 8)
         − Quiet Time
         − Sharing

12.30   Lunch

 1.30   Prayer and music

 1.45   Meditation
         − 'Nehemiah: Prayer and Action' (*Building the Temple*, Part Two, Section 5)
         − Quiet time
         − Sharing

 3.15   Prayer and music

 3.30   Eucharist

Closing remarks, tea and disperse.

Tony White − leader

3 Two-day retreat experience based on *Light out of Darkness*

It is understood that those participating in this retreat on *Prepare the Way* have already experienced *First Steps*, either in a previous two-day retreat or in a parish group. Two-day retreats are a very condensed form of the whole *Light out of Darkness* material. Nevertheless, they are a growth experience for the participants. Usually they lead to an experience of the six-day retreat, and sometimes to the additional two-day training workshop.

In introducing this two-day retreat, leaders need to ensure that participants clearly understand the concepts of faith-sharing and contemplative silence. It is necessary to stress that each one needs time, space and silence to be able to listen to God. The use of music, for example a Taize chant, may help to create an atmosphere of peace, of quiet and facilitate the deepening of *stillness*. Breathing exercises also help.

Sufficient time is necessary to allow for prayer and reflection on each presentation of material. Leaders need to cover the whole retreat with prayer before, during and after the retreat. It is helpful to have prayer support from those who are willing or who have such a ministry.

Programme for a two-day retreat using material from *Prepare the Way*

SATURDAY

10.00	Arrival and coffee
10.30–11.00	Welcome and introduction to retreat, including opportunity for retreatants to briefly introduce themselves.
11.00–11.30	Prayer and reflection followed by: **First presentation** – Section 1 – My Relationship with God
11.30–12.30	Quiet time to pray and reflect on presentation
12.30–1.00	Faith-sharing in small groups
1.00	Lunch
2.00–2.30	Prayer and reflection followed by: **Second presentation** – Sections 2 and 3 Communication – I speak to God: God speaks to me

| 2.30–3.30 | Quiet time to pray and reflect on presentation |

3.30–4.00   Faith-sharing in small groups

4.00–4.30   Tea

4.30–5.00   Prayer –
Third presentation – Section 4
Preparation for prayer
(To be used for prayer and reflection during the evening)

Concluding prayer and reflection

SUNDAY

10.00   Arrival and coffee

10.30–11.00   Welcome and prayer, and opportunity for brief faith-sharing on previous evening's prayer.

11.00–11.20   **First presentation** – Section 5
God's goodness revealed in me

11.20–12.30   Quiet time to pray and reflect on presentation

12.30–1.00   Faith-sharing in small groups

1.00   Lunch

2.00–2.30   Prayer and reflection followed by –
Second presentation – Sections 6 and 7
God's tenderness in my struggle; God's love for my neighbour – My love?

2.30–3.30   Quiet time to pray and reflect on presentation

3.30–4.00   Faith-sharing in small groups

4.00–4.30   Tea

4.30–5.00   Prayer –
Third presentation – Section 8
Am I trustworthy? (For prayer and
reflection at home)
Concluding prayer and reflection
                              Eilish Heath – leader